Black Achievers in Science and Technology

ASI Fellows

Editorial Management

Justin Ahanhanso

Lisa Cain

Lee O. Cherry

George Cooper

William ("Bill") Harris

James L. Hope

Carlos Kimathi

L. Rodney Maxwell

Albert Nzoko Moleka

Eddie Neal

Wiley Pierce

© 2011 by the African Scientific Institute, P.O. Box 12161, Oakland, CA 94604, 510-653-7027.

No part of this book may be reproduced, stored in a retrieval system, or transmitted by any means, electronic, mechanical, photocopying, recording, or otherwise, without written permission from the African Scientific Institute, or its representative thereof.

Black Achievers in Science and Technology

ASI Fellows

Third Edition, 2011 (The first edition was issued in 2006 to ASI Fellows only, resulting from ASI Fellows' 2006 Induction Ceremony.)

ISBN: 978-0-578-07755-0

Cover photo and design by Paul Wellington Smith, http://pwellingtonphoto.com

About this book

Contents of this book is continuously updated. New persons are added. The biographies of existing *ASI Fellows* change, as people engage in new activities. Some *Fellows* change their place of employment; some retire from being employed. There are some *Fellows* who have passed away.

We will retain the names and bios of deceased *Fellows* in this book to always remember them and their contributions.

Thanks to

Edgar Goff, who inspired the initiation of the ASI Fellows Program.

Foreword

The Objectives of the ASI Fellows Program is to facilitate a boundless roundtable of accomplished individuals who serve as a think tank, addressing issues relating to the world of science and technology. ASI Fellows is a collective which shares experiences, contacts and knowledge. This unique group of noted individuals, which has boundless potential and is always organic, also serves as a standard of accomplishments and encourages minorities to further engage in science and technology. Our youth can identify with these individuals and be encouraged that they too, as a young person, start their journey towards high accomplishments, knowing that others have achieved such goals.

Initially, this group of Black people in science and technology came from about 10 countries. *Now, about 470 ASI Fellows come from 32 countries throughout Africa and the African Diaspora, where there are more than 1.3 billion Black people.*

Over the years, the African Scientific Institute (ASI) has produced the *Blacks In Science Calendar* (11 years), *Science and Technology Awareness Fair* (more than 3,500 children each year for 10 years), *Technology and Environment Camp, SciTech News Paper* (25,000 national distribution for 8 years), *Africa Focus Series* (annual conference), *Constituents for Science and Technology Awareness*, and the *African Relief Fund*. ASI has partnered with diverse organizations such as Public School Districts, the National Association of American Americans in Human Resources (NAAAHR), Department of Energy's BASTEC Program, Bay Area Urban League, and many many more. We have co-founded and assisted in the establishment of several noteworthy and active organizations, which like ASI is dedicated to assisting African Americans.

Today, core ASI persons travel internationally, engaging in conferences and participating in projects. We continuously expand our efforts to maintain excitement among our network of professionals, while exciting our youth to pursue careers In science and technology.

The following individuals represent a very talented group of people in the world of science and technology........................individuals who the African Scientific Institute is proud to have as *ASI Fellows*.

Biographies

Shaukat Ali Abdulrazak, Ph.D.
Exec. Sec., National Council for Science and Technology; AgriScience

Prof. Shaukat Ali Abdulrazak is the Executive Secretary of the National Council for Science and Technology (NCST), which is the focal point on Science, Technology and innovation in Kenya. As the Executive Secretary to the NCST, Prof. Abdulrazak is the technical and administrative head of the NCST and is responsible for its day to day management of financial and physical resources as well as the management of human resources and programmes. He also guides the Council in the development and advocacy of Science and Technology policy popularization and promotion of science and technology as a tool for national development. Prior to joining the NCST, Prof. Abdulrazak was the Deputy Vice-Chancellor of the Research and Extension unit of the Egerton University in Njoro, Kenya, a position he held from 2002 – 2007. He also worked as a Senior Lecturer and Associate Professor at this university from 1997-2001. Since 2005, he worked as Professor of Animal Science at Egerton University.

Adigun Ade Abiodun, Ph.D., P.E.
Satellite Remote Sensing; Space Sciences; Civil & Hydraulics Engineering

A native of Nigeria, Dr. Abiodun served as the United Nations expert on space applications and chief of the Space Applications Section of the U.N.'s Outer Space Affairs Division from 1981 through his retirement in 1999. He holds a Ph.D. in civil and hydraulics engineering from the University of Washington, Seattle. He began his career at the U.N. in 1977 as a remote sensing specialist. During the course of his career, he initiated, designed, implemented and supervised the U.N. Space Applications Program. Since his retirement, Dr. Abiodun has served as the senior special assistant to the president of Nigeria on space and science technology (2000-2003); as a member of the College of Commissioner for the United Nations Monitoring, Verification and Inspection Commission (2000 to present); and chairman of the Committee on the Peaceful Uses of Outer Space (2004 to 2006).

Babagana Abubakar
Geology

Babagana has addressed issues relating to the effects of climates changes in rural Nigeria and the Sahelian areas in general. He is Vice-President of the Kanuri Development Association, non-governmental and not for profit making indigenous peoples organisation working on indigenous, human rights as well as climate change issues in Nigeria, Niger and some part of Chad Republics and is the current Head of Department of intellectual property and genetic resources, traditional knowledge and research.

Albert Cosmas Achudume, Ph.D.
Toxicology

Dr. Achudume is a Professor in the Institute of Ecology and Environmental Studies, serving as a lecturer. He earned his AA, BA, MS and Ph.D. degrees in the United States in Biology. From 1983 -1993, Dr. Achudume was a lecturer at a few universities teaching Principles of Genetics Engineering, Advanced Biotechnology, Biomass Utilization, Nutritional Biochemistry Biophysics - Isotopes and Radiation. During this time he also worked West African School Examination Council, Test Development and Research Office (TEDRO) from 1987 – 91. Currently, he is a lecturer in the Institute of Ecology where he teaches Biodeterioration and Biodegradation, Ecological Effect of Chemical in the Environment, Industrial Effluents: Treatment and Utilization, Biotechnology and its impacts on the Environment. Dr. Achudume has authored several publishings and is a member of professional societies and has amazingly found time to be a soccer coach.

Ebenezer A. Adebowale, Ph.D.
National Universities Commission; Animal Science

Dr. Adebowale serves on Nigeria's National Universities Commission, Abuja. He is Pro-Chancellor of the private Bowen University and Chairman of its Governing Council. From 2003 – 2008, he was the Executive Director of Obafemi Awolowo University's Institute of Agricultural Research and Training, Ibadan. He led in the development and accreditation of all courses by the National Universities Commission (NUC). He taught and performed research in Ruminant Nutrition in England, Scotland, Austria, Japan and Germany, resulting in over 25 publications. Dr. Adebowale was the Editor –in-Chief for the Nigerian Journal of Animal Production (Volume 12-14).

Jimmy Adegoke, Ph.D.
Geosciences

Dr. Adegoke is an award winning environmental scientist whose research focuses on understanding the relationships between changing land surface processes and diverse indicators of environmental change. He uses climate diagnostic tools, satellite remote sensing, and regional climate models to investigate these interactions at local and regional scales. Dr. Adegoke is a faculty member in the Department of Geosciences, where he conducts research in the Laboratory for Climate Analysis and Modeling (LCAM) and teaches courses in physical climatology, satellite remote sensing, environmental science and Geographic Information Systems (GIS). Dr. Adegoke is a member of several professional societies including the American Geophysical Union (AGU), Association of American Geographers (AAG), and American Meteorological Society (AMS). He is a Council Member of the African Association for Remote Sensing of the Environment (AARSE) and serves on the Technical Advisory Board of the UNESCO crosscutting project on the Application of Remote Sensing for Ecosystem and Water Resources Management in Africa. His recent work focuses on societal impacts of environmental change, including air pollution studies in rapidly changing mid-latitude urban areas, climate impacts on water resources, and coastal ecosystem dynamics in the Niger Delta region of Nigeria.

Adetunji Adelekan, MD, FACP
Nephrologist, Internal Medicine

Dr. Adelekan has practiced internal medicine for more than 40 years. He earned his MD at Harvard University and has practiced primarily in California. "Tunji" now lives primarily in Nigeria. Not only has he provided services through his private practice, he headed an Emergency Services Community Clinic. He now resides in Nigeria where he still provides healthcare services.

Sunday Adeniji Adesuyi, Ph.D.
Chemist

Dr. Adesuyi has been successful in higher education for about thirty years. He is a Professor of Chemistry and Chairman of the Department of Natural Science and Mathematics. He has also served in such capacities as Interim Provost/Vice-President for Academic Affairs and Acting President of the college where he is currently employed. He is the recipient of numerous honors and awards that include: Sears-Roebuck Faculty of the Year, UNCF Distinguished Leadership Award, Most Outstanding Science Faculty Award, U.S. Department of Commerce Appreciation Award. He was also named to Who's Who Among African Americans and to Outstanding Young Men of America. Dr. Adesuyi has also held or holds memberships and offices in numerous organizations that include being the President of the CIAA, Parliamentarian of NCAA Division II Management Council, Editor-In-Chief of the National Newsletter of the National Association of Minority Medical Educators (NAMME), and Executive Committee Member of the CIAA Basketball Tournament since 1990. Dr. Adesuyi is originally from Igbajo, Nigeria. He is married to the former Olayemi L. Adedeji; and they have one daughter, Adeola Ojuolape. Dr. Adesuyi is also an Ordained Minister, An Associate Pastor, and the Superintendent of Sunday School at First Baptist Church, Lawrenceville, VA.

Mayen Adetiba, P.E.
President of Association of Consulting Engineers of Nigeria; Civil Engineering

Mayan says her study of engineering was a stroke of luck. When she left secondary school in the 60s, she began to do a little bit of journalism, modeling and acting. She was also writing for *Lagos Weekend* which was part of *Daily Times*. She also was with *Radio Nigeria* and television. She modeled for Lintas and most of the big companies. Mayan then left for the United States to further her education. She found herself studying computer science. A Nigerian professor told her to go into Electrical Engineering as opposed to Computer Science which she was already studying; she agreed. Two years later, a counselor later suggested Mayen pursue civil engineering which would be a more stable field of engineering in Nigeria. When she returned to Nigeria, she had to fight to be respected as a female engineer and secure employment as an engineer. Many of these jobs were given to foreign white engineering contractors who took the design of the job abroad, then brought it back to Nigeria. Nigerians were not benefitting, both in knowledge and financially. Eventually Mayan became the President of the Association of Consulting Engineers of Nigeria (ACEN) where she believes that the government should be engaged to provide jobs to Nigerian engineers, which will increase Nigerians knowledge "because the more you design and build, the more perfect you become".

Clement O. Adewunmi, DVM, MSc., FCVSN, FICTM, KSM
Parisitologist; African Medicinal Plants; Executive Secretary, WANNPRES

Dr. Adewunmi is a Professor of Parasitology with over three decades of research into African medicinal plants with potential anti-infective properties. He has served as the Director of the Drug Research and Production Department of the Obafemi Awolowo University, Ile-Ife, Nigeria for seven years. He is currently the Executive Secretary of the Western African Network of Natural Products Scientists (WANNPRES) and the Editor-in-Chief of the *African Journal of Traditional, Complementary and Alternative Medicines*. He has received several fellowships in the past and collaborated extensively on plant molluscicides. Some of his courses have included chemotherapy, pesticides and molluscicides, African medicinal plants, Medical Parsitology, advanced human biology, physiological basis of phytomedicines, toxicology of natural products, and principles of drug evaluation. For thousands of years, spices have been a source of wealth and improved food taste and added health benefits to our diets. In West Africa, the plant *Tetrapleura tetraptera* (locally known as Aridan) is used as a spice, a medicine and as a dietary supplement rich in vitamins. His research in using this plant has determined that water extracts of *Tetrapleura tetraptera* were found to be highly effective in killing snails (for 28 days) carrying Bilharzia, the disease caused by Schistosomes.

Olanike Kudirat Adeyemo, DVM, Ph.D.
Veterinary Medicine, Aquatic Pathobiology

Dr. Adeyemo is an Associate Professor, in the Department of Veterinary Public Health and Preventive Medicine, University of Ibadan, Nigeria. She is the pioneer female in the Field of Aquatic Veterinary Medicine in any Faculty of Veterinary Medicine in Nigeria. Her research interest includes Ecotoxicology, aquatic toxicology, aquatic Pathobiology, Biochemical & Molecular Toxicology (Biomarkers), Identification of biological effects of environmental contaminants using fish as models, Environmental risk assessment, Evaluation of contaminants with respect to their relevance to environmental and human health. She has therefore conducted integrated research to understand and solve emerging and known infectious and non-infectious disease problems affecting fish for the purpose of providing scientific support to Nigerian aquaculture industry and to assist the Government with legislation development and implementation. She is a Fellow of Leadership for Environment and Development (LEAD) International, London and a Fellow of Norman E. Borlaug fellowship for African Women in Science. Currently Dr. Adeyemo is researching tetracycline residue in feral and cultured fish and their products in Nigeria, Trace metal speciation in selected freshwater systems in Nigeria, and Ultrastructural studies on the effects of lead nitrate on the gonads of *Clarias gariepinus*.

Aeyinka A. Adeyiga, Ph.D, FASEE; FAIChe
Professor of Chemical Engineering Director of DOE-Massie Chair of Excellence

Dr. Adeyiga's experience spans more than 25 years in Chemical Engineering practice and Engineering education. His research includes vapor-liquid equilibrium for acid gas constituents in natural gas, oil, and coal-derived fluids; and mathematical modeling of chemical processes and heat transfer, catalytic and non-catalytic gas-solid reactions, environmental and waste management. He has held research engineering positions with E.I. DuPont and De Nemoir Company, reservoir engineer with Shell Petroleum (International), and was Chief Consultant for Padson Engineering in Nigeria. Dr. Adeyiga was the founding Chair of the Department of Engineering at Hampton University, where he has spent the last eighteen years and has been awarded more than 10 research projects exceeding $4 million dollars since coming to the University in 1985. He also has performed research for the Department of Energy, NASA, and NSF. During his tenure as the Engineering Department Head, he oversaw construction of a new 5.2 million dollar Olin Engineering Building with state-of-the-art facilities for Engineering instruction and research. He led the Hampton Engineering programs to hosting the first ABET/EAC visit, which resulted in receiving the first accreditation for all of Hampton University's engineering programs in 1992.

John Afele, Ph.D.
Plant Breeding/Biotechnology

Dr. Afele obtained his doctorate in crop improvement (plant breeding/biotechnology) from the University of Guelph (Ontario, Canada) in 1990; Master's degree (1986) from the Catholic University of Leuven, Belgium (in tropical agriculture/ biotechnology); and undergraduate (1984) at the University of Ghana, Accra, Ghana. Recently, he was a consultant at the World Bank, where he helped deliver technical assistance to WB clients in Africa. His tasks included helping to implement WB facilitation of Ethiopian and Ghanaian immigrant professionals in the North American health and education sectors to deepen their self-organized delivery of basic services to their countries of origin. Prior to joining the World Bank, John was director of International Program for Africa (University of Guelph); an executive member of the Global Knowledge Partnership; Fellow at the Science and Technology Agency of Japan; research associate at the University of Guelph and McGill University (Montreal, Canada). John is author of *Digital Bridges – Developing countries in the knowledge economy (Hershey, PA: Idea Group Inc., 2003)*. The Cleveland Council on World Affairs, which organizes Model UN Conferences for thousands of area high school students, selected John's book as part of the core literature for the 2007 Model UN Conference (Economic and Social Committee).

Kouadio Affian, Ph.D.
GeoScience

Prof. Kouadio is Director, University Center for Research in Applied Remote Sensing (CURAT), University of Cocody, Cote D'Ivoire and Director of UFR Terre and Mineral Resources. He served as Vice Dean of the Faculty of Earth Sciences and Mineral Resources from 1997 to 2000. His expertise covers the areas of Marine Geology, Ocean Science, Geomorphology, the Integrated Coastal Management, Remote Sensing and Geographic Information Systems. He dealt with aspects of carrying out assessment of coastal resources, using appropriate indicators such as physical-chemical and ecological parameters, socio-economic and cultural issues as well as environmental considerations. He emphasizes using Global Positioning System (GPS), satellite and air photos, and Geographic Information Systems (GIS) as examples of tools that should be used to assess coastal processes including coastal erosion. GIS and satellite images in can be used for beach profiling and the assessment of pollution by heavy metals and hydrocarbons in coastal waters.

Godwin Kwaku S. Aflakpui, Ph.D.
Crop and Plant Physiology; Agronomy

Dr. Aflakpui is the Rector, Wa Polytechnic, Wa, Ghana. His past duties included serving as Head of the Resource and Crop Management Division, Crops Research Institute (CRI) of the Council for Scientific and Industrial Research (CSIR) from 2003-2006, and Deputy Director of CSIR-CRI (2005-2007). As a crop physiologist/agronomist, he has extensive field and laboratory experience in the areas of maize, legume-root, tuber crops, and vegetable crop-based cropping systems on farmers' fields. Some of the areas of his research include reclamation of degraded or abandoned lands with cover crops, investigating nutrient uptake and partitioning in crop-weed interactions using stable isotopes, appropriate use of fertilizers, and integrated nutrient management in cropping systems. He has also designed and conducted surveys of the perception of farmers to climate change, circumstances of farmers, input suppliers, agro-processors and how they relate to crop production, processing and storage. Not only does Dr. Aflakpui have management skills, he has written several scientific papers and is a member of national and international organizations.

Abolade S. Afolabi, Ph.D.
Plant Biotechnology & Molecular Virology, Bio-Safety and Diagnostics

Dr. Afolabi is a well-trained Plant Biotechnologist/ Plant Molecular Biologist, certified Clinical Laboratory Scientist and Plant Virologist with broad experiences. He earned his Ph.D. in Plant Molecular Biology, 2003, University of East Anglia, U.K.; MS degree in Bacteriology, 1984, Wagner College, New York; BS in in Medical Technology, 1982, St. John's University, New York. Currently, Dr. Afolabi works at the Biotechnology Advanced Laboratory, Abuja, Nigeria as Deputy Director (Research & Policy), responsible for program formulation and management (scientific and policy), synthesizing and editing of research findings, technical data and determining data relevance, conduct background research topics and write proposals for new studies, molecular cloning including promoter and gene construct development and evaluation, design and production of transgenic plants, molecular characterization (using all the gamut of molecular biology), and statistical analysis, biosafety regulation and Intellectual property, tissue culture including large-scale micropropagation and meristem culture thermotherapy for virus removal. Dr. Afolabi has worked for the Nigerian Academy of Science; Bay Bioassay & Biotechnology; West African Rice Development Association; Nigeria State Hospitals. He has authored several publishings and is a member of professional societies.

Abel Afouda, Ph.D.
Mathematics

Dr. Afouda is a Professor of Mathematics and President of the National IHP Committee in Benin and Board Member of UNESCO-IHE Institute for Water Education. He handles data collection management and use, highlighting the African Monsoon Multidisciplinary Analysis, which aims to improve understanding of the African monsoon, to provide guidance on methodologies, tools and approaches for adaptation. Regarding the current state of data collection at the national level, he lamented, *inter alia*, a decline in size and quality of hydrological services, poor dissemination of data, and repetition of data acquisition. Dr. Afouda has called for strengthening and consolidating the capacity of conventional hydrological data collection systems, and integrating adaptation to climate change into primary and secondary school curricula.

Georges A. Agbahungba, Ph.D.
Forestry Agronomist; Soil Science

Valentin Agon
Green Medicine

Using plants and bees (honey, pollen, royal jelly, bee venom and salivary enzymes of bees) eventually lead to natural remedies by Valentin Agon. He also promotes local knowledge and wealth of African plants. He says, "In Africa, nature has given us everything for the care of our health". Valentine Agon, a native of Benin, is a health practitioner (specialist green medicine) who earned a degree from AMCC-CANADA and trained at the Faculty CALIXTO GRACIA CUBA. He continues his studies for a sustainable development expertise to Maine in France and a specialty in pedagogy of social change and development at the University of Ouagadougou. He is the CEO of API-Benin and President of the International NGO Initiatives and Strategies for Development (ISD), an NGO working for the promotion and enhancement of natural remedies.

Louzolo (Augie) Agostinho
Senior Petroleum Engineer

Louzolo Agostinho ("Augie") had earned a Master's Degree in Petroleum engineering from the Colorado School of Mines and worked for several years for Chevron Overseas Petroleum (COPI) in Angola.

Jones Fairfax Agwata, Ph.D.
Environmental Science and Policy

Dr. Agwata is an environmentalist, specializing in water resources management and climate change impacts and adaptation. He has written about the characteristics of hydrological drought in the upper parts of the Tana Basin, Kenya. Curently, he serves as a Senior Lecturer in Environmental Policy, Centre for Advanced Studies in Environmental Law and Policy, University of Nairobi.

Justin Ahanhanzo
Physical Oceanography; Coordinator and Team Leader, UNESCO's GOOS-AFRICA Program

Justin is an Oceanographer and Team Leader of the Global Ocean Observing System in Africa (GOOS-Africa coordinator). He is the Technical Secretary of the GOOS Regional Alliances, GOOS-AFRICA Coordinator and Team Leader of the UNESCO Crosscutting Project on the Applications of Remote Sensing for Integrated Management of Ecosystems and Water Resources in Africa.

Joseph Owolabi Ajayi, Ph.D.
Hydrogeology, Engineering Geology

Dr. Ajayi received his doctorate in water resources from the University of Arizona and is a Professor in the Department of Geology at Obafemi Awolowo University in Ile-Ife, Nigeria. He has a varied career in academic, consulting and professional services in the technical areas of hydrogeology, water resources evaluation, and environmental engineering. He is consultant expert to several professional firms and multi-national corporations and has provided expert services to state and federal agencies in West Africa. A principal area of expertise is in the area of groundwater exploration and management in hard rock aquifer systems.

Kemji B. Ajoku, Ph.D.
Technology Management; Microbiology

Dr. Ajoku has worked for Nigeria's Raw Materials Research and Development Council since 1988. During this time, he served as Secretary to the National Multi-disciplinary Task Force on the techno-economic Survey on Textile, Wearing Apparel and Leather in 1988/89; pioneered the establishment of New Materials Division in the Council in 1992. Participated as a member of the negotiating team to Czech Republic on Lead-Zinc Project in Nigeria with collaboration of UNIDO-Czech Joint Programme on Metallic Industries, Prague, Czech Republic; during which he prepared the Memorandum of Understanding (MOU) in 1992. Presently, a Senior Chief Scientific Officer in charge of Investment Promotion Projects. Dr. Ajoku served as a consultant to Group of 77 Countries (G.77) through UNDP in Nigeria for an International Study on the Establishment of a Raw Materials Information Network for Africa between 1992-93.

Gboyega Aladegbami
Civil Engineering

While Mr. Aladegbami has experiences as a civil engineer, he founded AEKO Consulting in 1994, a multi-faceted company that has developed into a multi-million dollar systems integration company. AEKO has provided various services for the State of California and various counties and cities throughout the United States. He recently coordinated the design and subsequent deployment of an integrated cost control web-based application, PROMIS. Mr. Aladegbami recently coordinated the team formation for the provision of a county's enterprise resource planning (ERP). This PeopleSoft-based project has both financial and human resources modules. In addition, he provided overall project leadership on a network security study for the county and the subsequent implementation of an enhanced VPN project allowing secure communication between the county and some its partners. Furthermore, he led the AEKO team that was responsible for designing a converged network (VoIP) for a county's school district covering its entire 60 schools and 3 administrative facilities. For another school district, it designed and installed wireless and structured cable technology for its 100 schools and administrative facilities.

George E. Alcorn, Ph.D.
Physics

Dr George Alcorn is an Asst. Director at NASA's OSSMA. At NASA he has served as Deputy Proj. Mgr. for Space Station Adv. Dev., Chief of the Technology Commercialization Office, Proj. Mgr. for the Airborne Lidar Topological Mapping System (ALTMS), Mgr. of the In Step Flight Experiment Program, Deputy Mgr. for Center's Code R research program, and Deputy Div. Chief for NASA's Technology Integration Div. He earned his BS degree in Physics with honors while earning eight letters in basketball and football. He earned his MS in Nuclear Physics in 1963 from Howard Univ., after nine months of study. In 1967, he earned a Ph.D. in Atomic and Molecular Physics. Dr. Alcorn has earned over 20 patents. He is a pioneer in using particle techniques like plasmas, ion beams, and sputtering methods to make high performance semiconductor devices. He invented a radical x-ray spectrometer using thermomigration of aluminum. Among Dr. Alcorn's numerous awards is a NASA medal for his work in recruiting minority scientists and engineers and helping small businesses have successful research programs. In 2010 he received the NASA Exceptional Service Medal and the Robert H Goddard Award of Merit, GSFC highest Honor Award: Cited was his exceptional innovational and contributions to NASA, space science and technology.

Sam Olatunji Ale, Ph.D.
Mathematics

Prof. Ale has been re appointed for a 2nd term of five years as the Director General and Chief Executive of the National Mathematical Centre, Abuja. He has been commended by the Minister of Education for contributing immensely to the transformation of the Mathematical Science and Mathematical Sciences Education in Nigeria and other areas of human endeavour; for introducing new methods for demystifying mathematics as well as making mathematics simple, real and scintillating to pupils and students and for promoting the image of Nigeria in Mathematical Sciences internationally, especially in the scientific activities in the International Mathematics and Sciences Olympiads. Prof. Ale has produced over 99 publications in learned journals both local and foreign, mostly in Pure Mathematics and Mathematics Education. He has authored 8 published text-books and co-authored 14 others with MAN. He has tutored to graduation over 7 Ph.D's and 15 M. Sc. students and examined the Thesis Defense of over 11 Ph. D. and 150 M.Sc. graduates.

Edward Cleve Alexander, Ph.D.
Chemistry

He served as Chairman, Department of Chemistry in academia for 8 years and has been a Professor of Chemistry for thirty six years. He is sited as one of the seven "founding fathers" of Organic Chemistry at his prestigious institution. He was appointed Coordinator of the Third College Science and Technology Program, a program that was designed to encourage and enhance the success of African American and other underrepresented minority students in the sciences and mathematics. Dr. Alexander conducted research in the areas of organic photochemistry and on the synthesis and chemistry of highly strained ring compounds. His efforts also helped place numerous African American and other minority students into medical, graduate, and pharmacy schools. Using photochemistry, Dr. Alexander developed the most effective method known to date for synthesizing 2-substituted bicyclo[1.1.1.] pentanes. These compounds have been synthetically challenging and possess a very unique ring structure which has sparked special theoretical interest over the past fifty years. He is currently the P.I./Director of the "Bridges to the Baccalaureate Program" at San Diego Mesa College/UC, San Diego. This program is funded by the NIH is designed to increase the number of underrepresented minorities in the biomedical sciences.

Aliyageen M. Alghali, Ph.D.
University Vice Chancellor; Agricultural Entomology

Dr. is a Professor of Crop Protection (Entomology) and Vice Chancellor and Principal of Njala University. He is an agricultural entomologist with considerable professional research experience in tropical food crops pest management and practical University teaching, establishment, administration and management. He served as Liaison Research Scientist for the International Centre for Insect Physiology and Ecology (ICIPE) at the International Institute of Tropical Agriculture (IITA) working on integrated pest management for cowpeas. Other crops he has worked on are rice, sorghum and sweet potatoes. He has numerous peer review journals and conference publications and has served on the Editorial boards of several international journals. As Vice Chancellor and Principal who served in two public universities in Sierra Leone, he was able to successfully superintend over the splitting up of the old university (1972) including its assets and liabilities into two autonomous corporate bodies (2005), establish one of them from scratch (i.e. Njala University), tackled resource mobilization and strategic visioning. He was chair for the implementation and establishment of the first two public Polytechnic Institutions in Sierra Leone.

James E. Allen
Ret'd Mgr., Lab Space Flight Operations Facility.

(- 2006). Former manager of the Jet Propulsion Laboratory's Space Flight Operations Facility (SFOF) wass responsible for providing for the maintenance and operation of the SFOF environmental and utility equipment in support of Space Flight Mission Operations. Professionally, Jim has been employed in almost forty years of progressive engineering and management experience from aeronautical engineering to mechanical engineering; from electrical engineering to computer science; and from marketing to technical management. Over the last thirty five years, Jim has been a pioneer in the Space Exploration program at the Jet Propulsion Laboratory since the late fifties and has worked on the design and development of space craft with missions to the Moon, the Planet and beyond. He was Operations Project Engineer for Worldwide Deep Space Tracking Station in support of the space flight missions to Mercury, Venus, Jupiter and Saturn. He was involved with the Europeans in their Giotto mission to Halley's Comet and the planned Ulysses mission over the poles of the Sun.

Joan Olubunmi Amarteifio, Ph.D.
Biochemistry

Dr. Amarteifio is Acting Head, Department of Food Science and Technology and Associate Professor in Chemistry at Botswana College of Agriculture (BCA). She is currently researching the chemical composition of indigenous foods. She has authored and co-authored several refereed publishings that has covered such subjects as "The nutrient and mineral composition of Bambara groundnut landraces (*Vigna subterranea* (L.) Verdc.) cultivated in Southern Africa" and "*Promoting the use of underutilized crops in Botswana: the case of pigeon pea (Cajanus cajan)*".

Reginald L. Amory, Ph.D., F.ASCE
Civil Engineering

In addition to his expertise in civil engineering in the fields of structural engineering and structural mechanics, Dr. Amory has conducted research, provided consulting, and been a decision-maker in professional endeavors which include education, civil infrastructure, land development, defense, energy, transportation, labor affairs, and government affairs. He is also the recipient of many honors and awards including the 1999 Outstanding Civil Engineering Educator Award from the Maryland Section of the American Society of Civil Engineers (ASCE) for sustained and unusual contributions to the advancement of the civil engineering profession and service to mankind. A Fellow of ASCE, he is the first African-American to receive a Ph.D. in engineering from Rensselaer Polytechnic Institute. He is currently working on the development of a transportation technology curriculum that will prepare minorities, women, and disadvantaged individuals for transportation careers in the 21st century and beyond. His future research is focused on conducting fundamental studies aimed toward developing constitutive equations which describe the mechanical behavior of composite materials at the micro- mechanics-materials interface.

Gloria Long Anderson, Ph.D.
Professor Emeritus; Chemistry

Chair Emeritus of the Chemistry Department in academia, Gloria Long Anderson taught, administered, fundraised, and conducted as much research as her limited financial support made possible. She earned her M.S. degree at Atlanta University in 1961 and her Ph.D. in Organic Chemistry at the University of Chicago in 1968. Despite offers from scientifically well-equipped universities, she never went back on her 1968 pledge to stay in black schools. Dr. Anderson has performed extensive research in fluorine-19 chemistry and related areas of pharmaceutical development. Her research also included the study of amantadines, used in the prevention of viral infection. She also studied the use of propellants for rockets for the U.S. Air Force Office of Scientific Research. In 1990 she became a research consultant for BioSPECS of The Hague, Netherlands. Dr. Anderson encourages students, as she herself was mentored by her own parents and teachers.

Kenneth R. Anderson
Electrical Engineer

He is the Executive Director of The Anderson Group (TAG) Consulting for Information Technology and Digital Audio. From 1994-2003, Ken Anderson has been an Instructor at Burlington County College (BCC) /New Jersey Institute of Technology (NJIT), Technology & Engineering Center in Mount Laurel, NJ, where he taught courses in Electrical Engineering Technology and Computer Engineering and Linux Operating System. From 1979-1995, he was a Senior Member of the Technical Staff of SIEMENS Corporate Research, where he performed research and development of testing techniques for Very Large Scale Integrated Circuits (VLSI) semiconductor circuits, digital components and systems; Modeling and Simulation of Queuing Networks for exploring rapid modeling and analysis techniques for medical diagnostic imaging support systems, computer integrated manufacturing and information systems; He also served as a member of the start up team that began research in Test Technology for SIEMENS research activities in the US (SIEMENS is the fifth largest Electrical Engineering Company world wide). Ken has been very active in the IEEE Computer Society, the largest society of electrical an computer engineers with 100,000 members world wide (he was President 1988-91).

Tikisa M. Anderson
Electronics Engineering

Tikisa Anderson used his expert knowledge of systems engineering in the areas of high-speed digital design, fiber optics, satellite and ground network communications, data handling protocols (FDDI, 1773, 1553B, SONET, ATM), algorithm development, systems architecture, trade studies, planning, and risk assessments. He has managed engineers, in design and simulation of data-compression hardware algorithm, simulation team to verify fiber optic communications controller designs, and the design of 125 MHz, fiber optic communications bus controller ASIC. Tikisa designed Mil-Std-1553B Data Bus for satellite data handling networks and prepared satellite test compliance and verification documentation. He monitored satellite integration and test activities to ensure acceptance of test results according to system integration schedules, designed low-cost laser diode substitute for gas lasers in Navy test-bed Ordnance Unit, low-cost laser diode substitute for gas lasers in Navy test-bed Ordnance Unit and linearly predictive data compression hardware algorithm (DPCM). Tikisa was a past President of the Northern California Council of Black Professional Engineers (NCCBPE), a very active civic and community leader, taught in local colleges and universities and raised two wonderful children.

Kweku Andoh, Ph.D.
Ethnobotanist, Botanist, Proprietor

Ghanaian, British-educated ethnobotanist, Fellow of the Linnean Society of London and author of many books on ethnobotany and natural healing, is the son of the late J. E. Andoh, Africa's foremost botanist, and the descendant of a long line of herbalists and traditional healers. He pioneered the development of the Botanic Gardens at the Kwame Nkrumah University of Science & Technology at Kumasi, Ghana. Dr. Andoh has developed a line of natural healing products, Harbinger Herbal Nutrients, and promotes a healing paradigm, the Nebedaye Self Healing System. His herbal formulas are based on ancient and traditional remedies passed down in his family and used widely in Ghana and West Africa. Many herbal formulas are based on his vast knowledge of healing plants from around the world. As of June, 2004, Andoh completed a plant inventory project to assess the non-timber forest products available on the 660 acre training facility of the Federation of Southern Cooperatives, in the African American farm belt of Southwestern Alabama, that will lead to the development of many new market products for the Black farmers. He is the Executive Director of the North Scale Institute, an Education and Research Group in Ethno-botany and Traditional Medicine based in rural Georgia, just outside of Atlanta.

Ediang O. Archibong
Meteorology and Marine Expert

His background in applied Meteorology is from the Federal University of Technology Akure, where he also has two Post Graduate Diplomas, both in Computer Science and GIS/Remote Sensing (Africa Regional Centre for space and Science Education in English-Nigeria). He got a fellowship to study at the World Maritime University, Malmo, Sweden where he has a Master of Science in Maritime Affairs specializing in Integrated Ocean and Coastal Management. Ediang, also has a Master of Business Administration degree in Maritime Management from Concept University College London. He has publish over 30 Research Journals, Proceedings in the applications of meteorology in health, coastal and water resources, pollution, transport, energy, waste, aviation, agriculture and telecommunication, remote sensing for integrated management of ecosystems, water resources and reducing vulnerability to weather and climate extremes. He is the Secretary General of West Africa Quaternary Research Association (WAQUA). He has an Honorary Doctorate Degree Of Philosophy In Business Administration from the Cornerstone University Seminary, Jerusalem, Israel. He is presently in the Marine Division of the Nigerian Meteorological Agency where he is in charge of Research in Marine Accidents, Weather and Climate Extreme Marine events like Ocean Surges etc along the Coastline of Nigeria and West Africa.

Shem Arungu-Olende, Ph.D.
Secretary General of the African Academy of Sciences

He is Secretary-General of the African Academy of Sciences. He has a background is in electrical engineering. From 1968 to 1971, at the University of Nairobi, he conducted research on electrical power systems, their mathematical analysis, planning, design and operation. From 1971 to 2000 he was an expert on energy at the United Nations, where he provided technical advice on interconnection of power systems, bulk transfer and distribution of electricity; and on the design, rehabilitation, strengthening and operation of electricity systems in different parts of the developing countries, such as Ghana, Indonesia, Jamaica, Liberia, Namibia, Sierra Leone; prepared of reports on rural energy development as part of overall integrated rural development strategies. He is also the Chairman and CEO of QUECONSULT Ltd, which provides professional consultancy services in Engineering, Energy and Sustainable Development, Environment, Economic Development, Science and Technology, and Software Development to the U.N., UNDP, the African Development Bank, UNESCO, and the World Bank.

Modupe Fisayo Asaolu, Ph.D.
Toxicology and Clinical Biochemistry

Dr. Asaolu is an Associate Professor, Department of Biochemistry, teaching Biochemistry, Microbiology, Plant Science and Zoology. During 2008-2009, she was a Visiting Associate Professor, Department of Chemical Pathology, Obafemi Awolowo University, Nigeria. Her current research involves the use of some medicinal plants in the treatment of some diseases in Nigeria. She also researches various issues relating to conditions of pregnant women. Dr. Asaolu just completed her research on proximate analysis and phytochemical screening of the leaves and bark of *Mangifera indica*.

Moses T. Asom, Ph.D., MBA
Wireless Technology and Opto-electronics devices

Senior Vice President of Marketing, Sales and Business Development and Co-founder of SyChip Inc (Recently sold to Murata Electronics). SyChip designs and markets modules for wireless internet appliances, based on micro-system integration technology (MSIT) developed at Bell Labs. The company solution targets semiconductor segments that are difficult or too expensive to integrate monolithically (RF passives, embedded memory). Recently, Dr. Asom was a Director in the Lucent New Ventures Group overseeing photonics and semiconductor startups. He was the Marketing Manager for optoelectronics components covering Asia-Pacific and South America. Dr. Asom was also Product Manager responsible for developing optical transceivers for broadband access. He holds 3 patents (issued and pending).

Ojonigu Friday Ati, Ph.D.
Climatology/Physical and Biogeography, Remote Sensing and GIS

Dr. Ati is a Senior Lecturer in Nigeria. He has taught general and Tropical Climatology, GIS and Remote Sensing, and Cartographic Methods. He has researched on the rainfall characteristics in drought prone of the sudano-sahelian zone of Nigeria. Not only has Dr. Ati authored and co-authored publishings, he has also received several awards and his expertise has often been sought by prestigious organizations.

Donna Auguste
Software Engineering, Electrical Engineering, Renewable Energy, E- learning

Co-founder of Freshwater Software, Inc. (acquired for $147M in 2001), Ms. Auguste is an extraordinary computer scientist. In 1984, she joined Intellicorp, a Silicon Valley start-up with a vision to commercialize "expert systems", using artificial intelligence. Ms. Auguste then joined Apple computer, where she managed the elite team of programmers who helped create the industry's first PDA, Apple's pen-based/hand-held computer called the Newton. In 1996 Ms. Auguste co-founded Freshwater Software in Boulder, Colorado. Her team developed a product called SiteScope which is used by systems administrators who manage business-critical web servers. Ms. Auguste is also a devoted Catholic Christian and Gospel musician, primarily playing bass guitar. After Freshwater was acquired, Ms Auguste devoted more of her time to her non-profit Global Outreach organization, Leave a Little Room Foundation (http://www.LeaveaLittleRoom.org), installing solar electricity and building schools in African villages, and building hospitals and houses in Mexico. She does research in renewable energy and e-learning. Ms. Auguste is a graduate of the University of California at Berkeley, with a B.S. in Electrical Engineering and Computer Science, and she completed graduate studies at Carnegie Mellon University.

Osama Awadelkarim, Ph.D.
Engineering Science and Mechanics, Nanotechnology

Dr. Awadelkarim is Professor of Engineering Science and Mechanics and the Associate Director for the Center of Nanotechnology Education and Utilization at The Pennsylvania State University. He earned his B.S. in Physics from the University of Khartoum, Sudan, and his Ph.D. from Reading University in the UK. His research interests are in electronic materials, nano/microelectronics, and nano/microelectromechanical systems. Dr. Awadelkarim has authored/coauthored nearly 200 journal articles, book chapters, books, and conference proceedings. He is a recipient of Shell and the University Prizes from the Sudan, and Fellowships from the International Seminars in Physics and Chemistry (Sweden) and the International Center for Theoretical Physics (Italy). Dr. Awadelkarim worked in the Office of Public Diplomacy and Public Affairs at the Bureau of African Affairs and the Office of Science and Technology Cooperation in the Bureau of Oceans and International Environmental and Scientific Affairs. His assignment in the two offices was to promote interaction and collaboration between African, Arab, and Moslem scientists and scientists in the U.S. He presented talks and seminars at various scientific meetings and workshops in African and Islamic countries and developed a number of science and technology agreements between U.S. government agencies and their African and Islamic counterparts.

Gregory P. Bagley
Research Engineer

He designed, developed and supervised procurement or fabrication of numerous power systems and electronic controls for accelerators at the Brookhaven National Laboratory (1968-1993). These systems included a shunt regulator and other servo control systems for the Main magnet Power System and three different beam extraction pulse current supplies for the Accelerating Gradient Synchrotron, a proton accelerator. Mr. Bagley was responsible for the design, development and build of the 200 power supplies which powered the guide field magnets of the National Synchrotron Light Source, an electron storage ring. He designed and developed various systems for the building and testing of the superconducting magnets used in the Relativistic Heavy Ion Collider, a heavy ion storage ring. He also redesigned the controls of a 5KA, 50V magnet power supply to achieve a ripple output of 0.1 ppm (IEEE Trans. On Nuclear Sci., 6/83). Gregory Bagley designed and developed control systems of inertial navigation components for ship and space applications, including a battery powered inverter with an associated battery charger and server control circuitry of Pulsed Integrated Pendulum Accelerometer (PIPA) used on the Lunar Lander built by Sperry Gyroscope (1962-1968).

Shelly N. Bailey, P.E.
Civil Engineering

Mr. Bailey has approximately 50 years of civil engineering experience. He Headed the Concrete Laboratory for 11 years, where all Calif. concrete materials were evaluated. This work that led to the ASTM specifications and testing methods used in the several billion dollar California Water Project. For 10 years, he Headed California Dept. of Transportation's QC/QA Unit of the Materials and Research Laboratory. Mr. Bailey has provided engineering design services that included the installation of a 11,390 feet of 72" and 66" diameter feeder line to the Sacramento Regional Sewage Treatment Plant; one-quarter of the cable system for Sacramento Cable Television; light rail line starter systems; and cathodic protection systems. He has recertified over 160 PG&E's distribution substation's Spill Prevention Control and Countermeasure (SPCC) plans; developed a system of roof repairs for H.U.D.'s experimental housing; and provided survey and design services for several highway projects. Mr. Bailey is Co-Founder of the Northern California Council of Black Professional Engineers (NCCBPE) and two-term President; 1997-98 ASCE President, Sacramento, CA Section; and past President of the Amer. Concrete Inst. (ACI), North. Calif. Chapter. He has served as an Expert Examiner for California to register Quality Engineers.

Virgil A. Baker
Geotechnology

Virgil has more than thirty years experience in geotechnical and environmental engineering and site exploration. He has extensive knowledge and experience in the areas of in-situ testing, soil mechanics, geotechnical instrumentation, onshore and offshore site exploration, foundation engineering, deep foundations and dynamic pile driving analysis. His hands-on involvement in many onshore and offshore investigations greatly aids his clients in designing exceptional and innovative site investigation.

Olusanjo A. Bamgboye, Ph.D.
GeoScience

Dr. Bamgboye, acting executive director of the National Water Resources Institute, which is in charge of integrated water management in Nigeria. This organization has undertaken capacity building for water governance for legislators. It creates standards and models for Nigeria and the region and has the best equipped water analysis unit in the country for both physical and biological aspects.

Gaurdia Banister, R.N., Ph.D.
Executive Director and Specialist in Psychiatric Nursing

Dr. Banister is the first Exec. Dir. of the newly established Institute for Patient Care at the Massachusetts General Hospital in Boston. She is responsible for advancing the Institute's new vision for interdisciplinary education and research which is centered on a commitment to meeting or exceeding patients' needs and advancing professional practice. Dr. Banister is also co-Director of the Clinical Leadership Collaborative (CLC) to Diversity Nursing, a partnership with the University of Massachusetts, Boston that financially supports and mentors diverse nursing students in becoming registered nurses. Prior to this position, Dr. Banister was the Senior VP for Patient Care Services and Chief Nursing Officer at Providence Hospital in Washington, DC. She received the District of Columbia Nurses Association Practice Award in 1998. In 2001, Dr. Banister was selected as a Robert Wood Johnson Executive Nurse Fellow and currently serv es as an advisor for current fellows in the program. In 2006, she was selected as Johnson and Johnson Wharton Nurse Fellow. In 2009, Dr. Banister received the Distinguished Alumni award from the University of Wyoming School of Nursing and in 2010; she received the Distinguished Alumni Award from the University of Texas at Austin, School of Nursing.

Sharon J. Barnes, Ph.D.
Chemistry, NOBCChE National Secretary

Dr. Barnes is the National Secretary and local chapter President of the National Organization for Black Chemists and Chemical Engineers (NOBCChE). She has been featured in the book *"Black Stars – African American Female Scientist and Inventors"* by Dr. Otha Sullivan and appeared on two magazine covers: *SWE* (Society of Women Engineers) – *"Female Inventors"* and *Spotlight on the Golden Triangle of Texas – "Fabulous Females"*. Besides her many awards Dr. Barnes was a gubernatorial appointee to the Texas Medical Board, District Review Committee and gubernatorial appointee to the Texas Health and Human Services Council. In 2004, she was listed as one of US Black Engineer magazine's *"50 Most Important Blacks in Research Science"*.

John Barnett
Geology

Nabil H. H. Bashir, Ph.D.
Entomology, Pesticides & Toxicology

Dr. Bashir has been Head, Pesticides and Toxicology Department (1999 - 2007), Faculty of Agricultural Sciences, specializing in the metabolism of insecticides (in relation to resistance. He has taught General Entomology, Pesticides and Economic Entomology; Analytical Chemistry& Separation Techniques; Chemistry of Aromatic Compounds; Insecticides; General Toxicology; Applied Toxicology; Systemic Toxicology; Formulation & Residue Analysis; Environmental Pollution with Pesticide, and Research Methodology (for Pesticides& Toxicology Specialization, faculty of Pharmacy, faculty of Medical Laboratories). Dr. Bashir has authored several publishings (some in Arabic) and belongs to many professional organizations. Dr. Bashir areas of interests include: 1.Toxicology: *Residues*, *POPs* (Persistent Organic Pollutants) & *PTS* (Persistent Toxic Substances), Resistance to Insecticides, Mode of action, Metabolism and Fate in the Environment (soil, water, plant and animal tissues, *etc.*), Site of action, *Aflatoxins* and *Plastics*; 2. Pesticides: IPM-Compatible Compounds; Formulations, Natural Products, residues, Persistent Organic Pollutants (POPs); 3. Insect Physiology, with special emphasis on metabolism, the nervous system & endocrinology; 4. Economic Entomology: Cotton Pests; Fruit Flies of mango & cucurbits; *Agromyzidae* Leafminers & Termites, mosquitoes.

Gibor Basri, Ph.D.
Vice Chancellor for Equity and Inclusion; Astronomy

Dr. Basri is Vice Chancellor for Equity and Inclusion, UC Berkeley Campus. He is also a Professor of Astronomy at UC and was Acting Chair, Astronomy Department (2006-2007). He was Co-Investigator, Kepler Mission (NASA), a 1-meter telescope whose purpose is to detect transits caused by terrestrial planets around other stars. It will watch 100,000 stars continuously (every 15 minutes) for at least 4 years, with a photometric precision of one part in 50,000. It should see all the inner planets whose orbital planes cause eclipses for us, and also reflected light from giant inner planets. It is capable of finding "true Earth analogs" (planets with 1 Earth mass in 1 year orbits around Sun-like stars). While observing the stars, Dr. Basri also spends a lot of time helping our youut here on earth to interest them in science and math. He also served as a Board Member, Chabot Space and Science Center (1998-2007), the new incarnation of the Chabot Observatory, which has been serving Oakland since 1883. This is now a $65M facility in the Oakland Hills, with 3 telescopes (among the largest public ones), a state-of-the-art planetarium, and megadome theater. Its primary function is to enhance science education in the Bay Area, and it holds a lot of classes, teacher training, and other educational functions. It also has some exhibits, aimed at using Astronomy as the gateway to Science.

Harry S. Bass, Jr., Ph.D.
Biology

Dr. Harry Bass is currently a tenured Associate Professor of Biology in the Department of Natural Sciences at Virginia Union University. He has served as Chairperson of the Department of Natural Sciences for fourteen years and Head of the Division of Natural Sciences and Mathematics for five years at Virginia Union University. In these capacities, he assisted the University in securing numerous external grants to improve the curriculum in the sciences and to provide research opportunities for the faculty. Dr. Bass has been able to recruit outstanding faculty, building a strong academic department in the Natural Sciences at Virginia Union University. Under his direction the department of six faculty members has raised over eleven million dollars in funds from either federal agencies or private foundations. These monies were used to improve the science curriculum, provide fellowships for faculty and students, and purchase state-of-the-art equipment for biotechnologically oriented laboratory experiments. As a result of his efforts as chairperson, the number of majors increased, retention of students improved, and graduation rate of biology and chemistry majors doubled. His teaching specialties include Parasitology, Cell Biology, Histology, Research Techniques and Research. Dr Bass' research includes Enzyme purification and histochemistry of larval parasites. (trematodes).

Clayton W. Bates, Jr., Ph.D.
Material Science, Electrical Engineering, Physics

Dr. Bates worked for several engineering and scientific companies including Varian Associates, AVCO, Sylvania Electric Products, the Ford Instrument Company and RCA. He worked on projects ranging from low-level light detection and x-ray image intensification to the design of the nuclear reactor controls of the first SEA WOLF, the second atomic powered submarine. In 1972, Bates left Varian and accepted a position in Stanford University's Materials Science and Engineering and Electrical Department. He continued to work at Stanford for the next twenty-two years, where he helped to organize the Society of Black Scientists and Engineers. In 1994, he accepted the position of Associate Dean for Graduate Education and Research at Howard University's College of Engineering, Architecture and Computer Sciences Bates has been committed to increasing the number of African Americans in the science and engineering fields and the number of scientific research projects at predominately Black colleges and universities.

Gerald Bauldock
Chemical Engineering

With 23 years in the chemical industry, Gerald decided to start his own company, B-dock Educational Products. What started out as a desire to teach his sons chemistry, has turned into a growing company that is developing numerous products and services. At present, his products consist of books, a game, posters, a CD and math products. They are providing several services, Kids for Chemistry workshops, Chemistry Concepts for Operators and Technicians and Kids for Chemistry Clubs -- all are designed to make learning chemistry and math easier. Kids for Chemistry I teaches the first 20 atoms on the periodic table, ions, acids and bases, oxidation and reduction, organic chemistry and electrochemistry. Kids for Chemistry II takes you up to hydrogen fuel cells and is a work in progress. The Kids for Chemistry series is an ever growing work in progress. Gerald Jr. and Justin have been the motivating factor for the development of Kids for Chemistry. They are proof that young children can learn the chemistry concepts that are provided in the program and are dedicated to sharing that knowledge with others. Along with lecturing about chemistry to students of all ages, Gerald and Justin (and eventually Jacob) have been learning the ins and outs of running a business. They are actively involved in the production of our products and services.

Dankyi Augustine Beeko, M.D.
Consultant Neurosurgeon

He received a scholarship by the German Academic Exchange to study medicine, at the John Gutenberg University in Mainz, Germany in 1965 and earned his Degree in Medicine in 1971. After the required one year internship, he worked four years in General Surgery, before embarking on Neurosurgical Training which he finished at the Heinrich Heine Medical Academy in Duesseldorf, Germany. The King Fahd Specialist Hospital in Jeddah, Saudi Arabia enrolled me to set-up a Neurosurgical Center, in 1984. I remained in this position until July, 2003. Then he returned to Ghana, and was instrumental in setting up the Neurosurgical Center of the Komfo Anokye Teaching Hospital in Kumasi, in the Ashanti Region. Since 2008, he has been in private practice in Kumasi, and to some extent in Accra. Throughout the years, he has presented some twenty-eight scientific papers at international as well as local conferences in Neurosurgery. His interest has been in Pediatric Neurosurgery, Neuro-traumatology, and transplantation Surgery. He is a columnist with the Ghanaian Chronicle, where on weekly basis he writes about Science, Neurosurgery, as well as medicine in General.

Carl C. Bell, M.D.
Psychiatry

Dr. Bell is President & C.E.O. - Community Mental Health Council (CMHC) & Foundation, Inc. in Chicago. CMHC is a large multi-million comprehensive community mental health center, employing 200 social service geniuses. Dr. Bell is also Clinical Professor of Psychiatry & Public Health, and Director of the Institute for Juvenile Research (IJR) - University of Illinois at Chicago (UIC). He serves on the National Mental Health Advisory Council of the National Institute of Mental Health. During 40 years, he has published more than 450 articles, chapters, & books on mental health and authored The Sanity of Survival. He has been interviewed by Ebony; Jet; Essence; Emerge; New York Times; Chicago Tribune Magazine; People Magazine; Chicago Reporter; "Nightline"; ABC News; NPR; "CBS Sunday Morning"; The News Hour with Jim Lehrer; the Tom Joyner Morning Show; Chicago Tonight; & the "Today" show. A 1967 graduate of UIC, he earned his MD from Meharry College in Nashville, Tennessee in 1971. He completed his psychiatric residency in 1974 at the Illinois State Psychiatric Institute/Institute for Juvenile Research in Chicago.

Adolfo O'Biang Biko, Ph.D.
Civil Engineering

Born in Igombegombe, Rio Benito (Rio Muni), Equatorial Guinea; Dr. Biko earned his university education in the United States, with advanced degrees in civil engineering & mathematics. He worked as a structural engineer with a private engineering firm; computer graphics designer with N.Y. C. Department of Environmental Protection, and taught mathematics at Saint St. Francis College and New York City College of Technology (formerly New York City Technical College) of the City University of New York. Dr. Biko is fluent in Spanish, English, French, Portuguese, Fang & Lingala. He has written three books: his first book, "Fernando Poo, the Myth of Spanish Colonialism", was written in Spanish. His second book, "Equatorial Guinea: from Spanish Colonialism to the Discovery of Oil", was written in English and translated into Spanish and French. His third book, "Naked Like the Others, in Prison in Gabon, Africa" was written in English and translated into French.

Lawal S. Bilbis, Ph.D.
Biochemistry

Dr. Bilbis is a Professor of Biochemistry at Usmanu Danfodiyo University, of which he was Dean of this department from 2003-2007. He is President Nigerian Society of Biochemistry and Molecular Biology. Earlier in his career (1987-88), he was Head of the Chemical Pathology Department of General Hospital, Gusau and Head of the Biochemistry unit at General Hospital, Katsina (1986-87). Dr. Bilbis is Editor-in Chief of *Nigerian Journal of Basic and Applied Sciences*. He has authored and co-authored more than 60 technical publishings.

Harriette Howard-Lee Block, Ph.D.
Molecular Biology

Dr. Block is the Department Head of Biology at Prairie View A&M University and Program Coordinator for Curriculum Development Award. In 2008, she was a proposal reviewer for the Environmental Protection Agency STAR/GRO Research Program in Washington, DC. She was funded to develop the "Center for Microbial and Cardiovascular Studies" at Prairie View A&M University. In 1981, Dr. Block earned her Ph.D. from Atlanta University in Molecular Biology.

Damase Bodzongo, M.D.
Director General of Health, Thorasic Surgeon

Dr. Bodzongo is second in command of the Ministry of Health, serving in a non-politically appointed position. He also serves as Chair of his country's foremost University School of Medicine. Through his many hours of hard work, he still finds time to speak out about the need for a better healthcare delivery system.

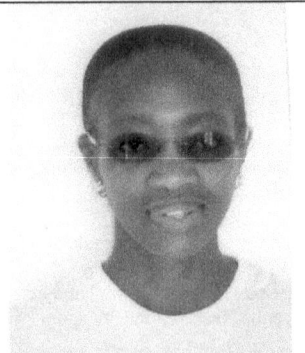

Ntseliseng Bohloko, Ph.D.
Pharmacy

Dr. Bohloko is a Manufacturing Optimisation Specialist. In this capacity, she provides input on working formula and generation of method of manufacture for new and transferred products; generate validation protocols and reports; and evaluate analytical laboratory results generated during execution of validation processes. Her experiences have included working as a Production Pharmacist, serving with her country's Drug Regulatory Authority, and being a Pharmacist while serving as Head of a Pharmacy Dept. Dr. Bohloko also served as a pharmaceutical sector expert (UNIDO project on strengthening of local production of essential generic drugs in least developed countries - LCDs - through the promotion of SMEs, business partnership, investment promotion and South-South Cooperation).

Hamilton V. Bowser, Sr., P.E.
Civil Engineering, Construction Co. Executive

Founded in 1968, of one of the largest black-owned general construction contracting, construction management and engineering design-build firms in the U.S. and provided engineering services as Bowser Engineers and Associates. Mr. Bowser is a national spokesman on minorities in construction and procurement issues. Past President of the National Association of Minority Contractors, he received the U.S. Commerce Department's National Advocacy Award for small and minority business development. His completed projects have included manufacturing facilities, commercial offices, hospital and laboratory, multi-family residential buildings, water treatment plant and chemical plant contracts. His company has provided construction management services for a $570 million dollar sewage treatment plant; 3,500 car garage; 2,400 bed prison; churches, recreation facilities and high rise apartments. Prior to 1968, Mr. Bowser was a structural and project engineer for a large New Jersey consulting firm, where he advanced to Vice President, Engineering. He is a licensed Professional Engineer in several states. With his brother Edward, R.A., he designed radiant heated chick hatcheries in Ghana that increased chick survival from 40% to above 90%. Mr. Bowser has more than 25 years of alternate dispute resolution experience as an Arbitrator with the panel that arbitrates claims up $10,000,000.

Christopher S. Boxe, Ph.D.
Environmental Science and Engineering

His interdisciplinary focus is on regional and global biochemical and physical evolution of planets on geological and shorter timescales by modeling, laboratory, and remote sensing techniques. Dr. Boxe serves on the African American Resource Team (AART) at NASA's Jet Propulsion Laboratory, contributing to JPL's Diversity Programs Initiative, which seeks to foster an inclusive environment, where the differences and similarities of individuals are valued and respected, ensuring full utilization of the talents and capabilities a diverse workforce. On a voluntary basis he gives scientific presentations basis to elementary schools and professional organizations about his work. Dr. Boxe works on collaborative practical science projects and field trips with a multitude of select elementary, junior high, and high schools in Los Angeles with the main goal of gearing underrepresented peoples towards the hard sciences (*i.e.*, with a special emphasis on Earth and Space Sciences).

Clarence A. Boyd, Jr., M.D.
Orthopedic Surgeon

Dr. Boyd not only practices as an Orthopaedic Surgeon, he first graduated as an Electrical Engineer in 1973. He earned his Medical Degree from the **University of Michigan (Ann Arbor)** in 1977. He completed his Internship in 1978 and Residency in General Surgery in 1979 and his Residency in Orthopaedic Surgery in 1982 from **University of California in San Francisco (UCSF)**. Dr. Boyd now serves at Eden Medical Center in Castro Valley, CA, where he is also on the Trauma Mortality & Morbidity, Surgery and Infection Control Committees. His professional interests include Orthopaedic Trauma and Computer Science Application to Medicine. His Additional Interests includes being the Co-Owner and Chief Programmer for Atrium Medical Software. While he has accomplished a lot professionally, Dr. Boyd is an excellent family man and works hard in his education district as an advocate for his and our children.

Adenike Omotunde Boyo, Ph.D.
Physics

Dr. Boyo is a Physicist teaches Classical Mechanics, Optics, Electronics, Heat and Thermodynamics, Solid State Physics, Electricity and Magnetism, Solar Energy Physics, Environmental Physics, and Materials Science. Her research has included construction and analysis of Solar Still, Solar Dryer, Solar Hot Water Heater and Cookers; Electrical Properties of Iron Clay Composite Resistors; Solar Electrification of Rural Villages; Thermodynamics properties of Binary Alloys; and Thermodynamics properties of Ternary Alloys.

Haruna Braimah, Ph.D.
Crop Pest Management/Biological Control

Dr. Braimah is a Senior Scientific Officer, (Pest Management/Biological Control), Head of Biological Control Unit. CSIR-Crops Research Institute, Kumasi Ghana. He has worked on the development and use of biologically based pest management strategies for pest management in Ghana and provide technical backstopping to the Plant Protection and Regulatory Services Directorate (PPRSD) of Ministry of Food and Agriculture (MOFA) in the areas of pest management and Pest Risk Assessment (PRAs). Dr. Braimah has a wide range of experiences dealing with crop pest management, some of which include times when he served as Team Leader of Horticulture Export Industry Initiative (HEII) Mango group, researching into mango development and pest management and developing extension materials for the guidance of farmers (2005 -2008); Team Leader, AgSSIP IPM project on Banana weevil, Cosmopolites sordidus (2004 -2007).

Robert "Pete" Bragg, Ph.D.
Univ. Prof. Emeritus, Material Scientist, Physicist

When someone says"carbon", what do you think of? Coal, right? Or maybe diamonds. But when the nose cone of a space shuttle withstands heat and impact upon reentry into the earth's atmosphere, that's carbon, too. When you enjoy the resilience of a graphite tennis racquet or the purity of water filtered by some new system, you may gain insight into the applications of Dr.Robert H. Bragg's forty-plus years of research on the structure and physical properties of carbon. In his research in x-ray diffraction and small angle x-ray scattering techniques, he collaborated with scientists in several laboratories in the U.S., as well as in Japan, France, Germany, Algeria, and Nigeria. Prior to joining academia, Dr. Bragg was a manager of research in metallurgy at the Research and Development Laboratory of the Lockheed Missiles and Space Company, Palo Alto, California. He was responsible for research activity in solidification, metallurgical composites, mechanical and thermophysical properties of refractory compounds, phase diagrams determinations, as well as research in the metallographic, x-ray diffraction, and electron microscope laboratories. Dr. Bragg was a Fullbright Scholar at Olafemi Awolowo University, Ife, Nigeria (1993-4). He also worked with the Collaborative Access Team at the Advanced Photon Source, Argonne National Lab (Fall, 2000).

Albert Bridgewater, Ph.D.
Particle Physics

A retired member of the Senior Executive Service, National Science Foundation (NSF), where his experiences included managerial, budget and science policy/planning responsibilities for hundreds of millions of dollars of physics, astronomy, atmospheric sciences, earth sciences, oceanography, Arctic and Antarctic research and human resources development. He served NSF as Acting Assistant Director, Deputy Assistant Director, Executive Assistant and Acting Program Manager. Dr. Bridgewater's experience includes being a Peace Corps volunteer in Cameroon, and the developer of many special projects supporting minority participation in science, engineering and mathematics, including: Former member of the Advisory Board of the Ana G. Méndez Educational Foundation, Jackson State University and Lawrence Berkeley Laboratory Science Consortium; Involved in development and management of Research Careers for Minority Scholars, Alliance for Minority Participation, Model Institutions for Excellence (MIE), and Collaboratives to Integrate Research and Education (CIRE); Involved in developing Together We Can Make It Work: An Action Plan to Provide Quality Education for Minorities in Mathematics, Science and Engineering; and Recipient of NSF grant to prepare Tribal Colleges and Universities to submit Major Research Instrumentation proposals.

Randolph W. Bromery, Ph.D.
Geophysics Professor Emeritus, Former Chancellor

Dr. Randolph W. Bromery is former Chancellor of the University of Massachusetts at Amherst. He served with the all-black unit of the U.S. Army Air Corps, Tuskegee Airmen during World War II. After the war, he earned his bachelor's degree in mathematics and physics from Howard University. From 1948 to 1967, Dr. Bromery was employed as an airborne exploration geophysicist while earning master's and doctoral degrees part-time and at night. In 1969, he accepted a faculty position at the University of Massachusetts in Amherst. He became department chair in 1969 and then moved up to Vice Chancellor for student affairs in 1970 and Chancellor in 1971 He recently completed nearly 55 years in higher education and government service, having previously served as president of Springfield College, Chancellor of the Board of Regents for Higher Education under Governors Dukakis and Weld, and as president of Westfield State College. He has been re-appointed by President Bush to a three-year term on the President's Committee on the National Medal of Science. He has honorary doctorates and eight others from around the world. He was named Outstanding Black Scientist by the National Academy of Sciences and received a Distinguished Service Award from the Geological Society of America of which he is a former President.

Delroy Brown
Biology, Nutrition Research

William T. Brown, Ph.D.
Physics

Dr. William Brown is a Principal Scientist with a research organization where he has worked since 1992, serving as a Senior Scientist and Group Leader. Prior to this position, he was a Senior Member of the Technical Staff at Sandia National Laboratories where he conducted research in diverse areas, including piezoelectricity and ferroelectricity. Dr. Brown has more than 30 years experience in diverse areas of applied science and project management. He has expertise in the formulation of high pressure equations of state and constitutive models, and in computational physics. He is a recognized expert in fracture generated field emissions (Fracto-emissions). Dr. Brown has also authored or co-authored more than 80 journal articles, conference proceedings, and reports. He is member of the American Physical Society (APS), and of the APS Topical Group on Computational Physics and the Topical Group on Shock Propagation in Condensed Matter. He has previously served on the Board of Directors of the National Technical Association and the National Consortium for Black Professional Development.

Lee F. Browne
Science Educator Emeritus, Chemist

Dr. Browne was born and raised in North Carolina, and educated in schools in West Virginia, including West Virginia State College (BS, 1944) and at Syracuse University (MS, 1960). After moving to Pasadena he taught chemistry at Muir and Blair High Schools for many years, he was recruited to Caltech in 1971 to serve as Director of Caltech Secondary Schools Relations Office, CalTech, CA, assisting to identify and bring local students, including minorities, to Caltech. Lee Browne was always at Caltech in one way or another. He often came to the school's lecture series and taught the children of the faculty. In fact, Lee Browne and his wife were the only two African Americans in the audience when Dr. Martin King, Jr. came to speak at Caltech on February 25, 1958. Lee felt that something needed to be done about the lack of cultural awareness at the institute. He helped to create the Student Support Program (SSP) which was designed to help underrepresented students to survive at Caltech. For six weeks before the school year began, about ten students, who were selected from the freshman class, attended an intense program in mathematics, physics, chemistry, and English. Over the years, the SSP proved to be very effective. Whereas only 17% of all incoming underrepresented students were graduated from Caltech, 58% of all underrepresented students that attended the program graduated.

Aaron L. Brundage, Ph.D.
Mechanical Engineering, Nanoscale & Reactive Processes

Dr. Aaron L. Brundage is an engineering scientist at Sandia National Laboratories where the scope of his work covers research, development, and application. These activities include the following: computational modeling and code development, energetics and microenergetics modeling, atomistic scale energetics modeling, thermal analysis and model-based quantification of margins and uncertainty. He is also an Adjunct Professor of Mechanical Engineering at the University of New Mexico. He received a B.S. and M.S. in Mechanical Engineering from The Pennsylvania State University and his Ph.D. in Mechanical Engineering from Purdue University. While at Purdue, he conducted research in gas turbine heat transfer and fluid mechanics.

Herbert L. Byrd, Jr.
IT Management

Lisa Cain, Ph.D.
Neuroscience and Cell Biology

Dr. Cain earned a doctoral degree in anatomy from the University of Mississippi Medical Center, from which she was the first African American female to receive a Ph.D. from the Anatomy Dept. At Robert Wood Johnson Medical School she was a postdoctoral fellow in the Dept. of Anatomy from 1989-90 and was a postdoctoral fellow in the Center for Advanced Biotechnology and Medicine from 1990-1992. Dr. Cain is an Assoc. Professor in the Dept. of Neurosciences and Cell Biology, where she teaches medical and graduate students. She is the Minority Afairs Representative for UTMB Galveston to the Association of American Medical Colleges and the Director of the Medical School Enrichment Programs. She served as Vice Chair of the Curriculum Committee of the School of Medicine from 2006-2008, and is presently Director of the Cell Biology Course, an Osler Student Society Mentor, and Vice President of the Minority Faculty Administrative Professional Council. Dr. Cain is a neuroscientist whose research has involved investigating agents that protect spinal cord neurons against the effect of glutamate toxicity and other insults. She is a 2007 graduate of the Scholars is Education Program, designed to develop leaders in the area of medical education. She is also a folk artist whose work is presently exhibited at several galleries throughout the U.S. and has been exhibited in New York, City.

Kevin Canada, P.E.
Civil Engineering

Kevin Canada, a ret'd supervising administrative engineer, has been practicing civil engineering, project management, and construction management for 30+ years.

George R. Carruthers, Ph.D.
Astrophysics

Dr. Carruthers held a position of Rocket Astronomy Research Physicist from 1964 to 1982. An inventor as well as physicist, he was instrumental in the design of lunar surface ultraviolet cameras, using the color spectrum of substances to detect their constituent parts. In 1969, he patented an image converter for detecting far ultraviolet electromagnetic radiation, which was first used in sounding rocket flights, including one in 1970 which made the first detection of molecular hydrogen in interstellar space. He then invented the Far Ultraviolet Camera/Spectrograph, a device which would examine both the Earth's upper atmosphere and deep space from a location that would avoid the distortions created by Earth absorption of ultraviolet radiation. By 1972, Dr. Carruthers's camera/spectrograph was constructed. Cdr. John W. Young carried the device aboard the Apollo 16 mission and placed it on the surface of the moon. Over 200 pictures of the Earth's atmosphere and geocorona, as well as of the Milky Way and deep space, were taken from this observatory. He also invented photometry ultraviolet cameras and spectrographs for rockets and satellites, several electronic imaging devices and other detectors for space astronomy and upper atmosphere physics research. In 1986, one two of Carruthers' inventions instruments captured an ultraviolet images and spectra of Halley's Comet.

Benjamin S. Carson, Sr., M.D.
Pediatric Neurosurgery

Dr. Carson is director of the division of pediatric neurosurgery and a professor of neurosurgery, oncology, plastic surgery, and pediatrics at the Johns Hopkins Medical Institutions. In 1987, Carson made medical history with an operation to separate a pair of Siamese twins. The Binder twins were born joined at the back of the head. Dr. Carson agreed to undertake the operation. A 70-member surgical team, led by Dr. Carson, worked for 22 hours. At the end, the twins were successfully separated and now survive independently. Carson's other surgical innovations included the first intra-uterine procedure to relieve pressure on the brain of a hydrocephalic fetal twin, and a hemispherectomy, in which an infant suffering from uncontrollable seizures has half of its brain removed. His special interests involve craniofacial reconstructive surgery, neuro-oncology (brain tumors), skeletal dysplasia, seizure surgery, and on the adult side, trigeminal neuralgia. Dr. Carson holds numerous honors and awards, including more than 40 honorary doctorate degrees. His three books, *Gifted Hands, THINK BIG*, and *The Big Picture* provide inspiration and insight for leading a successful life. Dr. Carson has been married for over 30 years to his wife, Candy, and is the father of three sons. And yes, his mother, Sonya Carson, who made all this possible, is alive and well.

Hattie Carwell, Ed.D.
Health Physics

Hattie Carwell is a retired health physicist and head of operations at one of DOE's site offices. From 1980-1985 she worked as an inspector/group leader for the Int'l Atomic Energy Agency. She earned a Bachelors of Science degree in Chemistry and Biology from Bennett College and a Master's degree in Health Physics from Rutgers University. Hattie is co-founder and Chairperson of the Development Fund for Blacks in Science and Technology. She has authored the several books, *"Blacks in Science - Astrophysicist to Zoologist", In pursuit of Excellence: Dr. Warren Henry World Class Scientist*, and *African American Achievements in Air and Space*. She is the Immediate Past President of the Northern Calif. Council of Black Professional Engineers. Hattie is the President Director and co-founder of the Museum of African Americans in Technology (MAAT) Science Village. She is the 2010 President of the National Technical Association (NTA).

Les E. Casher, Ph.D., F.R.E.S.
Medical Entomologist

Dr. Casher teaches and did lab and field research on Lyme disease (UC at Berkeley as a UC President's Fellow and Staff Research Assoc. - 1987-1997). He has research interest in entomological medicines. He has published papers in refereed journals on: i) acquiring, maintaining and transmission of the Lyme disease spirochetes; and on ii) plant-insect interactions in the USA and in West Africa. Dr. Casher was Asst. Professor of Biology at Cuttington University, Liberia, West Africa (1975-1982), where he did research and published on the host and parasitoids of Mylothris spp. (Pieridae). He was sponsored by UNESCO's International Cell Research Organization (ICRO) to study "*Development and Gene Expression in Drosophila melanogaster*" at Tata Institute of Fundamental Research (in Bombay, India); and sponsored by the Commonwealth Institute of Entomology (CIE) to study "*Applied Taxonomy of Insects and Mites of Agricultural Importance*" (in London, England). He worked several years in the states of Guanajuato & Michoacan (Mexico) as Project Director with the Conference on Inter-American Student Projects (CIASP). He works as an Asst. Technology Specialist at the very first *Center for Independent Living* (CIL), which provides services for people with disabilities; and also with the *Upward Bound Program* which assists disadvantaged H.S. students prepare for college.

Gilbert B. Chapman II, Ph.D.
Physicist, automotive materials and product specialist

Gil worked as a senior manager, senior specialist, project engineer and senior research engineer in advanced materials and materials characterization at two automotive manufacturers and NASA. This provided an extensive background of challenging assignments in research, development, and engineering. His specialties include specifying and selecting automotive materials and processes, nondestructive evaluation (NDE), emission spectrochemical analysis, high-energy fuels, supersonic propulsion, artificial intelligence, composites quality, the implementation of technical innovations in manufacturing systems, processes and products, as well as managing four testing laboratories, part-time college teaching and the establishment and management of several cross-functional teams. Before employment in the automotive industry, he was employed at NASA in a wide range of R&D assignments, such as developing computer automated emission spectrochemical analysis methods, supersonic propulsion and high-energy fuels. Gil's work has resulted in US patents, 56 publications and 110 conference presentations on subjects in which he specialized. Gil has BS, MS, MBA and Ph.D. degrees, and has been elected a Fellow in two technical societies. His list of 34 awards include the 2002 MKL Professor of Physics at Wayne State University and Black Engineer of the Year in 1999.

Lee O. Cherry
Executive Director, African Scientific Institute; Engrg.; Proj. Mgmt.

Co-founded Science and Technolgy based organization in 1967 as an outgrowth of distinctive African American efforts to enhance their images and our interests in scientific and technical areas. He has worked as an electric power distribution design engineer for a large utility company, a project manager of over $1 billion of projects, and curently works as an environmental engineer. Projects managed includes concepts, designs, and construction of hospitals; hyperbaric facilities; HEMP, Tempest, and SCIF facilities; missile research and test facilities, physical security projects; flight simulation facilities; antenna projects; aircraft hangars. He also developed "Blacks In Science Calendar", published "Technology Transfer" magazine and "SciTech" newspaper. He is Co-Founder of the Northern California Council of Black Professional Engineers (NCCBPE) and its 2006 President.

Bwire Chirangi, MSc, MPH
Medical Superintendent - Designated District Hospital & Public Health Specialist

Since 2004, Bwire Chirangi has offered diverse health services as a general Medical Practitioner in Tanzania at the Rorya Designated District Hospital (*Shirati KMT Hospital*) to both outpatient and inpatients, including counseling and care for People living with HIV/ AIDS. He is a renowned Doctor who travels from house to house treating the Elderly, Orphans of HIV and those who cannot afford attending to the Hospital due to economical and or physical disabilities. He is also a Board Member of *African Immigrants'& Social Services* (USA), which runs essential developmental projects including a Vocational School, in Tanzania. Experienced in strategic Management in Tropical Medicine and Public Health, Dr.Chirangi has been actively involved in planning, managing and continuous quality assessment of Health and Community Development Projects in Tanzania such as the *JUA Project* for Integrated Health care; a non-profit Bethsaida Health Centre with Home Based Care Initiative; *Jamii- Imara- CBHPP-* on Reproductive Health Outreach Services; Youth games and Sport (*Kabwana Soccer Team*). He is the founder and Facilitator to the Memorandum of Understanding with Shirati Hospital for Senior Medical Students from Maastricht University of the Netherlands (Elective practicum).

Bernard E. Chove, Ph.D.
Food Science and Processing

Dr. Chove is Head of Department, Department of Food Science and Technology at Sokoine University of Agriculture, Tanzania, where he is also Associate Professor, teaching Food Science and Engineering and Processing. Over the years, he has performed research with others as a team member on projects as "Development of appropriate interventions to enhance livestock, meat marketing, preservation and consumption in rural areas of the Eastern zone of Tanzania"; "Development of low-cost technology for processing fish waste from Lake Victoria. A regional project (Lake Victoria Research Initiative -VicRes)"; "Enterprise Development in Solar dehydration of Fruits and Vegetables for youth employment creation"; "Enhancing Child Nutrition and Livelihoods of Rural Households in Malawi and Tanzania through Post-Harvest Value-Chain Technology Improvements in Groundnuts".

Yvonne Y. Clark, P.E.
Professor, Mechanical Engineering

In 1947, Mrs. Clark was accepted at the University of Louisville but was not allowed to attend because of her race. Instead, the State of Kentucky paid her tuition to attend Howard University. She was the first woman to graduate from Howard University's Mechanical Engineering Program and to be hired at Ford Motor Company's Glass Plant, Nashville, TN, and first African American woman to earn the Master of Science Degree from Vanderbilt University's Engineering Management Program. In 1952, Mrs. Clark became the first African American member of the Society of Women Engineers (SWE). In 1956, she became the first woman engineer ever hired as an Instructor at Tennessee State University in the Mechanical Engineering Dept. She has been a faculty member since 1956, Head of Mechanical Engineering, and now Assoc. Prof., after 50 years!! Her research projects, funded by the Department of Energy, include "Energy Usage Monitoring of Residential and Commercial Structures" (1984 - 1987) and "Experimental Evaluation of the Performance of Alternative Refrigerants in Heat Pump Cycles" (1987 - 1996). She has been Director of NASA's National Aerospace Fellowship Program. At TSU, Yvonne has chartered student chapters for ASME, SWE, ASRAE, pi Tau Sigma National Mechanical Honorary chapter. She is a TSU link of the "Order of the Engineer".

Xernona Clayton
President and CEO, Trumpet Awards Foundation

Xernona is President and CEO of Trumpet Awards Foundation. Previously, she was Assistant Corporate Vice President for Urban Affairs with CNN, where she served as liaison between the corporation and civic groups across the country. She exemplifies the level one can achieve in electronic communications and communications technology. While not directly tied to the physical areas of communication technology, Ms. Clayton represents what is required to bring communications into the office place and our homes. She was the nationally-acclaimed host of The Xernona Clayton Show, a regular feature on WAGA-TV, CBS affiliate in Atlanta. Beginning her broadcast in 1967; she became the South's first Black person to have her own television show. In 1966, she coordinated the activities of Atlanta's Black Doctors in a project called "Doctors' Committee for Implementation", which resulted in the desegregation of all hospital facilities in Atlanta. This project served as a model and pilot for other states throughout the country, resulting in her receiving a national honor from the National Medical Association for its impact. She serves on the Boards of the Martin Luther King Center, Atlanta Urban League, and Southwest Community Hospital. She is also a member of the National Issues Forum of the Jimmy Carter Presidential Library.

Milton L. Cofield, Ph.D.
Chemistry

Cofield was a member of the research staff of the Eastman Kodak Company where the focus of his work was magnetism and magnetic resonance spectroscopy. His work centered on the structure and color of photographic dyes and the properties of thin magnetic films. Later he became professor of photographic technology management at the Rochester Institute of Technology where his interests were focused on imaging and graphic communications services, marketing and technology management. He was named a Fulbright Scholar in the Graduate Institute of Innovation and Technology Management at National Chengchi University of Taiwan in 2001. He is currently on the faculty of the Tepper School of Business at Carnegie Mellon University where he maintains his interest in technology management and entrepreneurship.

Timothy W. Conner, Ph.D.
Plant Genomics

Dr. Conner was a postdoctoral research fellow at the University of Georgia in the Botany Department until 1990 when he accepted the position as Senior Research Biologist at Monsanto Company in the Plant Gene Expression Group, part of the Corporate Research's R&D in the New Products Division.. Since 1990, Conner has been involved in a number of research and development projects as a research scientist, project leader, program and team leader, and director for gene discovery and expression, and structural and functional genomics. Throughout his career, he has worked on a number of agronomic, quality, and enabling technology projects covering a variety of crops including corn, and soybean. He was more recently Vice President of Oilseeds and Food Technology where his division was responsible for.strategy, project advancement, technology portfolio management through product launch of many biotech products. Currently, Conner is Vice President and Technology Lead for Latin America. Conner sees advances in biotechnology and genetic engineering as the only realistic solution for a majority of the food and environmental issues that man will face.

Edward S. Cooper, M.D.
Medicine

In 1992, Dr. Cooper, became the first Black President of the American Heart Association (AHA). He has now been retired for 15 years. Early in his medical career, Dr. Cooper served as chief of medical services for the U.S. Air Force Hospital in the Philippine Islands. He also served as president and chief of medical services at the former Philadelphia General Hospital, and as co-director of the hospital's Stroke Research Center. Dr. Cooper eventually joined the medical staff of the University of Pennsylvania Medical School in 1958. In 1972, Dr. Cooper became the university's first Black tenured medical professor. He has been an active member in many professional organizations and was founding member and chaired the executive committee of the American Health Education for African Development and the American Foundation of Negro Affairs. A native of Columbia, S.C., Dr. Cooper comes from a family of medical specialists. "In the South, there were usually teacher families, minister families, or in our case, doctor families," he says. Cooper's father, the late H.H. Cooper St., was a dentist, so are his two brothers. His late wife, Jean Wilder Cooper, was a retired physician for the School District of Philadelphia, and their children have followed the family tradition. The Coopers' oldest daughter, Lisa, is a pediatrician; daughter Jan is an endocrinologist, and their son, Charles, is a clinical psychologist.

George Cooper, Ph.D.
Chemistry

George Cooper is a Research Scientist at NASA-Ames Research Center. Since 1998 he has been a Principal Investigator doing research on molecular and stable isotope analysis of meteoritic organic compounds to determine their cosmochemical origins. He has co-authored articles published in a number of journals, including Science and Nature. From 1995-1998 he was a Principal Investigator at the SETI Institute, and from 1993-1995 he was a National Research Council (NRC) Postdoctoral Fellow within the Exobiology Branch of NASA-Ames Research Center. He received his Ph.D. in chemistry from Arizona State University in 1993. Dr. Cooper is interested in exploring areas in which a chemistry background may contribute to improving scientific infrastructure in developing countries (initially in Africa) to promote sustainable development.

Lois Louise Cooper, P.E.
Civil and Transportation Engineering

After working 38-1/2 years at the California Department of Transportation (Caltrans), Ms. Cooper retired. She was the first Black women hired in the engineering field for the Division of Highways (currently Caltrans) in Los Angeles. She is the first African American woman in California to earn her Professional Engineers License in Civil Engineering in 1978. Lois is also a Fellow in the SWE. When Lois retired, she was a Project Manager in the Project Development Services Branch of Caltrans, responsible for the oversight of many of the consultant projects in the Los Angeles/ Ventura County areas. Prior to this position, Lois had been a Project Manager for a portion of the Glenn Anderson (I-105) (Century) Freeway and the liaison between Caltrans and the Los Angeles County Transportation Commission (currently MTA), the Agency who constructed the Light Rail System in the median of the I-105 freeway. She has participated in the design of many of the freeways in Los Angeles and Orange County areas, such as the San Diego freeway, the Long Beach Freeway, the San Gabriel River Freeway and the Riverside Freeway. Lois joined the Los Angeles Council of Black Professional Engineers (LACBPE) in 1971, in which she served as the President, Vice President, Secretary and Treasurer from 1973-1976.

Walter Cooper, Ph.D.
Chemist, State University Regent Emeritus

Regent Emeritus of NY area comprised of the counties of Cayuga, Livingston, Monroe, Ontario, Seneca, Steuben, Wayne and Yates. He began his career as a research chemist at Eastman Kodak's Research Laboratories in 1956. He was promoted to Senior Research Chemist in 1961, Research Associate in 1966, and to the rank of Technical Staff Associate in 1981. Afterwards, Regent Cooper was appointed Manager of the Office of Technical Communications at Kodak's Research Laboratories in 1985. In this position, he was responsible for the supervision of the publications and technical reports of 2,300 Eastman Kodak scientific and research personnel. Additionally, Dr. Cooper managed a special Office of (research) Innovation. Dr. Cooper has published papers in the fields of physical chemistry and the chemistry of photographic film and is the holder of three patents. He retired from Eastman Kodak in 1986. Besides holding numerous honors and awards, writing in several technical journals, and belonging to several professional organizations, Regent Cooper has a life-long volunteer service to the Rochester community, which includes that of Associate Director of the Rochester and Monroe County Anti-Poverty program, a founding member of the Rochester Urban League, Rochester Area Foundation, and the Genesee Regional Health Service Agency.

Mildred Crear, RN, MPH
Nursing, Maternal & Clild Care

Retired Director of Maternal and Child Health (MCH), Mildred began her 41 years of service to DPH in 1963 as a public health nurse. Through her visionary leadership, several programs evolved that improved the health of diverse populations in San Francisco, including Family Planning, Black Infant Health, Fetal Infant Mortality Review, Child Care Health Consultant Program, and the Universal Home Visiting Program that offers every new mother a home visit from a public health nurse. Under Mildred's direction, Nutrition Services have also improved the health of women, infants, children and families. As Director, she created new programs to outreach to pregnant women and their children; programs placing public health nurses in child care programs and Foster care programs. Ms. Crear continues to work in the healthcare arena organizing community health screenings to reduce the health disparities in the African American Community.

Frank Alphonso Crossley, Ph.D., Met.E.
Material Science

Dr. Frank Crossley is a pioneer in the field of titanium metallurgy. He began his work in metals at Illinois Institute of Technology in Chicago after receiving his graduate degrees in metallurgical engineering. In the 1950s, few African Americans were visible in the engineering fields, but Dr. Crossley excelled in his field. He received six patents, five in titanium base alloys. His research greatly improved the aircraft and aerospace industry.
He has published over fifty papers in journals and symposia. He is listed in several who' who including Who's Who in America, 41st, 1980-81 through 61st, 2007 Editions.

Lesia Crumpton-Young, Ph.D.
Industrial Engineering

Dr. Lesia Crumpton-Young earned her Ph.D. in Industrial Engineering, with her major area of specialization: Ergonomics/Human Factors Engineering and minor areas of specialization: Safety Engineering and Statistics. Her research specialty areas include Human Performance Modeling, Industrial Ergonomics, Ergonomic Design for Special Populations, Prevention and Control of Cumulative, Trauma Disorders, Occupational Safety and Health, Virtual Reality, Human Reliability, and Information Security. Cureently, she teaches Industrial Ergonomics, Occupational Biomechanics, Ergonomic Design for Special Populations, Safety Engineering, Work Physiology, Work Design, and Human Factors Engineering. Dr. Lesia Crumpton-Young has many journal publishings, as well as co-authoring the book "Industrial Engineering Research Solutions". She has worked on several industrial research projects with companies such as UPS, IBM, Caterpillar, Intel, Garan Manufacturing, and Southwest Airlines.

Hardiman D. Cureton II
Science Education

Hardiman Cureton II received his B.S. degree from MacMaster University in Ontario, Canada, and his M.S. degree from National University in San Diego, CA. He has taught secondary science for fifteen years and is presently an instructor of science and Director of Educational Opportunities for at-risk students in Rocklin, CA.

Richard H. Djoble D'Almeida, FGCP, MFTM RCPS (Glasg.)
Chief Medical Officer

Dr. D'Almeida is a Fellow of the Ghana College of Physicians and a Member of ISTM (International Society of Travel Medicine). He is a Family Physician and a Consultant Travel Medicine Specialist. He is also a Member of the Faculty of Travel Medicine of the Royal College of Physicians and Surgeons of Glasgow. Currently he is the Chief Medical Officer of the renowned Nyaho Medical Centre. He presented a paper at the Corporate African Partnership for Prevention and cure of HIV, Tuberculosis and Malaria international conference held in Accra in April 2007. He has developed a proposal titled 'Safe Ghana Health Initiative' aimed at improving the safety of the travelling public to Ghana. He is a Consultant to Japan International Cooperation Agency in Ghana. He has recently authored the '**Safe Africa Travel**, a handbook of health tips to help the iterant traveller cruise safely through the continent. His career objective is to become a pioneer of high standard Family Health and Travel Medicine practice in Africa and helping to raise the standard and delivery of vaccination practice in Africa. Ultimately, he aims to help reduce the burden of vaccine preventable diseases and tourist morbidity in Africa through research and effective travel medicine interventions, advisory, and prompt treatment.

Dennis E. Daniels, Ph.D.
Epidemiology

Dr. Daniels has been named director of the Undergraduate Medical Academy at Prairie View A&M University and at the College of Medicine at Texas A&M University. Previously, he was deputy director with the Fulton County Department of Health and Wellness in Atlanta. Dr. Daniels earned his bachelor's degree from the University of Texas at Austin, and master's and Ph.D. degrees from the University of Texas School of Public Health at Houston.

Christine Darden, Ph.D.
Ret'd Senior Project Engineer, NASA

Her work has included extensive work in supersonic wing design, low-speed flap design, and sonic boom minimization and prediction. Dr. Darden was an engineering group leader in NASA's High Speed Research Program, which for the last few years focused mainly on addressing three major environmental concerns associated with supersonic flight: eliminating the threat of ozone depletion, ensuring "acceptable" engine noise levels, and minimizing sonic boom--the crashing sound generated by pressure disturbances when an aircraft flies faster than the speed of sound. During this period she has authored or co-authored over 51 technical papers or articles. Of particular note is her work in sonic boom minimization where she developed a computer algorithm, used widely by engineers working in this field. Dr. Darden attended Hampton Institute, now Hampton University, where she earned a bachelor of science degree in mathematics. After years of teaching at the high school level, she earned a master's degree in applied mathematics from Virginia State University and a doctorate in mechanical engineering from George Washington University.

Rufus Benton Darden, Ph.D.
Civil Engineering

Dr. Darden has over 30 years experience in the water/wastewater areas of civil engineering, including 2 years as a U.S. Air Force Base Utility Engineer. His experience is summarized as follows: Designed a stormwater detention system for the San Francisco International Airport North Field Air Cargo Facility development. The detention system for the 45-acre site consisted of drain pipes, pump stations and a detention pond designed for a 5-year storm. Approximately 45,000 cu. ft. of initial (contaminated) runoff was detained, and subsequent runoff was pumped to San Francisco Bay using two 250 horsepower pumps. He utilized the Haestad Methods' Stormcad program for obtaining flows and analyzing hydraulics. Dr. Darden has designed 1200 horsepower recycled water pump station with hydropneumatic tank for Napa -American Canyon Water Recycling Facility expansion. His many other experiences include managing the design of a 70,000-GPD wastewater pump station and collection system and construction assistance services for three wastewater collection and treatment facilities in Tulare County, CA; as well as preparing 10% design of grading, drainage, utilities, and roads at six sites along the San Francisco Hetch Hetchy water system. He served as Project Engineer preparation of wastewater master plans for the cities of Santa Maria and Taft, CA.

Calvin A. Davenport, Ph.D.
Professor Emeritus of Microbiology, CA State U., Fullerton, CA

Distinguished for his work in higher education, Dr. Davenport retired after more than forty years in College and University classrooms. He was a mentor for pre-medical students and dozens of his former students now serve in medical professions. He developed and taught a popular course on the "Biology of Sexually Transmitted Diseases" in 1975, a time long before this subject was addressed by other universities. Apart from teaching, many of Dr. Davenport's activities revolved around programs for students. These included a tutoring program for the retention of women and minorities in Engineering/Computer Sciences and Liaison and Director, Incentive Grants Program of the National Action Council for Minorities in Engineering. Active in local, state and national organizations related to education, he served on the Senior Accrediting Commission for the Western Association of Colleges and Universities and as a consultant/evaluator for a number of companies and institutions including NIH, NSF and the Danforth Foundation. Dr. Davenport also served as Chairman of the Board of Trustees, Orange County/Long Beach (CA) Health Consortium, an organization of health care educators, providers and consumers that was designed to coordinate and improve delivery of health care. His research was in the area of antimicrobial resistance of pathogenic bacteria.

Carolyn S. Davis
Biology

She has 25+ years of combined fine arts and teaching experience and expertise. Her background is comprised of an extensive educational foray that includes a BS in education, a Master's of Fine Arts and a wide variety of leadership and curriculum development experience. I currently use my 20 years as a visual information specialist to assist me in developing teaching aids for a diverse group of 10th grade biology students including students who are currently learning to speak the English language.

Ifeyinwa Davis
Environmental Scientist

Ms. Davis started her career in 1981 as a Research Scientist at the Institute of Oceanography and Marine Research in Nigeria from where she visited the Bedford Institute of Oceanography (BIO) Dartmouth, Canada and RUTGERS Marine Field Station at Tuckerton, New Jersey in 1989 as a visiting scientist. In 1991, she was accepted at the University of South Florida, in the Marine Science Program and completed the Master's Program courses before accepting a job with the U.S. Environmental Protection Agency in 1998. Prior to this appointment, she worked as an intern with the U.S. Geological Survey in the Water Resources Division laboratory in Ocala, FL through the Environmental Career Organization (ECO). Some of her interests include increasing awareness for energy development through rural pilot projects; knowledge management through development of credible academies and science foundations in developing countries; Information Systems Education and human capital development in the use of Geographic Information Systems (GIS) for data management.

John H. Day, Jr., Ph.D.
Chief, Electrical Engineering Div., Physics

John is NESC Chief Engineer for Goddard Space Flight Center (GSFC) at National Aeronautics & Space Administration (NASA), where he serves as the liaison between GSFC and the NASA Engineering & Safety Center (NESC), maintaining proactive involvement with programs and projects and providing technical expertise and technical resources. From 1999-2010, he was Chief, Electrical Engineering Division GSFC, when he led an organization of engineers, technicians, managers, and support staff engaged in developing electronic components, subsystems (power, data, & communications), electrical systems (flight & ground), and related technologies for NASA's earth & space science missions. He was Branch Head of this organization during 1992-1999. A former physicist in the isotope branch of the U.S. Geological Survey, he is author of many scholarly scientific publications. He is a member of the American Institute of Aeronautics and Astronautics, the Institute of Electrical and Electronic Engineers, the National Society of Black Physicists, and the American Physical Society.

Joseph Debro
Chemistry; Engineering, Project Dev.

Mr. Debro is a Co- Founder of Transbay Engineering and Builders, the National Association of Minority contractors and the Founder of the first and only minority owned surety company in the country, Builders Mutual company. Earlier, he worked for NASA as a bio-chemical Engineer at Moffete Field, on the environment of the first space capsule. We were tasked with designing systems to dispose of waste in space. Joe Debro has written several publications. He earned an AB in bacteriology and an MS degree in biochemistry from the University of California at Berkeley.

Peter J. Delfyett, Jr., Ph.D.
Trustee, Chair, Professor, Optics, ECE, & Physics

Dr. Delfyett is the University of Central Florida Trustee Chair Professor of Optics, EE & Physics at The College of Optics & Photonics, and the Center for Research and Education in Optics and Lasers (CREOL). Prior to this, he was a Member of the Technical Staff at Bell Communications Research from 1988-1993. He served as the Editor-in-Chief of the IEEE Journal of Selected Topics in Quantum Electronics (2001-2006), and served on the Board of Directors of the Optical Society of America. He served as an Associate Editor of IEEE Photonics Technology Letters, and was Executive Editor of IEEE LEOS Newsletter (1995-2000). Dr. Delfyett is currently serving as President of the National Society of Black Physicists (2008-2012). Additionally, he has been awarded the NSF's Presidential Faculty Fellow Early Career Award for Scientists and Engineers, which is awarded to the Nation's top 20 young scientists. He has published over 500 articles in refereed journals and conference proceedings, and has been awarded 30 United States Patents. He helped found Raydiance, Inc., which is a spin-off company developing high power, ultrafast laser systems, based on Dr. Delfyett's research, for applications in medicine, defense, material processing, biotech and other key technological markets.

Cheick Modibo Diarra, Ph.D.
Chairman for Africa at Microsoft Corp., Aerospace Engineering

Dr. Diarra studied mathematics, physics, and analytic mechanics in graduated from Pierre & Marie Curie University in Paris. He went on to earn his Ph.D. in mechanical and aerospace engineering from Howard University, Washington DC., where he later taught for six years. In 1998, he was recruited by Caltech's Jet Propulsion Laboratory where as an interplanetary navigator, he was involved in five NASA missions, including the *Magellan* mission to Venus, the *Ulysses* mission to the poles of the Sun, the *Galileo* mission to Jupiter and the Mars Observer mission. He then served as the public outreach manager for the Mars Pathfinder mission. In 1999, Dr. Diarra obtained permission from NASA to work part-time in order to devote himself to education development in Africa, founding the Pathfinder Foundation. He took a further sabbatical in 2002 to found a laboratory in Bamako, Mali for the development of solar energy. In 2000 and 2001 he also served as a Goodwill Ambassador for UNESCO. In 2002 and 2003 he served as CEO of the African Virtual University, based in Kenya. Dr. Cheick Modibo Diarra is currently the chairman of Microsoft Africa. He has also been awarded the African Lifetime Achievement Award and voted one of the 100 Africans of the 21st Century by Jeune Afrique.

Lincoln I. Diuguid, Ph.D.
President, Chemical Lab & Mfr.

Proprietor of a chemical lab & manufacturing company. After working as an analytical chemist and teaching in Pine Bluff, Arkansas, he finished his doctorate in organic chemistry in 1945. Two years ater he bought a building and converted it into a chemical lab. In addition to his chemical research, he took on teaching at Harris-Stowe State College. Although he retired from teaching after 33 years, he still works at his lab with as much energy, persistence and optimism as ever. In 2000 the American Chemical Society awarded him aspecial citation for his contributions to chemistry andmedicine. Never given credit for some of his discoveries before coming to St. Louis, he persists in working toward his primary goal, to find a cure for cancer. He says that he has several promising compounds that he believes to be revolutionary. " What keeps him going? He says his work gives him a reason to live. He could have made a much better living working for a big company, but money is not his motivator.Though his work could conceivably benefit all humanity, he sees his greatest contribution as his work with students. He became interested in chemistry when his own high schoolteacher pointed to the opportunities in the field - though at the time most were closed to his race. He did his best to set his students on the right track, and hears from some of them afteras long as 30 years.

Felix Djembo-Madingou, M.D.
Regional Director of Medicine

Dr. Djembo-Madingou is one of the country's regional Medical Director. In this capacity, he services patients throughout the region and oversees medical delivery systems in his region.

James A. Donaldson, Ph.D.
HU Dean of Arts and Sciences; Mathematics

In 1961, Dr. Donaldson graduated from Lincoln University with an AB degree in Mathematics (he later has become a member of this university's Board of Trustees). He earned both his MS degree (1963) and Ph.D. (1965) from the University of Illinois in Urbana-Champaign, after writing his thesis in differential equations. His interests in differential equations have continued and his research publications include numerous papers in analysis, differential equations, and applied mathematics. He has lectured widely on his research in North America, Africa, Asia, and Europe. It is Dr. Donaldson's view that the manner in which mathematics is presented to undergraduate students is pushing them away from mathematics. He is also interested in efforts to increase the participation in mathematics and science by members of underrepresented groups. Currently, he is a member of several Boards: TransAfrica and the Davis-Putter Scholarship Fund (providing 25-30 scholarships). During his tenure as Howard University Mathematics Department Chairman (1972-1990), the department developed the first and only Ph.D. degree program at an African American University. This program has become a major producer in America of African American holders of a Ph.D. degree in Mathematics. He was a member of the Science and Technology Commission of the Sixth Pan African Congress.

Raymon Dones
Engineering, Construction, Renewable Energy

He learned electrical and plumbing trades while working as a Pullman car porter in Denver, Colorado. After receiving his electrical contracting license, he established Dones Electric, which later became incorporated as Aladdin Electric in Oakland, California. Dones is a founding member of The National Association of Minority Contractors, a nonprofit trade association that was established in 1969 to address the concerns of minority contractors. Today the organization has chapters in 49 states, the Virgin Islands, England and South Africa. Ray Dones was instrumental in establishing Project Upgrade, one of the first construction trades apprenticeship training programs in the United States. As a contractor, Dones had a hand in building or subcontracting a large part of Oakland's landscape, including the MORH and Acorn housing developments in West Oakland, the West Oakland Health Center, and the early construction of Oakland City Center. In 1999, Dones was named one of the most influential people in the construction industry by Engineering New-Record Magazine.

Ikechukwu N.S. Dozie, Ph.D.
Public Health Microbiology and Parasitology

Professor Dozie is a Public Health Microbiologist and Parasitologist with research emphasis on tuberculosis, HIV/AIDS and other sexually transmitted infections (STIs), malaria, onchocerciasis (river blindness), environmental sanitation, hygiene and infection control etc. Professor Dozie has received several scholarships, honours and awards for distinctive contributions to science, technology and innovations for sustainable development. He is a consultant to several local, national and international organizations. He has successfully published many articles in reputable scientific journals nationally and internationally. He currently serves as a reviewer/editorial board member of many scientific journals as well as the managing editor of the *Journal of Innovations in the Life Sciences* (JILS).

Eddie Dunbar, MBA
Entomologist

Eddie is Founder & CEO of BugPeople. He possesses competencies in entomology and technology-based instruction. In 1990 Dunbar founded BugPeople, which he adapted to increase technical competencies in four efforts: University of California Cooperative Extension (Berkeley), where Dunbar served as an Insect Hotline Operator (1994-1996); the CityBugs program, which recruited Oakland students to the Berkeley campus, and where Dunbar was Project Coordinator (1996-1998); the Leadership Institute for Teaching Elementary Science, Mills College, Oakland, where Dunbar conducted continuing education workshops for science teachers (1998-2000); and the Lawrence Hall of Science, where Dunbar served as a field instructor (2000-2005). Today, Dunbar reaches learners through innovative curriculum hosted on California's most exhaustive entomology education website (www.bugpeople.org), through three insect field guides - including *Lake Merritt and Greater Oakland Insects* - and through photographs of thousands of California insect species. Currently, Dunbar is writing *Insects of the San Francisco Bay Area* to be published on CD-ROM in 2008.

W. Paul Dunn
Aerospace Engineering

As Principal Director, Launch Systems Engineering Directorate, The Aerospace Corporation, he has led the work on a number of vehicle systems, including medium launch vehicles, the Inertial Upper Stage, other upper stages, propulsive systems, vehicle systems integration, and launch systems analysis. Among his many honors is the Distinguished Graduate Award from the University of Texas at Austin in 1993, the highest award given by the College of Engineering.

James Ealey
Electrical Engineer, Computer Science

Mr. Ealey is an Electrical Engineer who worked for Naval Sea Systems Command (NAVSEA) for 21 years. He worked his way up to Command Data Management Officer/Alternate Chairman, NAVSEA DRRP. He also acted as the (former) Naval Material Command agent for all Naval level review and approval of all data item Descriptions submitted by all DoD activities. Mr. Ealey excercised approval authority for data requirements related to specifications and standards. He also served as the Command focal point for the Government/Industry Data Exchange Program (GIDEP). He has served as the Executive Chairman of the Naval Sea Systems Command (NAVSEA) Requirements Data Review Board and is a graduate of the DoD Data Management School at Wright-Patterson Air Force Base. He wrote NAVSEA Instruction 4000.6 (Data Management) and NAVSEA Inststruction 5200.7 (GIDEP). Mr. Ealey has worked in various positions in NAVSEA, including that of an Integrated Logistics Support (ILS) Engineer. After leaving NAVSEA, Mr. Ealey worked for various companies as a Senior Data Analyst, advising and assisting Project Managers in all areas concerning DoD Contract Data Management, Configuration Management and ILS. Mr. Ealey's career has been outstanding, earning many awards of achievement. He has led workshops in his field, taught courses and served as a consultant.

Archie W. Earl, Sr., Ed.D.
Mathematics

Former Naval Medical Research Center (NMRC) Faculty Research Fellow, he is presently an Associate Professor in the Mathematics Department, School of Science and Technology, at Norfolk State University. Dr. Earl earned his B.S. in mathematics, M.A. in mathematics, and Ed.D. in higher education, from Norfolk State University, Hampton University, and the College of William and Mary, respectively. He has written several articles and books about mathematics and the use technology in colleges and universities, e.g., <u>Probability and Statistics for Science Majors with Internet and Statistical Software Applications,</u> and <u>High Tech Higher Education</u>. Dr. Earl has over thirty years of experience in secondary and higher education. He has taught mathematics or statistics at both the undergraduate and graduate levels.

Julian Earls, Ph.D.
Ret'd Center Dir., NASA Glenn Research Center, Physicist

Dr. Earls retired in 2006 as Director of the National Aeronautics and Space Administration's Glenn Research Center at Lewis Field in Cleveland, Ohio from 2003 to 2005. Glenn Center is engaged in research, technology and systems development programs in aeronautical propulsion, space propulsion, space power, space communications, and microgravity sciences in combustion and fluid physics. While managing an annual budget of approximately $773 million, he oversaw a workforce of 1,920 civil service employees and 1,300 on-site support service contractors. The center consists of 24 major facilities and over 500 specialized research facilities. Dr. Earls has been a noted Health Physicist and Radiation Specialist. He authored the first Health Physics Guides within his institution; served as a member of the Launch Team for Apollo XIII Lunar Program; served as the first African American Radiation Specialist in the New York Regional Office of the U.S. Atomic Energy Commission (now the U.S. Nuclear Regulatory Commission). He is co-founder of an organization whose members make personal contributions to raise $1 million for scholarships to black students who attend black colleges. Dr. Earls has been inducted into National Black Colleges Hall of Fame, along with Justice Thurgood Marshall and Dr. Martin Luther King, Jr.

Omotayo Oluranti Ebong, Ph.D.
Pharmacology

Dr. Ebong is Member of the Senate and Governing Council of the University of Port Harcourt, Nigeria. She First Vice Chairman Member, Country Coordinating Mechanism (CCM) for HIV/AIDS, Malaria and Tuberculosis. She has been the Dean Faculty of Basic Medical Sciences, Niger Delta University (2006) and Head of its Department of Pharmacology and Dean of its Faculty of Basic Medical Sciences (2003 – 2005). Dr. Ebong researches the efficacy of phytomedicines and chemotherapeutic drugs in the treatment of malaria; Antimalarial Drug resistance; Immunology and Molecular Biology of Malaria; and Co-infection of HIV and Malaria.

Oghenetsavbuko Todo Edje, Ph.D.
Cropping Systems Agronomy

Prof. Edje, has served in universities and international research institutions for about four decades and has experiences spanning several countries and continents. During this period, he has conducted a wide range of research projects, mostly on cropping systems, livelihoods, food security and on drought, especially for small-scale farmers in Swaziland, Malawi, Tanzania and Zambia on cereals, grain legume crops, indigenous vegetables and root and tuber crops, including cassava and sweet potato. He has published over 100 scientific papers, has been editor of several journals, a member of several scientific associations and is the current representative for agriculture on the National Research Council of Swaziland. His research on the use of sunnhemp (*Crotalaria juncea* L) as a cover crop as well as a crop for soil fertility improvement and the control of nematodes is beginning to gain recognition and acceptance among farming communities. His on-farm research also includes conservation agriculture for soil fertility improvement, crop yields and carbon dioxide sequestration, as well as rainwater harvesting technologies for crop production. Prof also researches on the use of green manure crops [green weeds, sunnhemp (*Crotalaria juncea* L)] for crop production, especially for maize, dry beans and sweet potato production and researches on indigenous fruits and vegetables.

Robert V. Edwards, Ph.D.
Chemical Engineering

Prof. Edwards' research has primarily been in laser light scattering for dynamic measurements. The technique is used to measure fluid velocities, surface tension, particle size and many other dynamic phenomena. In the process of doing this research, he learned a lot of techniques for modeling stochastic processes and for designing instrumentation based on the results of the calculations. This involved numerical simulations and creating statistical data processing algorithms that were simply impractical to apply in the recent past. The advent of the PC changed all of that and made who new classes of computation available to engineers and scientists. This research resulted in over 50 refereed publications. He has spent 14 years in academic administration at Case Western Reserve University, having served as department chairman (twice), associate dean, and assistant to the President for Minority Affairs. Prof. Edwards is a fellow of the AIChE. His latest efforts have involved trying to transmit the statistical knowledge gained in his research to the average practicing engineer. Part of that effort is his book "Processing Random Data: Statistics for Engineers and Scientists."

Mustafa El Tayeb, Ph.D.
Dir., UNESCO Div of Science Analysis & Policy; Geophysics

Dr. El Tayeb holds an Engineering Diploma from St. Petersburg (Leningrad) Mining Institute, a Master and a PhD in Geophysics from Bordeaux I University in France. He started his career in 1974 as a mining engineer/geophysicist at the Geological Survey Department of the Sudan. His work covered the utilization of geophysics to civil engineering works, engineering geology and the exploration of mineral resources in the various regions of the country. His research covered areas such as marine seismic reflection, airborne gravity and magnetic surveys of the central Red Sea. Dr. El Tayeb joined UNESCO in 1981. In 1986, he assumed the post of the Chief of Section responsible for Arab States and then became responsible for both Arab States and Africa Sections; he supervised the development of a number of national S&T plans and projects. From 1989 – 1996, he was the Chief of Development Analysis and Operations; he assisted UNESCO Member States in formulating science policies, strategies as well as the development of partnerships between universities and industries and the evaluation of higher education institutions and universities. In 1996 Dr. El Tayeb was appointed Director of the Division of Policy Analysis & Operations of UNESCO and given the task of building UNESCO's capacity in this area.

Dimi Elisa, Ph.D.
Director, Research and Planning, Public Health

Dr. Elisa wass her country's Director of Public Health, charged with planning and implementing the country's healthcare delivery systems. Currently, she is the director of the hospital of Talanga.

Amani Eltayb, Ph.D.
Pharmacology

Dr. Eltayb is a researcher from Khartoum-Sudan. She has a Bachelor in Veterinary Science and a PhD degree from Karolinska Institutet, Sweden in pharmacology. Currently her research is mainly focused on antibiotic use and resistance and antibiotic residues in animal farming and their impact on human health and environment. She also works as a mentor for young girls with the African European Women Scientists Network. Recently, she has been active in the field of international public health concerning drug misuse, antibiotic resistance and HIV prevention. Dr. Eltayb is also interested in International affairs and health and is involved in several organizations working for scientific development in African countries. She is also Treasurer for both the Sudanese Swedish Association and NAWES (African European Women Scientists).

A. Egrinya Eneji, Ph.D.
Agronomy

Dr. Eneji is the Director of the West African Institute of Agricultural and Environmental Research (WAIAER). He is also Professor of Crop Science and Production Technology, China Agricultural University, Beijing and Adjunct Professor of Agronomy, Cross River University of Technology, Nigeria. His research interests include Soil fertility management, Ecological agriculture, Waste recycling, Bioremediation and Cropping systems/plant eco-physiology.

Andrew Achuo Enow, Ph.D.
Agricultural Sciences (plant pathology)

Dr. Enow is a Programme Specialist for Biological Sciences, International Council for Science (ICSU) Regional Office for Africa (ICSU ROA). During 1994-2000, he was a Research Officer at the Institute of Agricultural Research for Development (IRAD), Cameroon, where he used the Plant Growth-Promoting Bacteria (PGPB) to combat the cocoyam root rot disease; Assessed the risk of ground water pollution with agro-chemicals; provided characterization, epidemiology and control of major diseases of rubber; and screened of Rubber genetic resources for resistance to major leaf diseases. While working on his doctoral research fellowship during 2000-2005 at Ghent University, Belgium, he investigated the role of salicylic acid in the resistance of tomato and tobacco to biotrophic and necrotrophic fungi; investigated the effect of abscisic acid on plant defence responses to pathogen attack (using tomato as test plant against a necrotrophic fungus, biotrophic fungus and a soft rot (necrotrophic) bacterium, and tobacco as test crop against the two fungi); tested different combinations of various Cameroonian agricultural solid wastes in compost to derive cocoyam root rot-suppressive compost. Not only does Dr. Enow contributes to capacity for farmers, he also has written several technical papers.

Justin Epelu-Opio, Ph.D.
Secretary General, Uganda National Academy of Sciences (UNAS); Veterinary Medicine

Dr. Epelu-Opio is a Professor of Veterinary Anatomy, teaching subjects as gross/microscopic and developmental Anatomy . From 1993 – 2004, he served as Deputy Vice-Chancellor of Makerere University. During 1985 - 1990, he served as Head, Department of Veterinary Anatomy, but relinquished this position because he was appointed by His Excellency the President of the Republic of Uganda to serve as Chairman of the Presidential Commission for Teso (i.e. Soroti and Kumi districts together). Currently, Dr. Epelu-Opio is Chairman, Board of Trustees of the Joint Clinical Research Centre, treating HIV/AIDS and other related diseases. This center in now a well renowned institution worldwide and there are seven centers of excellence in the country as well as over fifty (50) outreach stations upcountry. In 2009, he was elected first Secretary General of Uganda National Academy of Sciences (UNAS) for a 3-year term. Dr. Epelu-Opio research interests include delving into the biology of the reproductive system in various animals, and the study of the reproductive behavior or pattern in the goat and cows by application of nuclear techniques. Dr. Epelu-Opio has been appointed Board Director with the Civil Aviation Authority, Uganda government parastatal which oversees aviation regulations in the country in July 2010, for a 3-year term.

Aprille J. Ericsson, Ph.D.
Aerospace Engineer, Educator

The majority of Dr. Ericsson's 20+ years engineering career has been at the NASA Goddard Space Flight Center (GSFC). Initially she worked in the Guidance Navigation & Control discipline, conducting spacecraft simulations and analysis to predict their dynamic behavior during flight and to determine the best spacecraft attitude and structural vibration control methods. Dr. Ericsson has also worked at NASA HQs as a Program Executive for the Earth Science Enterprise and a Resource Manager Space Science Enterprise. During the last 5 years, she has been an Instrument Manager (IM) in the GSFC Instrument Systems Branch, where she has led/managed teams of scientist and engineers on various instrument proposals and flight missions. Her proposal efforts include: the Lead for the Space Science Small Explorer Advanced X-Ray Polarimeter (AXP) mission, which was awarded an unsolicited $0.5M to further develop its new technology; telescope manager for the Jupiter Magnetosphere Explorer; and IM for the Vector Electro-Dynamics Investigation, Terrestrial Planet Finder Coronagraph Spectrometer instrument and for Dust Collector Experiment on SCIM, a proposed Mars Scout sample and return mission. Currently, Dr. Ericsson is the IM for the resubmission of the AXP proposal and Project Engineer for Lunar Orbiter Laser Altimeter Instrument which will provide topographic data to map the lunar surface in preparation for future moon exploration.

Augustine O. Esogbue, Ph.D.
Dir., Intelligent Systems & Controls Lab

His research interests include dynamic programming, fuzzy sets, decision making and control in a fuzzy environment, and operations research with applications to socio-technical systems such as health care, water resource management and disaster control planning. He is also the Director of the Intelligent Systems and Controls Laboratory which is currently investigating a hybrid approach to intelligent control via fuzzy sets, neural networks, and reinforcement learning theories as well as its application to various large-scale, nonlinear and uncertain dynamical systems. In addition to his research, Dr. Esogbue teaches courses in dynamic programming, stochastic operations research, engineering design, and neuro-fuzzy control.

Herman E. Eure, Ph.D.
Ecological Animal Parasitologist

Dr. Eure is Professor of Biology, Wake Forest University, and Associate Dean of the College. Host parasite interactions are the primary focus of his research. How these parasite interact with their hosts and the various factors that impact on that relationship is studied in vertebrate organisms ranging from frog, toad, turtles to fish. He is interested in determining how factors such as host diet, temperature, availability of infective intermediate host, host sex and age influence the seasonality of parasite populations. An additional interest lies in how these populations are regulated, both at the intermediate and definitive host levels. He has been the recipient of several awards during his academic career: Wake Forest's highest award for teaching, The 2001 Jon Reinhardt Award for Distinguished Teaching and the University's highest award for outstanding advising of students (1992); The recipient of the Yokley Faculty Service Award from the Beta Beta Beta National Biological Honor Society; and a 1997 recipient of NAFEO's Distinguished Alumni Citation Award from the University of Maryland, Eastern Shore. He was also the Chair of the Department of Biology at Wake Forest University for 8 years, from 1998-2006.

Fabian I. Ezema, Ph.D.
Physics

Dr. Ezema's interests include Solar Energy Physics, Materials Science & Crystal Growth, Nanomaterials - Synthesis & Characterizations, Photovoltaics, Climate change & Environmental Physics. He has co-authored to chapters in science books, covering subjects as "Solar and Stellar Systems" and "Energy Transformation in Physical Systems". He has authored extensively in various publications.

Jonathan D. Farley, Ph.D.
Mathematics

Seed Magazine named **Dr. Jonathan David Farley** one of "15 people who have shaped the global conversation about science in 2005." He won the Harvard Foundation's Distinguished Scientist of the Year Award in 2004. He obtained his doctorate in mathematics from Oxford University in 1995, after winning Oxford's highest mathematics awards. Jonathan Farley graduated *summa cum laude* from Harvard University in 1991 with the second-highest grade point average in his graduating class. Dr. Farley's field of interest is lattice theory. He solved a problem posed by MIT professor Richard Stanley that had remained unsolved since 1981. Dr. Farley's work applying mathematics to counterterrorism has been profiled in *The Chronicle of Higher Education*, in *Science News*, in *The Economist* Magazine, in *USA Today*, and on Fox News Television. Dr. Farley is co-founder of Hollywood Math and Science Film Consulting. Dr. Farley has been a consultant for the hit television shows *Numb3rs* and *Medium*. In 2001, *Ebony* named Dr. Farley a "Leader of the Future." Dr. Farley has been profiled in *Jet* Magazine and on the cover of the NAACP's *Crisis* Magazine. Dr. Farley has written for *Time* Magazine, *The New York Times, The Guardian, Essence*, and the hip hop magazine *The Source*. The city of Cambridge, Massachusetts officially declared March 19, 2004 to be "Dr. Jonathan David Farley Day".

Doudou D. Faye, Ph.D.
Entomology; Agronomy

Dr. Faye earned his degree as Agricultural Works Engineer with specialization in Entomology and Crop Protection from Bambey, Senegal National Agronomy School of Rural Engineers, before serving as a National Crop Protection Prospector (1975 - 1978), and the first Regional Phytosanitary Inspector of Diourbel Region, Senegal. He earned his advance university degrees in Entomology and Agronomy in the U.S. Dr. Faye served as Senegal Senior Integrated Pest Management Entomologist on Cotton and Food Crops with the Senegal Institute of Agriculture Research and as a rural development consultant project leader for West Africa Rural Foundation, Rodale International and USAID related missions in sustainable development project identification, implementation and evaluation. As a neem specialist, Dr. Faye has contributed in several Neem Foundation World Neem Conferences (Vancouver, Canada, 1999, Mumbai, India, 2002, Coimbatore, India, 2007 and serves in the Neem Foundation's International Consultative Committee. In the USA, as a co-owner, Dr. Faye served as Senior Scientist in charge of the Research and Development and EPA registration of Stet Corporation, maker of the WisEarth True Stop^{TM} organic Fire Ant (*Solenopsis invicta*, Buren) and Whitefly (*Bemisia tabaci* and *B. argentifolii* pesticides, soil amendment and plant nutrients.

Lloyd N. Ferguson, Ph.D.
Chemist, Professor Emeritus, author of 7 chemistry books

Is distinguished as a retired Professor Emeritus since 1986 from California State University at Los Angeles where he has been on its faculty since 1965 and served as Chairman of its Department of Chemistry during 1968-71. There is now a scholarship in his name at this institution. He has noteworthy accomplishments during his forty-plus years in chemistry. He taught chemistry at Howard University in Washington, DC for 20 years and served as head of its Dept. of Chemistry from 1958-65. Dr. Ferguson is an author of 50+ journal publications; he has written articles in Colliers encyclopedia and an Italian encyclopedia; he has also written seven chemistry textbooks. Not only is he a recipient of many awards and distinguished in several publishings, Dr. Ferguson has served the Black community well. He has provided assistance to minority youth in chemistry, as he participated in the formulation of the SEED program (Support for the Educationally and Economically Disadvantaged) of the American Chemical Society, but he is the most widely read Black author in chemistry. Of his seven chemistry textbooks, two has been translated into Hindi and Japanese. However, many readers of his books know that he is a Black author. A classic example occurred at the University of Mississippi. While it was keeping Blacks from entering the university, it was using Dr. Ferguson's book as a text.

Terry L. Few
Mechanical Engineering

Terry has designed Advanced Exhaust Sytems and is the Manager of Augmehto (augmentor) design for General Electric Corp., OH, which produces Marine Engines, Aircraft Engines, Aircraft Maintenance or Repair Materials, Executive Aircraft, Maintenance Services, and Non Destructive Test (NDT) Equipment or Systems. Early in his career, he worked as a Test Facilities Engineer and designed Aero Thermo Combination systems. Terry went on to work as a design engineer for Mechanical Simulator Development and serve as Manager for designing advanced fans and compressors.

Mark J. Finch, M.D.
Infectious Diseases

Dr. Finch graduated from UC Berkeley in 1975 and UCSF School of Medicine in 1979. He completed his internship and residency in Internal Medicine at University of Michigan in 1982, being board certified the same year. He was an Epidemic Intelligence Service (EIS) officer for the Centers for Disease Control from 1982 to 1984, specializing in the investigation of foodborne and diarrheal disease outbreaks. He completed his Infectious Disease fellowship at University of Maryland in 1986 with board certification in 1988. He also served as a Visiting Professor of Tropical and Infectious Disease at La Universidad Peruana Cayetano Heredia in Lima Peru. Dr. Finch has published approximately a dozen peer-reviewed papers on infectious disease and managed care topics. Dr Finch currently works as a Medical Director for a large California health plan and continues to practice hospital-based infectious disease part-time.

Essex E. Finney, Jr., Ph.D.
Agriculture Science

He received his B.S. from Virginia Polytechnic Institute, an M.S. from The Pennsylvania State University and was the first African-American to receive a PhD. in the Department of Agricultural Engineering at Michigan State University in 1963. Dr. Finney served as a military officer from 1963-65. He then accepted a position with USDA/ARS in 1965, where he has served as Chairman of the Agricultural Marketing Research Institute, Assistant, Associate and the Director of the Beltsville Agricultural Research Center, Senior Policy Analyst in the office of the Science Advisor to the President, and Associate Director of the ARS 12-state North Atlantic Area. In 1992, he was appointed to the number two post as Associate Administrator in the Agricultural Research Service (ARS), from 1993-94 he served as the Acting Administrator of this agency. ARS operates 375 research groups at over 100 locations in the United States and in seven foreign countries on an annual budget of $700 million. He continued with USDA until his retirement in 1995. His early research was on drying cereal grains and the physical properties of agricultural products. He continued with research on instrumentation and non-destructive techniques for measuring the quality of food and other agricultural products.

Edward G. Fisher, M.D.
Physician, Surgeon

Dr. Fisher, a brilliant professional, is quite active in the medical community and serves as Chaplain to the D.C. Medical Chirurgical Society and volunteers for many community activities in the medical and educational areas. He is a licensed and ordained minister of the Gospel and pastors a small church in SE Wash DC. The church has an outreach in Haiti. He is the co-author of "Human Sexuality - The Christian Perspective", and the author of "Moses and the Burning Bush". He is the President of the Mercy Outreach Ministry International, and VP of the Institute of Urban Living, a community nonprofit. He is quite active in the community and has been cited for numerous awards and commendations. He is a noted speaker on Medicine and Religion. He is married to the Rev. Dr. Judy A. Fisher, and has a blended family of 6 adult children.

Kweku David Fleming
Mechanical & Electrical Engineering

Fleming is a design consultant with expertise in engineering design. He also works to build manufacturing capacity in developing countries. Until recently, he was the Principal of Tek Designs International, an engineering design firm providing project management and design services in the IT, telecom and industrial design sectors. Fleming has consulted on wireless telecom projects in emerging markets, with projects in Africa Europe and the U.S. He currently serves on the Corporate Strategy team at Embarq. Kweku was the NSBE National Chairperson from 1989 to 1991. Credited with first instituting the NSBE International Committee, he returned in 1999 to serve as the International Committee Chairperson and presided over NSBE's global realignment.

Vernon C. Floyd
Broadcast Engineer

Vernon C. Floyd, founder of radio stations, WJMG, WORV, and WGDQ. He is a graduate of Tuskegee Institute; he studied at Dunbar Trade School, and Industrial Training Institute in Chicago. He held an M.O.S. of 078, (Electrician) and 648 (Radio Technician) while serving in the military services. He worked for electrical contractors in Mobile for two years; was chief engineer of station WMOZ (Mobile), for about twelve years, taught Advance Electronics at Carver State Technical Trade School for two years in Mobile. He holds a 1st Class F.C.C. Broadcasting Engineers, License; General Class Short Wave License, and Electrical Contractors License for the City of Hattiesburg, MS. He is the owner and operator of the first African American radio station that has been the voice for the black community in the Pine Belt area since 1969. His refusal to allow these stations to be purchased by corporate giants makes Vernon C. Floyd without a doubt, a great man. "What I am to be, I am now becoming."

Joseph Ibikunle Folayan, Ph.D.
Civil, Structural, Water and Geotechnical Engineering

Dr. Folayan is the Principal Partner and Chief Executive of Progress Engineers. He is responsible for the management of the firm and the works undertaken in the fields of Soils, Foundations, Geotechnical Engineering, Water Supply and Irrigation Engineering. He has managed and directed Geotechnical Engineering studies for major multi-storey buildings, commercial and industrial facilities; offshore and land reclamation projects in the United States of America and in Nigeria. Prior to Progress Engineers he was an Associate Partner in Dames & Moore, USA, a multi-national engineering consulting firm. Dr. Folayan has served on the Board of several organisations such as the Nigeria Building and Road Research Institute (1978-1980), The Royal Exchange Assurance (Nigeria) Limited (1980-1983). He is one of the founding members of the Association of Consulting Engineers, Nigeria (ACEN) and was elected President of ACEN between (1994 - 1997). Executive Committee of Federation Internationale des Ingenieurs Conseils (FIDIC) where he became the first third-world Engineer to be elected into the Executive body. Dr. Folayan has received numerous awards and recognitions for his contribution to the consulting engineering practice in Nigeria.

Regina Folorunsho, Ph.D.
Climatology and Remote Sensing/Geographic Information System

Regina Folorunsho is Chief Research Scientist at the Nigerian Institute for Oceanography and Marine Research. She has written about coastline erosion and implications for human and environmental security.

John W. Forje, Ph.D.
African Science and Technology Policy

Dr. Forje is a Prof Archie Mafeje Fellow, AISA Pretoria, South Africa. He obtained his education from the Universities of Lund, Sweden, Hull and Salford United Kingdom. He is a member of the Teaching Staff of the University of Yaoundé 11-Soa, and visiting Lecturer University of Buea, Cameroon Sub-Director Ministry of Scientific Research, Yaoundé. Member of the Cameroon Academy of Sciences. Dr. Forje is Founder and Research Director, Centre for Action-Oriented Research on African Development (CARAD) Cameroon. He is a member of the Validation Group on the 6th Conference of African Ministers for Public/Civil Service [CAMPS} under the African Union (AU). He is author of the following selected books: *Science and Technology in Africa. Vol.10, Longman World Series on Science and Technology {1989},Consolidating democratic Governance and Quality Management in Africa [2003], The Challenges of Administrative Political and Developmental Renewal [2009[2 vols. State Building and Democracy in Africa [2009]. Here the People Rule [2009]. Century of Change – Symposium on African Unity [2011] Nova Science Publishers Inc, New York, USA.* Contact Post Box 13429 Yaoundé – Cameroon.

Alvin G. Foster, DVM, Ph.D.
Veterinarian

Prior to his retirement in 1994, Dr. Foster was Director, Animal Science Research-Domestic Project Leader for the Ivermectin/Swine programs for Merck. He also assisted the Senior Director of Animal Science Research by developing Clinical Operating Plans and coordinating domestic and international activities to market animal products. Before his directorship, he was the Associate Director, Animal Science Research – International for Merck. Early in his career at Merck, Dr. Foster was a Senior Research Microbiologist, and Senior Research Fellow. He organized the Gastrointestinal Infections Disease area and studied the pathogenesis of bacterial initiated enteritis in domestic animals to develop compounds to overcome this disease. Not only has he received several honors and awards for his work, Dr. Foster has authored and co-authored several publications and articles in prestigious journals.

Norma Francisco, Ph.D.
Educator; Administrator

Dr. Francisco has dedicated her life to helping youth excel academically. Her career has spanned dental hygiene, public health, and educational psychology. She received BS, MPH, and PhD degrees from UC San Francisco (UCSF), UC Berkeley, and Stanford University, respectively. For years, she taught and chaired the Dental Hygiene and Preventive Dentistry Division at UCSF. Upon completing her PhD, she vowed to help level the playing field for inner city youth by opening a Kumon Math & Reading center in East Oakland, CA. There she taught and mentored hundreds of students ages 4 to 60. To help families afford the math and reading tuition, she established the Teach a Child to Fish Scholarship Foundation. She has received numerous honors including the UCSF Dental Alumni's Medal of Honor, an Echoing Green Foundation Fellowship, and the National Dental Society's Outstanding Role Model Award. Currently, Dr. Francisco is a senior academic advisor at Brandman University and executive director of Teach a Child to Fish Scholarship Foundation.

Renty B. Franklin, Ph.D.
Scientist

Dr. Franklin is a Professor in the Dept. of Biomedical Sciences, Dental School, University of Maryland, Baltimore. He is also the Director of the Molecular Cell Biology Track of the graduate program in Biomedical Sciences where he is actively involved in prostate cancer research. His honors and professional activities include: Grant reviewer for the NSF, the NIH, the American Osteopathic Society and the Department of Defense, Prostate and Breast Cancer Research Programs. Among his awards are a Porter Foundation Fellowship; Outstanding Research Award, Howard University; Howard Hughes Distinguished Scientist Award, 1994; and he was profiled in Distinguished African American Scientists of the 20th Century, Oryx Press, 1996. He is an ad hoc reviewer for *Endocrinology, The Prostate, American Journal of Physiology, Biochemistry, Journal of Andrology, Cancer Research, Journal of Clinical Investigation, Biochimica et Biochysica Acta and Journal of the American Association of Cancer Research*. He was a member of the Reproductive Endocrinology Study Section, NIH (1992-1996) and its Chairman (1994-1996). He was a member of the Reproductive Endocrinology Study Section, NIH (2002 - 2004) and was the chairman of the Integrative and Clinical Endocrinology and Reproduction Study Section, NIH (2004-2005).

Bert Fraser-Reid, Ph.D.
Chemistry

Distinguished Research Chemist and James B. Duke Professor (rec'd by only 43 out of 1400 professors) Emeritus, has written over 350 publications. He has lectured at universities, academies, companies, and prestigious institutions in 47 countries. He synthesized insect pheromones from glucose, and shown that many synthetic petroleum based products can be made from sugars. His lab has discovered reactions to make complex sugars, known as oligosaccharides, which are among nature's most important biological regulators, particularly for the body's immune system. He retired from Duke in 1996 and founded a private non-profit research Institute, with a goal to develop carbohydrate-based therapeutic agents for Third World infectious diseases, under the sponsorship of the World Health Organization. In May, 2000, Dr. Fraser-Reid was chosen as the only US member of a Consortium of six international interdisciplinary scientists, funded by the prestigious "Human Sciences Frontier Programme Organization" of Europe, to work towards a carbohydrate-based anti-malaria vaccine. His Institute accomplished the first syntheses of antigenic oligosaccharides associated with malaria and tuberculosis. Dr. Fraser-Reid has won the world's *premiere* award in Carbohydrate Chemistry, also national chemistry awards from societies in USA, Canada, Japan, the Alexander von Humboldt Senior scientist Award from Germany.

Edward H. Freeman, Ph.D.
Chief Technology and Technology Officer, Advanced Knowledge Sys. Research

Dr. Freeman has over 25 years of industry experience in public and private sector IT development, IT management, Artificial Intelligence/Expert Systems development, strategic planning systems, research & development, "shrink wrap" product development, and industry consulting. Prior to his current position with DPS, Dr. Freeman was Vice President of the Requirements Management Business Unit for Rational Software Inc.; founder and CEO of the Radiance Group Inc., a software engineering firm developing medical information and decision support systems; VP of Product Technology and various senior director-level positions with US West Advanced Technologies; Director of HRIS for Stanford Research Institute; and Adjunct Faculty member UCLA Graduate School of Management (MIS), and the Graduate School of Education, CU Denver. He joined the Denver Public School district in 2003 and now serves as its Chief Technology and Information Officer. Since that time, he has launched a number of major district-wide technology initiatives including, the development of a comprehensive teacher pay-for-performance system called ProComp; the design/implementation of an enterprise-wide data-warehouse & academic computing environment; and the ongoing development of district-wide performance metrics and student assessment systems.

Kamau Gachigi, Ph.D.
Material Scientist

He is a lecturer and researcher in the Department of Mechanical Engineering in the University of Nairobi, Kenya, where he has been since 1999. He obtained his undergraduate degree in materials science from the University of Bath (UK) and his MS and Ph.D. in Solid State Science from Penn State. His doctoral thesis was on antiferroelectric ceramics for electrical energy storage and delivery applications, for which he obtained a US patent. He worked for TDK in Narita Japan as a research scientist for 2 1/2 years, where he specialised in electro-ceramics for varistor manufacture. He currently teaches materials science to Mechanical and Electrical Engineering students, and his research includes the production of activated carbon for water filtration, the processing of titanium bearing heavy minerals sands, the recycling of waste plastics (in collaboration with the University of Kassel, Germany), and ferroelectric and antiferroelectric materials (in collaboration with Penn State researchers). He is also the founder of a student group which is designed to encourage entrepreneurship based on engineering and scientific knowledge, and to serve as an outreach to high schools and the community, which he intends to develop into a business incubator. He is also involved in the setting up of a Science Park at the University of Nairobi, and is a lay preacher.

Ilene P. Garner
Engineering Management, Chem/Math.

Ilene Garner has been a manager for over 25 years and held a number of positions in research and development, marketing and sales, project management, product management, and business development. She earned a BS Degree from Farleigh-Dickinson University, an MS Degree in Physical Organic Chemistry from New York University, and a Masters Certificate in Project Mgmt from George Washington University. In 1996, Ms. Garner came to the territory to assume the position of General Manager of AT&T Virgin Islands. She joined the University of the Virgin Islands in 2002 and was charged with creating the Community Engagement and Lifelong Learning Center which offers corporate training, professional development, continuing education and consulting services. In 2006, she assumed the additional position of Program Director for the Occupational Safety and Health Consultation Program for the Virgin Islands. Under Ms. Garner's leadership the Center has implemented over 300 courses and programs, secured endorsement from the International Association of Continuing Education and Training. In 2005 the unit was designated to manage Homeland Security training for the U.S. Virgin Islands. The Center has trained over 1500 students since inception and has launched an on-line program that provides 300 training opportunities, making the unit "globally interactive."

Julius W. Garvey, M.D.
Thoracic, Cardiothoracic Vascular Surgery; son of Marcus Garvey

Dr. Garvey continues to combine his busy surgical practice (Thoracic, Cardiothoracic Vascular) with community service. He is the youngest son of Marcus Garvey. Dr. Julius Garvey is a founding member, and is currently Chairman of the Marcus Garvey Committee International, Inc., an organization that serves to improve the economic, cultural, educational, and spiritual condition of Africans all over the world. Additionally, he serves on the Boards of various other organizations such as, The Board for the Education of People of African Ancestry, The Zumbi Foundation, and the Brotherhood. Over the years, he has worked in conjunction with the various Ministries, the Department of Corrections, and the University of the West Indies, on issues concerning the education of the Jamaican youth, the building of schools, the transfer of books and medical supplies, and a medical student exchange program. He lectures on African History and culture and on the legacy of Marcus Garvey, in the United States, Canada, and the Caribbean. His audience includes Junior High, High School, and college students, as well as, social communities, religious, political and national organizations.

Yaye Kene Gassama, Ph.D.
Director General of National Agency of Applied Scientific Research; biotechnology and plant physiology

Former Minister for Scientific Research, Senegal, Dr. Gassama has also been Chairperson of the African Ministerial Conference on Science and Technology (AMCOST); Vice chair of General Assembly of COMSTECH (Committee on Science and Technological Cooperation); National Coordinator of Biotechnology and Biosafety for Senegal. She has been Professeur titulaire in plant biology department, Faculty of Sciences and techniques University of Dakar, in charge of lectures in biotechnology, microbiology and plant physiology ; responsible of the laboratory of plant biotechnology. Dr. Gassama has also been the National coordinator for UNEP on biotechnology and biosafety and consultant for CORAF-WECARD (Conseil Ouest et Centre Africain pour la recherche et le dévelopment agricoles). She has authored and co-authored 38 scientific publications in international journals.

Diane D. Gates-Anderson, Ph.D.
Environmental Engineering

Dr. Gates-Anderson graduated with her doctorate in environmental engineering in 1991. First she worked in the Environmental Sciences Division at Oak Ridge National Laboratory in Tennessee on how to treat hazardous wastes that had contaminated the soil and groundwater. In one project she and her research team focused on toxic chemicals found in many fuels and solvents that commonly permeate the earth and flow into groundwater. In another project, she investigated a chemical means of leaching mercury out of radioactive wastes. Currently, she works in the Radioactive and Hazardous Waste Management Division, where she invented the process of sealing in laboratory and factory air filters and all their contaminants. The process is called IS*SAFE, for "in situ stabilization and filter encapsulation." Still another project involved disposing depleted uranium waste. Recently Dr. Gates-Anderson has turned to dealing with pesticide spills and preparing in the event of dangerous chemicals purposely unleashed into the environment by terrorists. She is a successful wife, mother and community activist as she serves on the Human Relations Commission in her city, and spends hours organizing and teaching workshops that encourage students to consider technical careers.

Akpa Raphael Gbary, M.D.
WHO Representative to Benin; Medicine

Dr. Gbary, a citizen of Côte d'Ivoire is an experienced health professional with extensive experience in human resources for health development. He obtained an M.D. in 1979 from the Faculty of Medicine at the Peoples' Friendship Patrice Lumumba University in Moscow. The same year, he obtained a diploma in Tropical Medicine and Hygiene at Faculty of Medicine, University of Aix-Marseille II of France. He started his career in 1980 as medical epidemiologist at the *Institut national de Santé publique* of Abidjan, Côte d'Ivoire. In 1985, he was seconded as a researcher and deputy Chief of Research Unit to Organization for Coordination and Cooperation of Major Endemic Diseases Control at Centre Muraz, Bobo-Dioulasso, Burkina Faso. His work as researcher involved applied field research on malaria and other tropical diseases. He earned his Ph.D. in Epidemiology and Community Health in 1995 at Faculty of Medicine, University of Montréal, Canada. Currently, Dr. Gbary is the WHO Representative to the Republic of Benin.

Andemariam Gebremichael, Ph.D.
Associate Dean, and Dean of Academic, Student, and Research Affairs; Medicine

Prof. Gebremichael is the Associate Dean of Orotta Schools of Medicine and Dentistry in Eritrea and Dean of Academic, Student, and Research Affairs. Through his hard work, he assisted in producing Eritrea's first 31 general medical practitioners and 8 specialized doctors who graduated in December 2009 on the basis of the Medical College's internal resources.

Mack Gipson, Jr., Ph.D.
Professor of Geology

(1931 – 1995) Was a Professor of Geology and research scientist in academia. His petroleum research activities focused on a number of areas including the petroleum potential and resevoir characteristics of hte East Slovakian and Danube basins of Slovakia, Purdue Bay (North Slope, Alaska), Pakistan, the Gulf of Mexico, Tanzania, Somalia, Senmark, and mass physical properties of saprolites in the South Carolina Piedmont. In June 1964, Dr. Gipson became Professor and Chairman of the Department of Geological Sciences at Virginia State University in Petersburg. He was also the Director of the National Science Foundation Summer Institute for High School Teachers for Earth Science (1965 - 73); he also directed an Academic Year Institute in Earth Sciences for two years. During this period he performed research investigations on the geology of Mars, which were sponsored by NASA. From 1973 - 74, Dr. Gipson was a visiting scientist with the Exxon Company in petroleum exploration. In 1975 he accepted a position in petroleum research with Exxon Production Research Company, where his work included investigations in seismic stratigraphy, unconventional methods in exploration, reservoir evaluation, and clastic diagenesis. He was the first African American to obtain a Ph.D. in Geology; Founding Advisor of the National Association of Black Geologists and Geophysicists (1981).

Lynford L. Goddard, Ph.D.
Physics, Electrical Engineering – Lasers and Photonics Research

Dr. Goddard is Assistant Professor of Electrical and Computer Engineering. His research group focuses on fabricating, characterizing, and modeling individual lasers and photonics-based sensors, instrumentation and integrated circuits, as well as developing new processing techniques and testing novel semiconductor materials and devices. Applications include hydrogen detection for fuel cells, thermal imaging for security, optical spectrum analysis for metrology and next generation fiber optic communication systems, and optical logic and memory for high speed data processing. His doctoral research focused on characterization and modeling of 1.5-micron GaInNAsSb/GaAs lasers. At Lawrence Livermore National Lab, he conducted post doctoral research on photonic integrated circuits, sensors, and data processing systems. Recently, Dr. Goddard was elevated to be a senior member of the IEEE for his significant professional achievements. Only 8% of the approximately 388,000 current members hold this grade. He is the recipient of a Presidential Early Career Award for Scientists and Engineers (PECASE) nominated by the Department of Energy in 2008 and awarded by President Obama at a White House ceremony in 2010. Dr. Goddard is an author or co-author of over 70 scientific publications. He has 1 issued U.S. patent, 3 pending patents, and 3 provisional patents.

Edgar Goff
Futurist, Research Development

Futurist, Project Manager, and Urban Planner, has provided project management services for thirty years in fields of architecture/ engineering, transportation, real estate development, product innovation, and technology transfer. His experiences span from the provision of an Industrial Development Formulation and Master Land Development Plan for U.S. mid-size cities to facilitating the luring of high-technology companies by providing business development in the Western United States, Great Britain, Saudi Arabia, Nigeria, Korea, Taiwan, Hong Kong, Mainland China, Mexico, and Costa Rica. Mr. Goff is also well experienced in areas of high-technology development and marketing, as a result of working with major state-of-the-art research/development firms. He assisted these firms in commercializing their technology to create leading edge innovation technology in competitive environments. He identified how they could restructure and rejuvenate, thereby allowing them to exploit and create methods to introduce future/survival urban environments for emerging global competitive markets. Mr. Goff has been principal of Hollywood Design Ltd., a consortium of former Hollywood Film Industry movie sets designers and craftmen. He is the grandnephew of Ms. Hattie McDaniel, 1940 Academy Award Winner - Gone With The Wind.

Ernest J. Goodson, DDS
Orthodontics

Dr. Goodson is the proprietor of a private practice of orthodontics. He was the Director of Dental Services in various North Carolina counties and a Lecturer of Mathematics in two universities. After earning his Bachelor of Science in Dentistry from the University of North Carolina 1976, he went on to earn his Doctor of Dental Surgery Degree at UNC's School of Dentistry in 1979. Ernest continued educating himself at the University of London, England; University of California, San Francisco; and Harvard University. He has written several publications and performed research, while giving many lectures relating to orthodontics and dentistry in general. While practicing long hours at his office, Ernest finds time to be a husband and father to his two sons and perform public service throughout his community. He also serves on the University of North Carolina's Health Science Board, which manages the entire medical campus at UNC-Chapel Hill. Along with the North Carolina Medicaid Dental Director, he created and designed a program for orthodontist in this state to treat underserved children.

Odell Graham, Ph.D.
Physics, Electrical Engineering

Dr. Graham, former Chief Scientist at Hughes Aircraft, where he was involved in electronic component design for tactical guided missiles. He was involved in nearly every radar-guided seeker head developed at Hughes. Through all his technical developments, Dr. Graham has earned a well deserved reputation for being an exceptional role model and mentor. He was involved in Minority Engineering Programs (MEP) at various universities. In 1991, he was named Black Engineer of the Year for Outstanding Technical Achievements. Additionally, he has taught courses in electro-magnetic theory, antenna theory, and microwave engineering. He earned his BS degree in Applied Physics, then his MSEE and PhD in Engineering, specializing in electro-magnetic theory, with minors in Applied Math and Solid State Electronics.

Bradford C. Grant, , AIA, NOMA
Associate Dean of the College of Engineering, Architecture, and Computer Sciences, and the Director of the School of Architecture and Design

Bradford Grant is Professor and Director of the School of Architecture and Design and Associate Dean of the College of Engineering, Architecture and Computer Sciences at Howard University. As a registered architect, Grant has extensive experience in urban and community design, universal design, contemplative practices in design education and cultural identity in architecture. His community design work, research on the role of African American architects and his work on "Drawing as Meditation" has earned him the Universal Design Education Award, the Virginia Downtown Development Association Award, AIA Education Honor Award, the AIA Institute Honor for Collaborative Achievement and the Contemplative Practice fellowship. Bradford is past president of the Association of Collegiate Schools of Architecture (ACSA), HBCU liaison to the board of the National Organization of Minority Architects (NOMA) and is currently a board member of the Center for Contemplative Mind in Society. He completed his graduate studies at the University of California at Berkeley and undergraduate degree from California Polytechnic State University, San Luis Obispo.

Julius Grant
Machinist, Research Technician

Julius earned his BS and MS degrees in Physics from Howard University in 1993 and 1999, respectively. His research interests include magnetic properties of solids, health effects of iron particles and long-term storage devices for nuclear waste. Julius currently serves as a Research Technician/Machinist, in the Department of Physics, where he repairs, modifies, and/or constructs laboratory and experimental research equipment and apparatus; develops instructional laboratory experiments; fabricates equipment for new research in close collaboration with the research team; and constructs innovative and new scientific equipment to enhance the learning process. Earlier, he worked as a Laboratory Manager in the Magnetism Laboratory, where he supervised student workers and their projects within the laboratory. Julius has co-authored several publications in his areas of interests in the field of physics.

Clarence C. Gray, III, Ph.D.
Agriculture Research

(1917-2001) Clarence Gray was a VA Tech Professor Emeritus of International Studies, a retired Foreign Service Officer of the US Agency for International Development, a retired US army officer--veteran of WW II and the Korean War, and a retired principal officer of the Rockefeller Foundation. His specialty is international agricultural research management. His public service career began as a high school instructor in rural Virginia, continued as an agronomist and chemist at Virginia State College--a historically Black institution, extended across several continents, wound down as a consultant to leaders in governments and international agencies and ended as head of CCG Associates. He was a member and Chairman of the Board of Trustees of the renowned International Rice Research Institute in the Philippines. From 1970 to 1983 he was a leader in the Green Revolution that freed Asian nations from frequent famines and became the engine of growth that changed the course of history in the world's most populous region. He was Editor: Crop Germplasm Conservation and Use in China, 1980; Strategies for Agricultural Education in Developing Countries, 1974. For his service, he received many honors, including monetary rewards and honorary degrees. He is listed in Who's Who in the World.

Gerald Green
Mechanical Engineering

Gerald Green is a retired Gas/Reservoir Engineer from Pacific Gas & Electric Company. He survived tongue cancer in1995, neck cancer in 1997, and prostate cancer in 2008. He released his memoir, *Life Constricted: To Love, Hugs and Laughter* in 2010. He and his wife, Monica, own Green Consulting Service, an alternative energy and management solution company, and Each 1 Teach 2 Books, a publishing company. He has tutored adult literacy through Oakland's Library Second Start Program, and has mentored young African Americans males in a fatherhood program at the Mentoring Center in Oakland for over six years.

James L. Green, M.D.
Clinical Associate of Ophthalmology and Visual Science

Dr. Green specializes in medical and surgical treatment of vitreal-retinal diseases. He has expertise in surgical treatment of retinal holes that directly affect vision.

Barbara Green-Ajufo, DrPH
Epidemiologist

Dr. Green-Ajufo is an epidemiologist who has worked in public health for more than 20 years at the local and federal levels. She currently works for the Alameda County Public Health Department managing the HIV/AIDS Epi Surveillance Unit, Alcohol and Drug Program and HIV/AIDS-related special epidemiologic projects. Ms. Green-Ajufo has a long-standing commitment to improving the health of women and infants. In 1995, she served as an Epidemic Intelligence Service (EIS) Officer at the Centers for Disease Control and Prevention (CDC), Atlanta, GA. Her research there focused on the roles of race, racial-esteem and racism on reproductive health outcomes and the role of race/ethnic-specific research in explaining the gap in disease disparity. She has worked as an adjunct professor, published a number of articles and presented at a number of national and international conferences on a range of topics.

Kevin C. Greenaugh, Ph.D.
Nuclear Engineering

Dr. Greenaugh is a senior manager at the National Nuclear Security Administration (NNSA) in Washington, DC, where he manages close to a billion-dollar program in nuclear deterrent research and development. He is Director of the Office of Military Application and Stockpile Operations of the National Nuclear Security Administration, and part-time Howard University professor. He discusses the importance of deterrence as well as the benefits to society that have come from the development of nuclear weapons, including supercomuters capable of analyzing energy needs and tracking natural disasters, and the design of peaceful applications of nuclear technology. He is responsible for the development of computer models using the fastest computers in the world and for conducting research and testing at world-class experimental facilities. He has developed national policy for NNSA. He is one of the highest-ranking officials involved in the nuclear deterrent. Formerly, Dr. Greenaugh worked at Los Alamos National Laboratory as a scientist/engineer and the National Institute of Standards and Technology. In addition, Dr. Greenaugh was the president of the National Technical Association from 1988 to 1989. He has been an adjunct professor at Howard University for over fifteen years. He has numerous scientific publications and has been keynote speaker for a number of events.

Lionel O. Greene, Jr., Ph.D.
Research Scientist

He was a scientist in the aerospace industry from the early 1970's through the early 1990's. During this period, he earned his doctorate from Stanford University in Neuropsychology/Computer Science, and completed a post-doctorate at the MIT in Bioastronautics. The aerospace neurophysiologist, who worked with NASA, AT&T Bell Laboratories, and Lockheed Missiles & Space Co. Laboratories. He ended his involvement with the defense industry at the conclusion of the Cold War, and began pursuing a career in education, educational management, and community outreach. He was an Army Officer, with a specialty in air defense artillery systems, coupled with his academic training in the brain sciences and aviation, lead to assignments on projects such as the Strategic Defense Initiative ("Star Wars") Space-Based Command Center, the Army Experimental Light Helicopter Development Program, and Brain Controlled Cockpit Automation Technology. Dr. Greene plays drums and flute, and has worked with artists such as Dexter Gordon, Eddie Henderson, and Charles Earland. He has several publications in the sciences and engineering, and has founded or co-founded several educational programs targeting the underprivileged.

Henry Randall Grooms, Ph.D.
Engineering Manager, Civil Engineer

Since 1969, Dr. Grooms has occupied a number of key technical positions, including his position as senior manager, Strength Structural Analysis and Design for Boeing Integrated Defense Systems. He was responsible for an 80-member stress analysis staff that supported the Delta IV, X-37 and various other programs. He has been honored with awards for his distinguished work in structural engineering on the Apollo, Skylab and Space Shuttle programs. Dr. Grooms is the author or co-author of more than 20 technical articles and papers with many related to space shuttle operation, including "Preliminary Spacecraft Design—The Case for Complete Vehicle Analysis" (1993), "What is an Optimal Spacecraft Structure?" (1990), and "Structural Analysis of the Space Shuttle Orbiter" (1984). The father of 12—many of whom are in college or advanced degree holders—Dr. Grooms' accomplishments also include efforts to help at-risk, inner-city youth as the co-founder of Project Reach. Dr. Grooms is the author or co-author of "Why Are There So Few Blacks in Engineering," "Reaching Out to 'At-Risk' High School Students," and "Trying to Influence 'At-Risk' High School Students."

Ameenah Gurib-Fakima, Ph.D.
Pro-Vice-Chancellor and Professor of Organic Chemistry

She is Professor at the University of Mauritius, works in the department of Chemistry at the Faculty of Science. Her main line of research has been on the pharmacological properties of the endemic medicinal plants of Mauritius. She has published four books on the Medicinal Plants of Mauritius and Rodrigues, 2 CD-ROMs on the Medicinal Plants of the South West Indian Ocean, 2 books on Mauritius through its medicinal plants (English and French version), and an Illustrated Guide to the Flora of Mauritius and the Indian Ocean Islands. She is co-author of another major book entitled Medicinal Plants of Mauritius and the Indian Ocean Islands (MedPharm Scientific, 2004). Elected Fellow of the Linnaean Society of London and of the World Islamic Academy of Science in Jordan, she won the l'Oreal-UNESCO Prize for Women in Science for Africa in 2007, the National Economic and Social Council Prize for Mauritius in 2007 as well as the Special Prize of the CTA/NEPAD/AGRA/RUFORUM for 'African Women in Science' April 09 and the African Union Award for 'Women in Science' for the Eastern African Region in September 2009. She has been elevated to the Order of the Commander of the Star and Key of the Indian Ocean by the Government of Mauritius in 2008 and to the Order of the 'Chevalier de l'Ordre des Palmes Academiques' by the Government of France in 2009.

Arif Gursel
Software Development at Microsoft

Arif is a technical evangelist at Microsoft Corp. He drives technical strategy and platform adoption with strategic software partners that create and deliver software and service solutions for audio, video, and imaging on Microsoft platforms such as Windows Vista, Xbox360, and Zune. He specializes in digital media technologies and their impact on the entertainment industry. Arif is the technical voice of Microsoft's Audio Music Partner (AMP) Alliance. AMP is a group of multi-media industry partners working together to develop, manufacture, and support products and services that inter-operate with Microsoft platforms. He is also the CEO at Invisible Man Entertainment, a production company specializing in audio production, technical deal negotiation, and consulting for the media and entertainment industry. Mr. Gursel is a Board Member of Seattle's NPR station KUOW 94.5.

Adugna Haile, Ph.D.
Entomology, Integrated Pest Management

Dr. Haile is the Head of Plant Sciences Department in one of Eritrea's universities. His specialties are Entomology and Integrated Pest Management. He earned his BS and MS degrees from the Alemaya College of Agriculture, Ethiopia and Ph.D. from the Agricultural University of Norway. Dr. Haile helps to produce scientists who are qualified to improve crop production and to manage plant resources and ecosystems. These graduates of agriculture science are involved with modern integrated crop protection techniques, plant pests and diseases assessment, and help restore natural woodlands and conduct forest research.

Robert Hammie
Mathematics, National Chess Master

Robert earned his BA degree in Mathematics for the University of California, Berkeley. While he hs instructed many Bay Area California youth in math, he is best known for his skills as a National Chess Master.

Ernest C. Hammond, Jr., Ph.D.
Physics

Dr. Hammond, works on organic dye lasers, absorption spectroscopy of EU 2 o3, scanning electron microscopy, transmission electron microscopy, photographic film studies in space, and lunar sample analysis using SEM & TEM from Apollo 11. He jointly developed a method and device to calibrate spectroscopic film according to certain spectral-photometric characteristics used in ground-based and rocket launched instruments by the Laboratory for Optical Astronomy.

Delon Hampton, Ph.D., PE
Civil and Structural Engineering; Program/Construction Management

Dr. Hampton's professional career encompasses a civil engineering professorship at Howard University fro 25 years, professional engineering registration in 18 states, and the District of Columbia, and the successful formation and continued growth of Delon Hampton and Associates (DHA), an award winning, top ENR 500 design and 100 program and construction management firm with offices in Atlanta, Georgia; Los Angeles, California; Champaign Urbana, Illinois; Baltimore, Maryland; Silver Spring, Maryland, and headquarters in Washington D.C. He earned several degrees from Purdue University and the New Jersey Institute of Technology and his Masters Degree in Civil Engineering in 1958 from the University of Illinois, his PhD in Civil Engineering in 1961 and an additional honorary Doctorate from Purdue University. He was the first African American President of the American Society of Civil Engineers (1999-2000). Dr. Hampton has authored over 40 papers and has received two honorary doctorate degrees for services to the engineering profession. He is a former Councilor of the National Academy of Engineering, a Fellow of the American Academy of Arts and Sciences; and is a recipient of the Edmund Friedman Professional Recognition Award and the James Laurie Prize, both given by the American Society of Civil Engineers.

Marc R. Hannah, Ph.D.
Past V. P. SGI and Chief Scientist

Dr. Hannah co-founded Silicon Graphics, Inc. (SGI) and spent 16 years there helping grow the company from a small startup to a multi-billion dollar computer hardware and software company with products from desktop workstations to large, multiprocessor supercomputers. At SGI, Dr. Hannah was chief architect for most of the company's low-end and mid-range graphics systems. He worked closely with Jim Clark to initiate projects to deliver SGI technologies into consumer applications, including the Nintendo-64 game machine for Nintendo and Orlando Interactive TV trial for Time-Warner. Since leaving SGI, Dr. Hannah has done consulting projects for SGI and other companies, and dabbled in a few start-ups, including Omniverse Digital Solutions, a minority focused, web-based media company, and Pulsent Corporation, a technology company developing compression technology for video delivery over the Internet. Dr. Hannah has been granted 13 patents.

Mark G. Hardy, Ph.D.
Biology

Dr. Hardy is Special Assistant to the Provost for Distance Education, Professor and Chair (2002 - present), Department of Biology. He earned his BS (1980) and MS (1982) degrees in Biology from State University, Jackson, MS and Ph.D. in Psychology from the University of Alabama, Tuscaloosa, AL, 1986. He is also the Program Director, Research Initiative for Scientific Enhancement (RISE) Program (2003 - present) College of Science, Engineering, and Technology. Dr. Hardy has been featured in *Who's Who in Science and Engineering* and *Who's Who Among Young American Professionals*, as well as several other citations. Not only has he authored several publishings, he also has been successful in getting several areas of his interests funded.

Anthony "Tony" Harris
Mechanical Engineer, Corp. **Executive**

Anthony "Tony" Harris is President and CEO of Campbell/Harris Security Equipment Company (CSECO), a manufacturer of contraband, explosives, and "dirty bomb" detection equipment. Primary customers include the US State Department, the Department of Homeland Security the US Customs and Border Patrol, and domestic and international law enforcement agencies. Prior to acquiring CSECO, Mr. Harris was VP of marketing for Calpine Corp., headquartered in San Jose, CA, where he was responsible for brand management, marketing strategy development and execution, new product development, advertising and sales training. Before Calpine, Mr. Harris was VP of National Account Services and Western Region sales at PG&E Energy Services in San Francisco. He has also been VP of marketing and sales for Pacific Gas & Electric Company, and President of Standard Pacific Gas Line, Inc. He has been Pres. and CEO of a Silicon Valley start-up venture, StyleChoice.com and has also been Pres. and CEO of Sonoma Ford/Lincoln Mercury. Mr. Harris is one of the founders of the National Society of Black Engineers (NSBE) and currently serves as Chair of its National Advisory Board. He earned his BS in mechanical engineering from Purdue in 1975 and an MBA from the Harvard Graduate School of Business in 1979. He was named a Purdue Outstanding Mechanical Engineer in 1999.

Gary L. Harris, Ph.D., PE
Electrical Engineering, NanoScience

Dr. Harris received his doctorate, masters and BSEE degrees from Cornell University in Electrical Engineering-Electro-Physics in 1980, 1976 and 1975 respectively. He is currently is Professor of Electrical Engineering and Director of the Materials Science Research Center of Excellence at Howard University in the School of Engineering, where he also serves as Director of the National Nanotechnology Infrastructure Network (NNIN) was Associate Vice President for Research from March 1995 to October 2000. Dr. Harris has published well over than 60 peer reviewed scientific articles; edited five books; presented over 100 papers at scientific conferences and was conference Chairman of the International Conference on Silicon Carbide and Related Materials; a participant and lecturer in the International School of Solid-State Device Research in Erice, Trapani, Sicily; received the 1987 Electrical Engineering Outstanding Teaching Award, the National Society of Black Engineers 1985-86 Scientist of the Year Award and was chairman of the Institute of Electrical and Electronics Engineers (IEEE) - Washington Section Electron Devices Group 1984-85. He has worked on several multimedia productions including "Chips are for Kids" and "Safety First" and was featured in the PBS Special "Stuff of Dreams", WNET.

Geraldine E. Harris, Ph.D.
Microbiologist

Science Coordinator, Division of Field Science, Office of Regulatory Affairs at the Food and Drug Administration (FDA). From 1975 - 1977, she became an assistant professor of microbiology at Winston-Salem State University. She went to work for FDA in 1980 where she served as a Consumer Safety Officer for ten years, compiling, generating and evaluating scientific and technical data which formed the basis for the determination of the safe and effective use of food additives. She also served as liaison between FDA's Center for Food Safety and Applied Nutrition (CFSAN) and food industry scientists, consumer groups and individual consumers explaining and interpreting scientific and consumer issues associated with food additives and GRAS (food ingredient: Generally Regarded As Safe) petitions. While serving CFSAN, Dr. Harris abstracted, summarized and evaluated data from Reproductive/Teratology (RT), chronic, and short term toxicology studies as part of the process for review and reappraisal of safety information on regulated food additives. Not only does Dr. Harris lecture, she has produced several publications and she has research interests in molecular mechanisms of staphyloccocal pathogenesis, post secondary allied health/science program development/ evaluation, health/biomedical aspects of aging, and quality assurance for clinical/non-clinical laboratories.

James A. Harris, Ph.D.
Nuclear Chemist and Researcher

(1932 – 2000) Recently retired from one of the Nation Laboratories, as Assistant Division Head, Engineering and Technical Services. While working in his laboratory, he achieved the development and application of Germanium Semi-Conducting Detector Techniques to Neutron Activation Analysis. He became quite famous as Co-Discoverer of heavy manmade chemical elements 104 and 105. Headed the lab's Heavy Isotopes production group. Also, while serving in this group, he was responsible for the control and handling of large quantities of radioactive products, as well as the principal investigator of the actinide elements.

Wesley L. Harris, Ph.D.
Aerospace Engineer and Educator

While at NASA from January 1993 to June 1995, Dr. Harris was responsible for strategy, planning, advocacy and direction of NASA's aeronautics research programs and for institutional management of NASA's Langley, Lewis and Ames Research Centers and Dryden Flight Research Center. From July 1990 until December 1992, he was Vice President of the University of Tennessee Space Institute. From July 1985 to June 1990, Dr Harris was Dean of the School of Engineering at the University of Connecticut, Storrs. He was Professor of Aeronautics and Astronautics at Massachusetts Institute of Technology (MIT) from August 1972 to June 1985. Following leadership service at NASA, Dr. Harris returned to MIT in July 1995 as Professor of Aeronautics and Astronautics. He has served in his current position as Head of the Department of Aeronautics and Astronautics, MIT, since June 2003. He has served on advisory groups of the National Research Council, the Army Science Board, the National Science Foundation, and the Princeton University Board of Trustees. Dr. Harris was elected to the National Academy of Engineering (NAE) in 1995. He has published technical papers on aeroacoustics, unsteady external transonic flows, theory of shock waves in gas mixtures, and hemodynamics. Dr. Harris is the recipient of several honorary doctoral degrees.

William "Bill" Harris
Nano-Technology, Computer Chip Processor

Bill co-founded the African Scientific Institute (ASI) in the mid-1960's and serves as its Executive Secretary. Mr. Harris was the Publishing Editor for two nationally distributed technical publications (1987 - 1993). He Processed Engineered the manufacturing of specialized computer chips for Fairfield Semiconductor Corp. and National Semiconductor Corp. for 19+ years. Currently, he continues performing as a Process Engineer in another company that uses micro-machining technology (10+ years).

Djuana M. E. Harvell, Ph.D.
Cancer Biology, Cell Biology

Dr. Harvell is a graduate of Clark Atlanta University where she earned her BS and MS degrees in Chemistry in1995. In 2001, she earned a Ph.D. from the University of Nebraska Medical Center in Pathology and Microbiology. As a postdoctoral fellow, Dr. Harvell developed an experimental *in vivo* model for studying mechanisms of estrogen and progesterone signaling in human breast cancers. She then translated that experimental work to the analysis of clinical tumors involving patients undergoing hormonal therapies for their breast cancers. Currently, she works in the laboratory of Dr. Kathryn B. Horwitz and teaches at the University of Colorado Health Sciences Center. Her research focus is to understand the actions of the ovarian steroid hormones, estrogen and progesterone, and their role in breast cancer development and progression. The long-term goals of her work are to understand how hormones control breast cancer growth, to understand how breast tumors become resistant to hormone treatment, and to devise ways through which the development of resistance to breast cancer treatment can be avoided. Dr. Harvell has received numerous awards and has spoken and published widely on the subject of issues relating to breast cancer.

L. Julian Haywood, M.D., MACP, FACC, FAHA, FAAAS, WAP
Cardiologist

Dr. Haywood is a Professor of Medicine at the University of Southern California Keck Schoole of Medicine. He developed one of the first coronary care units in 1966 and the first on-line, real-time rhythm monitoring system in 1969, reported acute MI with normal coronary arteries in 1974, acute MI in sickle cell anemia with normal coronaries in 1983, myocardial ischemia in sickle cell anemia, myocardial infarction in Blacks, cardiac dysfunction in sickle cell anemia, diastolic dysfunction measured by apexcardiogram, computer techniques for perfusion scan interpretation and LV function measurement by MRI, differential risks for myocardial infarction in blacks, importance of psychosocial and socioeconomic factors in myocardial infarction, race/sex determinants of cardiac enzyme levels, vector cardiographic measurement of atrial size, myocardial injury associated with bone marrow embolism in sickle cell anemia, differential risks of atrial fibrillation among racial groups. Dr. Haywood's areas of interest include Myocardial ischema, patho-physiologic mechanisms and clinical parameters; Cardiac arrhythmias-clinical mechanisms and management; Cardiovascular manifestations of sickle cell anemia; Noninvasive procedures for cardiovascular diagnosis; Psyco-social and socioeconomic factors in cardiac illness. He is author or co-author of over 257 publications.

David Rice Hedgley, Jr., Ph.D.
Mathematician

In 1985 he solved the decades old problem of computer graphics by developing the mathematical algorithm that would tell computers which lines on a computer screen could and couldn't be seen from various perspectives (or what we call today 3D). And if that wasn't enough, to ensure his position in the technology hall of fame, Dr. Hedgley then came back in 1999 and created a formal algorithm for routing traces on a printed circuit board, that is so complex it required the invention of new symbols to explain his work. Essentially what it does is cut down the time for finding a route on a circuit board exponentially Historically, most previous algorithms have been either very costly or very slow and usually both. This contribution will avoid both problems and as a result provide a framework for supporting the electrical parts and electrical components between circuit components. Dr. Hedgley explained to the readers of Ebony, that the road to success and acceptance had not been easy; "Computers were not on Hedgley's mind when he was growing up. He was interested in linguistics but majored in biology and chemistry at Virginia Union University. Math came later and he earned a second bachelor's degree in the discipline from Michigan State University. When we celebrate "Black History Month", remember that technology and computers would not be the same without Dr. Hedgley.

Nadia Hegazy, Ph.D.
Computer Science; Communications Engineering

Dr. Hegazi is a Senior expert for ICT strategic planning ministry of telecommunication and Information Technology and International Relations Ministry of Telecommunications and Information Technology since 2002. She has been a Professor of Computer Engineering since 1986. From 1986 – 1998, she served as Head of the Central Data Processing Department at the National Research Centre and from 1981 – 1993 she also served as Head of the Informatics Research Department. Dr. Hegazi is a Consultant to the Minister of Education since 1988. She has been Consultant to the Minister of Scientific Research during 1989 – 1994 and Consultant to the Head of the Parliament from 1991-2001. She has authored and co-authored approximately 100 publications. She is still very active in national and international ICT projects and activities.

M. Nidanie Henderson, Ph.D.
Chemistry, Molecular Biophysics

Dr. Henderson research is focused on deciphering how the Abl protein functions. Abl kinase is a protein whose unregulated activity is implicated in the pathogenesis of chronic myelogenous leukemia (CML). A subset of patients treated with a small molecule inhibitor of Abl activity relapses due to the emergence of drug-resistant mutations in the protein. Since analysis of mutant proteins often reveals insight into protein function, we hope that the study of these drug-resistant mutant proteins in addition to the native protein will teach us more about Abl function. Dr. Henderson also lectures in Chemical Biology.

Marvin B. Hendricks, Ph.D.
Genetics Research, Molecular Biology

Dr. Hendricks earned his BS degree from MIT in 1973 and his Ph.D. (1980) from John Hopkins University in Molecular Biology. He has been a Senior Research Scientist with Millennium Pharmaceuticals, Inc., Brigham and Women's Hospital and Integrated Genetics, Inc. He is a member of several professional organizations; co-authored books and written many articles in international journals on recombinant DNA molecules. He was also Valedictorian at Central High School, Newnan Georgia in 1969.

Hon. Olden Henson
Physicist, City Councilman

Hon. Olden Henson, a graduate of the University of Pennsylvania, holds both a Bachelors and Masters degree in Physics. He is also a graduate of the Federal Bureau of Investigations' Counterterrorism Academy as well as the FEMA Preparedness School. A former physicist for General Electric Corporations' Nuclear Division, he transitioned into the political arena by getting elected to the Hayward, California City Council in 1993. He utilized his training as a physicist as a member of the National League of Cities' Public Safety Committee Member in 1994 and making public safety technology, disaster preparedness, and interoperability key focus issues for the organization. Olden has given testimony before 7 U.S. Congressional and Senate committees on subjects ranging from the need to continue funding for local government technologies and the need for resources and information sharing in preparation and response to disasters natural and terror generated. He has hosted a CSPAN on Public Safety Technologies. Olden continues his role as an elected official in Hayward while chairing the technology committee in his city.

William Henson, Ph.D.
Ret'd Professor of Agriculture and University Administrator

Now retired, he has worked in most facets associated with poultry husbandry--- from poultry farm operator (general farm work) to researcher in poultry production and marketing. He has performed laboratory research on egg shell quality, served as egg and poultry inspector to enforce fresh egg laws and to ensure the wholesomeness of poultry. As a Senior Agricultural Economics Service Representative for the U.S. Department of Agriculture, Dr. Henson performed economic analysis of egg and poultry sectors and poultry and egg supply, demand and price analysis for the U.S. Northeast Region. From 1967 - the present, he was an Assistant Professor of Agricultural Economics. Twenty-two technical research bulletins or journal articles in the area of poultry and egg economics have been authored or co-authored by Dr. Henson. He contributed to seven major U.S. Department of Agriculture task force reports as a poultry and egg specialist. Until his recent retirement, Dr. Henson was Assistant to the Dean, College of Agricultural Sciences, Pennsylvania State University. In this position he was charged with graduate student recruitment and served as the Director of Minority Programs in the College of Agricultural Sciences.

Brandon L. Hewitt, P.E.
Civil Engineering, Const. Mgmt.

Brandon is the Vice President of KHAFRA which offers its clients engineering and design services for the following disciplines: architecture, civil engineering including water resources engineering, environmental, structural, mechanical, electrical, instrumentation and controls engineering, energy assessment, construction management and GIS.

Ray A. Hill, Ph.D.
Botany, Biology

Dr. Ray Hill, retired AP Biology teacher, has coached student teams to several successful "wins" in Department of Energy-sponsored Science Bowls and NSTA/Toshiba ExploraVision and Duracell Challenge competitions. Ray is the recipient of one of the first Siemens Advanced Placement Scholar awards and two Distinguished Einstein Fellow Finalist awards. He serves as an AP and SAT II consultant, a Development Committee member, and AP Biology Reader.

Lynne M. Holden, M.D.
Emergency Medical Physician

Dr. Holden is the President and Executive Director of Mentoring in Medicine. Dr. Holden provides the overall leadership for the team, recruits volunteers, facilitates program development, creates overall organizational strategy, and establishes collaborative partnerships. Dr. Holden attended Temple University School of Medicine and completed her residency in Emergency Medicine in 1995 at the Albert Einstein College of Medicine-Jacobi/Montefiore Emergency Medicine Residency Program in the Bronx, NY. She served as chief resident her final year. She is a board-certified Emergency Medicine doctor. For the past six years, Dr. Holden has served as a Co-chairperson of the Admissions Committee at the Albert Einstein College of Medicine and as Montefiore Residency Site Director of the Jacobi-Montefiore Emergency Medicine Residency Program. She is currently in her final year of the Healthcare Leadership Academy at Montefiore Medical Center in the Bronx, New York. Dr. Holden is also the coordinator for The Emergency Department Clinical Exposure and Mentoring Program. She is a Deaconess at the Abyssinian Baptist Church in Harlem and serves on the Scholarship, Health and Hospitality ministries.

Denise Holland
President, Black Data Processing Associates (BDPA); Computer Science

Denise Holland serves as the BDPA National President. In this position, she is responsible for leading the organization and ensuring that its vision and mission are effectively realized through quantifiable objectives. She has over 30 years of professional experience including Human Resource Management/HRIS, IT Project Management, IS Security Management, Change and Problem Management, and Financial Management Systems. Currently, she is the Director Information Technology - SAP for Amtrak. She is responsible for overseeing the Human Capital Management (HCM) mySAP Production System; managing Payroll, Human Resources, Time Management, and Training/ Change Management Teams; presenting system changes to senior management; ensuring departmental processes and procedures are developed; and participating in SAP project implementations.

Kerrie L. Holley
Software Development, CTO for IBM's Center of Excellence

Kerrie Holley is currently a Distinguished Engineer in IBM Global Services, a member of IBM's Academy of Technology, and a chief architect in the Business Consulting Services (BCS), Application Innovation Services (AIS) group. Kerrie is the CTO for IBM's Center of Excellence for Web services and Services Oriented Architecture (SOA). His areas of expertise are in software engineering best practices, end-to-end advanced Web development, adaptive enterprise architecture, conducting architecture reviews, Web services, service-oriented architecture, e-business solutions, information technology strategy, formation of partnerships among clients and vendors, and managing technical risks. In recognition of his sustained technical achievement and leadership, Mr. Holley was appointed an IBM Distinguished Engineer in 2000. In that same year Mr. Holley was elected to the prestigious IBM Academy of Technology which is comprised of 300 of IBM's top technologists. He received a Bachelor of Arts degree in Mathematics and a Juris Doctorate in law degree from DePaul University.

Franklin Hornbuckle
COO, Satellite Aerospace Corp., EE

Mr. Frank Hornbuckle is Vice President and Division Director of the CTA Spacecraft Special Payloads Division. In this role, Mr. Hornbuckle supports NASA/Goddard Space Flight Center in the design and development of its small satellite programs and all Shuttle Special Payload Systems. Before joining CTA, Mr. Hornbuckle was Vice President of Engineering at Fairchild Space Company in Maryland where he and his organization successfully completed the design and supported the launch of several satellites including Applications Technology Satellite - F, Landsat, Solar Maximum, Explorer Platform, and the TOPEX/ POSEIDON (US/French satellite). Mr. Hornbuckle was responsible for the manufacture of high performance fighter aircraft flight units such as the F-14 Stores Management System and the F-16 Solid State Data Recorder and Transfer Unit. Mr. Hornbuckle started his career at the RCA Astro Space Division in Princeton, NJ where he designed analog and digital components and subsystems for several RCA satellites including the TIROS Meteorological Satellite, NIMBUS Meteorological Satellite, Atmoshere Explorer, and several classified missions. As a senior Engineer, Mr. Hornbuckle developed RCA's first Direct Energy Transfer (DET) spacecraft power system which was first flown as a space military program. Derivations of this system are still being utilized today.

Napoleon Hornbuckle
Ret'd Corp. Vice President, Diversified Technologies, EE

Past Corp. VP at Motorola Corp., where he provided leadership for the Diversified Technologies Division, Motorola Space and Systems Technology Group. In 1984, he assumed the responsibility of the Tactical Communications Operations within the Communications Division, with the Marketing, Program Management and Engineering Departments reporting to him. During this time, he successfully led the introduction of a number of products into the military. One product was the AN/PRC-112 survival radio that was used by Captain O'Grady in Bosnia. Another product was the LST-5 satellite transceiver used by the military special operations, state departments, and others during times of crises. In 1990 he was asked to lead the Strategic Electronics Division that comprised all of Motorola's space-related products. In 1992, the division received the Goddard Space Flight Center Excellence Award for Quality and Productivity. Napoleon was selected in 1993 to lead the group efforts in diversification of its businesses. A new division was formed, Diversified Technology Division, which he led. This division consists of both military and commercial products. Some of the commercial products developed include those for electronic toll collection and the GPS/cellular phone for emergency messaging.

Norbert Hounkonnou, Ph.D.
Quantum Mechanics; Mathematical Physics

Professor Hounkonnou received his PhD from the Université catholique de Louvain (Belgium) in 1992. He has been professor of mathematical physics at the Institut de Mathématiques et de Sciences Physiques and at the Faculty of Sciences of the Université Nationale du Bénin since 1996. He is a leading expert on noncommutative and nonlinear mathematics in mathematical and theoretical physics putting special emphasis on generalized deformed quantum (oscillator) algebras including representations, coherent states, quantum orthogonal polynomials and special functions. He has worked at Orsay, Pennsylvania State, Montréal, Louvain, Université de Lomé, etc. Dr. Hounkonnou has published over 40 research papers on n-body problems in non-relativistic quantum mechanics, on scattering theory in non-relativistic and relativistic quantum mechanics using the von Neumann theory of self-adjoint extensions of symmetric linear operators, and on classical and semi-classical orthogonal polynomials. He has been the President and holder of the International Chair of Mathematical Physics and Applications (ICMPA - UNESCO Chair). Some of his memberships include the International Association of Mathematical Physics, African Academy of Sciences (AAS), New York Academy of Sciences, and UNESCO Scientific Board for International Basic Sciences Programme (IBSP).

Clifford W. Houston, Ph.D.
Microbiology and Immunology, Immediate Past President of the American Society of Microbiology

Dr. Houston **is** Associate Vice President for Educational Outreach and the Herman Barnett Distinguished Professorship in Microbiology and Immunology. He is also the past President of the American Society for Microbiology and is the former Deputy Associate Administrator for Education in the Office of Education at NASA Headquarters, where he provided oversight and guidance for divisions charged with developing space science programs, research opportunities, networking resources for students and faculty at all education levels and collaborated with science centers and museums to provide space science education to all ages of the general public. Dr. Houston earned his BS degree in Microbiology & Chemistry and his MS degree in Biology from Oklahoma State. In 1979, he earned his Ph.D. in Microbiology and Immunology from the University of Oklahoma Health Sciences Center. His research has focused on the role that bacterial toxins play in the pathogenesis of disease. Recently, he was appointed to the National Institutes of General Medical Sciences Advisory Council. A prolific author, he has published numerous articles and abstracts and has addressed prestigious audiences throughout the world. Dr. Houston has also established educational programs and activities throughout the country to enhance the interest of young students in mathematics and science.

Johnny L. Houston, Ph.D.
Mathematics, Computer Science

Is a Senior Research Professor in the Department of Mathematics and Computer Science in academia. Previously, he served as Vice Chancellor for Academic Affairs and Dean of the Faculty. Dr. Houston has served in several capacities as a Specialist in Mathematics and/or Computer Science. He is a co-founder of National Association of Mathematicians (NAM) and has been its Executive Secretary from 1975 until 2000. A very active and productive mathematical/computational scientist and educator (served on 3 doctoral committees, supervised 15 Master theses, supervised 10 undergraduate honor theses, coordinated 15 national conferences and has been the PI/Co-PI for several millions of dollars in grant money), Houston holds regular membership in several major professional organizations. Among other note-worthy accomplishments, he is the author of many articles on the history of African Americans in Mathematics, two bookss: The History of NAM, the First 30 Years; 1969-1999 (240pp), and the recently completed Profiles on American Mathematicians of Diverse Ethnicities, 1699 - 1999.

Samuel Hunter, M.D.
Physician and Biochemist

Dr. Hunter is a physician with a specialty in Internal Medicine. He earned his medical degree from Cornell University Medical School, and holds a Ph.D. in Biochemistry from the University of Illinois. He studied further as a Post-Doctoral fellow at The Albert Einstein College of Medicine. Before entering the practice of medicine, he was an assistant professor of Biochemistry at Rutgers University. For past seven years Dr. Hunter has studied shea butter extensively, both in the laboratory and clinically. He has traveled to over a dozen countries in Africa where he has studied the processing of shea butter by various methods. His most significant contribution to the industry was the discovery that the cinnamic acid content was a reliable indicator of the quality of a given batch of shea butter. In the U.S., Dr. Hunter is the foremost expert on the clinical usefulness of shea butter. He serves as consultant to companies and groups in both private and public sectors. Dr. Hunter is one of the founding members of the International Shea Butter Association. As the main speaker at The American Shea Butter Institute's Shea Butter Workshop, he shares rare and valuable information on shea butter, its ingredients as new solutions for important problems in nutrition, health care and material science; and promote the benefits of this product for solutions in various industries.

A. Chidi Ibe, Ph.D, DIC P.Eng, FGS, FOS
Physical oceanography, Geology, Ocean governance

After retiring from his service with the United Nations System in 2008, Prof Ibe became the Pro-Chancellor of Evan Enwerem University (former: Imo State University, Nigeria). While serving in the UN in 1990, he was the Senior Asst. Exec. Secretary and Head of the Marine Pollution Research and Monitoring Section in the Secretariat of the Intergovernmental Oceanographic Commission (IOC) of UNESCO, where he directed the Global Investigation Program for the Marine Environment (GIPME) as well as coordinated the global effort to study and clean up the pollution of the Persian Gulf (1991 – 1995) in the aftermath of the Gulf war. In 1995, he joined the United Nations Industrial Development Organisation (UNIDO), where he was responsible for the implementation of several environmental programmes including the role of Regional Director/Principal Technical Adviser on Persistent Organic Pollutants (POPs) and International Waters in Africa. In 2006, he was appointed the first Executive Secretary of the Interim Guinea Current Commission in 2006. Prof. Ibe is the author/co-author, editor/co-editor of 17 Books/Manuals on Coastal Areas Management, Near-shore, Dynamics and Environmental Pollution Control and published approx. 70 scientific/technical papers in reputable international journals.

Oyewusi Ibidapo-Obe, Ph.D.
Civil Engineering; Mathematics

Professor Ibidapo-Obe the President of the Nigerian Academy of Science. After earning his Ph.D. in Civil Engineering in 1976. In 1983, he became a full Professor of Civil Engineering at the University of Lagos. During 1991 -1995 he was Head of the Engineering Analysis Unit and the Dean of the Faculty of Engineering between 1995- 1999. He was subsequently the Deputy Vice-Chancellor in April 2000 and acted as Vice-Chancellor between September 2000 and April 2002. He was appointed substantive Vice-Chancellor on 1st May, 2002 and successfully served until 30th April 2007. He was the Chairman of the Committee of Vice Chancellors of Nigerian Universities. Prof. Ibidapo-Obe has published extensively in reputable international journals with some 60 papers. The focus of his research is on Control and Information Systems in a Stochastic Environment. He serves as an International Scholar-in-Residence at The Pennsylvania State University and a Visiting Research Professor at Texas Southern University.

Elham M. A. Ibrahim, Ph.D.
Commissioner for Infrastructure and Energy Of The African Union Commission; Electrical Engineering

In her position as a Commissioner with AUC Dr. Ibrahim is responsible for the promotion of strategies for accelerated development and sound management of transport, communications, tourism and energy sectors across the continent. A native of Egypt, she was also Egypt's first Under Secretary of State in Egypt, Ministry of Electricity and Energy. She has also served in numerous energy strategy and policy related positions, and led computer aided management for projects and electric network design and project management in electric networks, renewable energy, and testing facilities. She has a Ph.D. in Electronics and Communications from Cairo University.

Felix I. Ifeanyi, DVM
Biology; Veterinarian

Dr. Ifeanyi is an university Professor and Head of the Department of Biological Sciences. He also serves as the Director of the university's Research Initiative for Scientific Enhancement (RISE) Program, which enhances the competitiveness of its participants in gaining admission into graduate schools to earn Ph.D., or MD/PhD degrees and upon completion of the graduate programs, pursue careers in biomedical research.

Saidq Bello Ikharo, Ph.D.
Facilities Engineering and Management

Dr. Ikharo is Vice Chancellor of General Services in the Peralta Community Colleges District, providing leadership in the modernization of the District. During his tenure at Peralta, Dr. Ikharo, who recently reorganized the Department of General Services, has headed the construction of the new Berkeley City College, a $65-million project that is due to open later this summer. He has also overseen the design, development and construction of more than 25 District-wide projects, totaling some $150 million, including deployment and construction of the new 18,000 square-foot, $15 million Laney College Art Building. Prior to joining the Peralta Community Colleges District, Dr. Ikharo was General Manager for Purchasing and Contracts at the Oakland Unified School District, where he supervised the daily operations of a myriad of departments for 140 schools in the district.

Victor Akpan Inem, M.D.
Family Physician; Primary Health Care

Dr. Inem has been a consultant and visiting Professor in Family Medicine at the University of Lagos University Teaching Hospital teaching Primary Health Care, Primary Health Care, Integrated Management of Childhood illness and Lecturer on Refugee Health to the Masters Program in Humanitarian and Refugee Study. At this same institution, he has taught research Methodology-Qualitative & Quantitative, Community Paediatrics, IMCI, ELSSI for Doctors, post basic nursing in ophthalmology, paediatrics and community health officers. Dr. Inem has also been a Consultant to medicine residents in the supervision of house officers at the Delta State University Teaching Hospital in Warri, overseeing the general out-patient dept., setting up the national health insurances scheme clinics and conducting Ward and clinical rounds training. He was the Medical Director of Interface Medical Clinic, Shomolu (1990 – 1996); consultant and Deputy Medical Director of Jalupon Estate Hospital (1988 – 1990) where he performed administrative and clinical duties, in charge of the Obs and Gynae unit. During 2003-2004, Dr. Inem participated in UNICEF and WHO research studies

Peter Intsiful, Ph.D.
Physics

Dr. Intsiful is an Industrial/Engineering Physicist. His research interests include: Thermo-electro-mechanics and advanced energy systems. He is currently engaged in the investigation of magnetic properties of materials. Dr. Intsiful's post graduate work involved Neutron Activation Analysis of elements, such as Aluminum and Magnesium. Following his postgraduate work, he joined Bendix Field Engineering Corp., where he was engaged in spacecraft engineering and worked to maintain various subsystems, including payload instrumentation, altitude & control, power and communication. He later joined Allied-Signal Corp., where he was involved in Geodetic Engineering: tracking of satellite/spacecraft orbits, via Tracking Data Relay Satellite Systems (TDRSS). He eventually joined Ford Aerospace (later Loral AeroSys) as Research and Development Engineer. Here, he worked on major engineering projects such as, SpaceLab, Landsat, and InfoLan Gateway. Eventually, he led an effort to develop a Verification & Validation Plan for the Space Station Ground Information Systems Network. Presently, Dr. Intsiful is a Lecturer at Howard University and an Adjunct Professor at the University of the District of Columbia.

Adrian J. Isles, Ph.D.
Computer Science, Mathematics

Dr. Adrian Isles has worked on pioneering new methodologies and technologies in the area of static functional verification for RTL designs. He was one of the architects and chief developers of Solidify, Averant Inc.'s flagship static functional verification tool. Dr. Isles obtained his B.S. in Electrical Engineering from Howard University in 1993 and his M.S. and Ph.D. in Electrical Engineering and Computer Science from the University of California, Berkeley in 1997 and 2000, respectively. His research focus is in areas related to computer-aided design and formal verification of integrated circuits. Since 1990, he has also worked with Intel Corporation and Massachusetts Institute of Technology, Lincoln Laboratory. He has written numerous research papers in the field and holds several patents.

Saadou Issifou, M.D., Ph.D.
Head of Hospital Medical Research Unit; Medicine; Medical Parisitology; Molecular Biology

Since 2001, Dr. Issifou has been the Head of Medical Research Unit of the Albert Schweitzer Hospital, Gabon. He was the Head of Health Research Unit, Regional Centre for Development and Health (CREDESA/SSP) in Benin, serving as Coordinator of community based health research (1998 – 2001). Earlier, he served as the Research officer in malaria and public health at the Regional Centre for Development and Health (CREDESA/SSP) in Benin from 1988 - 1998. Dr. Issifou evaluated health centres of health service development project in three administrative areas in Bénin (LALO, OUAKE and TOFFO) in March1998. He has trained health workers (Nurses and Midwife) on the utilization of the "ordinogrammes" in the Atlantic, Ouémé and Mono administrative departments, organized by the CREDESA/SSP and financed by the FED (Fonds Européen de Developpement), June - September 1999 and November – December 2000. He provided documentary review on malaria and interventions for malaria control in Benin from 1992 to June 1999, financed by the UNICEF (22nd June to 28 th July 1999). He also served as WHO's National Consultant for National Vaccination Days (NVD) for poliomyelitis eradication. Dr. Issifou has authored and co-authored more than 50 publications.

Deborah Jackson, Ph.D.
Opto-Electronics Communications

Her research covers a wide range of topics in electromagnetic phenomena and solid state physics. Early on, she studied the materials properties of low temperature superconductors at MIT. Moving on, she studied materials using hard X-ray and vacuum ultraviolet radiation as the probe at the Stanford Synchrotron Radiation Project. She later joined the prestigious Schawlow/Hansch laser laboratory and began work in non-linear optics, where she used visible and mid-infrared lasers to study atomic spectra. One of her most cited papers was published while at IBM, when she documented, and correctly explained the presence of interference effects between different optical harmonics. While at the Hughes Research Laboratory, she initiated a photonic device development program aimed at integrating photodetectors, modulators, diode lasers and VLSI circuits on a common chip. At the Jet Propulsion Laboratory, she moved into the radio frequency portion of the electromagnetic spectrum to develop and deliver two space qualified radio frequency instruments, for the Cassini mission to Saturn. As an inventor, she has devised and patented a high bandwidth encryption interface for use in the telecommunications grid. She is currently a Program Manager in the National Science Foundation.

Keith H. Jackson, Ph.D.
Physics, X-Ray Optics, Sponsored Research

Dr. Jackson is now a university's Vice President of the Division of Research and Professor of Physics at Florida A&M University. Until recently, he has been a leader of lithography programs at the Center for X-ray Optics at the Lawrence Berkeley Laboratory. From hand-held supercomputers to synthetic enzymes that repair damaged cells in the human body, to self-assembling molecular-sized machines that clean up our environment, the future belongs to nanotechnology. A key to achieving this future is x-ray lithography, which can fabricate devices with features of about 100 nanometers, only a thousandth the thickness of a human hair. His work was primarily in the area of molecular dynamics and photo-dissociation. This work required the use of rare gas excimer lasers and synchrotron radiation as excitation sources in the vacuum ultraviolet. Earlier, he was involved with the development of Silicon Nitride ($Si_3 N_4$) as a potential gate insulator in NMOS, and CMOS technologies. His job was to develop the necessary processing techniques required to fabricate thin nitride films on silicon substrates. Later, in 1988, Dr. Jackson became a member of the Technical Staff at Rockwell International, where he established a facility for the growth and characterization of polycrystalline diamond thin films.

William Jackson, Ph.D.
Chemist. Photodissociation Dynamics with Velocity Ion Imaging

Dr. Jackson has 45 years as a chemist ranging from serving for the Martin Marietta Co., the National Bureau of Standards and NASA's Goddard Space Flight Center. He was a Professor of Chemistry for 11 years at Howard University and the University of California at Davis for 21 years, where he retired in June of 2006. While working for NASA, Dr. Jackson became an expert in studying the chemistry of comets. He is also an expert in the use of lasers to study photochemical reactions (he is the first person to using dye lasers to study photochemistry). His research interests included laser chemistry and photochemistry, cometary astrochemistry, and the photodissociation of ions and molecules. His studies in cometary astrochemistry included laboratory studies, theoretical calculations, and telescopic observations at the National Observatories. The laboratories studies use velocity-ion-imaging to determine the identity, velocity and angular distribution of the fragments. Four-wave-mixing techniques with lasers are used to generate vacuum-ultraviolet-wavelengths for both photodissociation and photoionization. The molecules that are being investigated are the ones that are important for understanding molecules that are present in comets, planetary atmospheres and the interstellar medium.

Assan Jaye DVM, Ph.D.
Veterinary Medicine; Viral Diseases

Dr. Jaye is the Interim Head Viral diseases Program, MRC (Medical Research Council Laboratories) unit, Gambia. Earlier, in 1998, he was employed as a Scientist in charge of HIV and Measles Immunology in the Viral Diseases Programme at this unit. He has authored and co-authored more than 50 papers that were published in distinguished scientific journals. After earning his Ph.D. in 1988 and researching for a short period in his final clinical year, where he identified a biochemical marker of susceptibility to cattle trypanosomiasis, he opted for a career in Veterinary/Medical Research. His work in Immunology and Molecular biology of trypanosomes was undertaken at the International Livestock Research Institute in Kenya and at Brunnel University in UK from 1989-93. From 1998, as a research scientist, his work extended to HIV immunology from 1998 and as head of the HIV immunology projects, he developed interest to understand the underlying immunological mechanisms responsible for long-term non-progression in HIV-2 infected individuals. Dr. Jaye is now being seconded by MRC to UCAD (Cheikh Anta Diop University, Senegal) to initiate a regional research collaboration on infectious diseases. He has also got a grant from the Canadian Global Health Research Initiative to coordinate capacity development in Senegal, Guinea Bissau and Gambia for a regional platform for HIV

Ambrose Jearld, Jr., Ph.D.
Chief of Research Planning and Evaluation, Marine Biologist

Chief of Research Planning and Evaluation Section of the Research Planning and Coordination Staff at Northeast Fisheries Center, National Marine Fisheries Service. This facility is a fore- runner to the starting of marine science in the U.S., approx. 1871. In his position, Dr. Jearld assures research products are sufficiently evaluated by the Center to meet user needs. Also, he identifies studies at various institutions that have potential to augment the Center's research. Previous to his current position, Dr. Jearld served as Chief, Fishery Biology Investigation, Resource Assessment Division. He developed advanced research techniques in the field of fishery biology to generate scientific information necessary to management policies and fisheries science; directed advanced and complex research investigations in such areas as fish and shellfish determination age and growth, maturity, fecundity (number of eggs female fish produce and carry), and behavioral studies important to assessments and to fisheries management; managed the production of yearly estimates of critical assessment parameters such as age compositions of 18-20 species.

Yemisi Adefunke Jeff-Agboola
Food Mycotoxicology/Phytopathology; Food Microbiology

Dr. Jeff-Agboola is a Principal researcher in the department of Food Science and Tecnhnology, School of Agriculture and Agrcultural Technology, Federal University of Technology Akure, Nigeria. She is involved in teaching and research in the area of Food Fementation Technology, Food Microbiology, Nutritional Evaluation of Food Processing , Meat and Meat technology, Dary Technology, Science Laboratory Techniques, Radioisotopy, and cell biology. She serves as article reviewer for many local and international journals and as a resource person for Irepodun Ifelodun Local Government in Ekiti State on Food processing and preservation Techniques, St Loise Secondary School in the area of importance of some essential minerals to the body and processing of fruit juices from the indigenous fruits.

Bill Jenkins, Ph.D.
Epidemiologist

Dr. Jenkins was a Supervisory Epidemiologist in the Div. of STD/HIV Prevention in CDC, where he served as an expert on minority issues in STD/HIV Prevention and Control through his research on issues, associations, and implications of STD (Sexually Transmitted Diseases) and HIV diseases on minority communities. He also instructs medical and undergraduate students and others in biostatistics, epidemiology and public health. Prior to this position, Dr. Jenkins worked for the National Center for Health Statistics (NCHS). After leaving NCHS he became a Consultant in Biostatistics and Epidemiology where some of his assignments included research and development of proposals in Health Services Research (KOBA Associates). From 1980-87, Dr. Jenkins served as a Mathematical Statistician and provided project management, data systems management and statistical consultation. He was President of the Society for Analysis of African American Public Health Issues (SAAPHI), comprised primarily of Black Epidemiologists and Biostatisticians working to improve the health status of African Americans. He is founder of Project Imhotep, a training program in Biostatistics and Epidemiology and co-founder of the Public Health Sciences Institute.

Anthony M. Johnson, Ph.D.
Distinguished Research Physicist; Photonics Research

Dr. Johnson has been Director of the Center for Advanced Studies in Photonics Research and Professor of Physics and Computer Science & Electrical Engineering at the University of Maryland Baltimore County since 2003. He received a B.S. in Physics (1975) from Polytechnic Institute of New York and a PhD in Physics (1981) from City College of New York. He was a Distinguished Member of Technical Staff at Bell Labs in Holmdel, NJ, where he spent 14 years before joining New Jersey Institute of Technology (1995), where he was Chair and Distinguished Professor of Physics until 2003. Current research interests include the ultrafast photophysics and nonlinear optical properties of bulk, nanostructured, and quantum well semiconductor structures and ultrashort pulse propagation in fibers. He served as a member of the Board of Directors of the American Physical Society (APS) [94-97], the IEEE Lasers & Electro-Optics Society [93-95], the Optical Society of America (OSA) [93-96 & 00-03] and the American Institute of Physics (AIP) [02-08] He was 2002 President of the OSA; Editor-in-Chief of *Optics Letters* (95-01); member of the DOE Basic Energy Sciences Advisory Committee (99-08); and Chair (09-10) of the IEEE Photonics Society Fellows Evaluation Committee. He is a Fellow of the APS, OSA, IEEE, AAAS, and the National Society of Black Physicists.

George W. Johnson, Jr., M.D.
Physician, Cardiothoracic & Vascular Surgery

Dr. Johnson earned his MD from Meharry Medical College, MD, 1976, then went on to earn his credentials from Baylor College of Medicine in General and Vascular Surgery in 1981 and Thoracic Surgery in 1983. His medical interests include Endovascular Surgery and Off Pump Coronary Artery Bypass. Dr. Johnson is a member of several professional organizations that help to keep him on the cutting edges of medicine. He is a member of COR Specialty Associates of North Texas, P.A. (CSANT), Texas' largest medical and surgical group practice providing cardiology, cardiothoracic surgery, vascular surgery and heart and lung transplantation services at over eighteen hospitals and twenty medical offices in the Dallas, Fort Worth, and North Texas region.

Denise L. Johnson-Miller, M.D.
Oncologist and Surgeon

Dr. Johnson-Miller is Director of the St. Francis Breast Surgery Program. Recently, she worked at Stanford University Medical Center, Calif., where she was director of cancer outreach and the melanoma surgery programs as well as practicing at Stanford Hospital and Clinics and Lucile Packard Children's Hospital. She also was Associate Professor of Surgery at the Stanford University School of Medicine. Additionally, she served as General Surgery Section Chief at Palo Alto Veterans Affairs Medical Center. She specializes in Melanoma Surgery and focuses on breast cancer and soft tissue sarcoma surgical treatment. She has numerous abstracts and publishing's about her expertise. Some of her recent Basic Science Research Projects include: Effects of Growth Hormone and GH Analogues on a Radiation Induced Pancreatic Tumor Cell Line, Analysis of Cellular Immune Response and Histocompatibility Expression in a Mouse Intracranial Sarcoma and Effect of Somatostatin Peptide Analogues in a rat sarcoma model. She has been listed among "America's Top Doctors for Cancer" (Castle Connelly); was the inaugural National Medical Leadership In Education Award winner, is recognized in Women of Color in Education, Health and Technology; is a member of the New York Academy of Sciences; and received the Minority Medical Faculty Recognition Award, Stanford University.

Marian C. Johnson-Thompson, Ph.D.
Director, Office of Institutional Development, Biologist

She is Director of Education and Biomedical Research Development, National Institute of Environmental Health Sciences, NIH. She identifies the environmental health research and training needs of underserved populations, coordinates the Institute's K-12 science education programs, chairs the NIEHS IRB and is a member of the NIH Human Subjects Research Advisory Committee. Her early research focused on the mechanism of simian virus 40 replication and conformation; and she later focused on the molecular basis of multi-drug resistance in breast cancer cells. She is Prof. Emeritus of Biology and Environmental Science, UDC and Adjunct Prof. at the School of Public Health, UNC-CH. She is a member of the American Association for Cancer Research, life member of the African Organization for Research and Training in Cancer, and a former member of the African American National Advisory Committee of the Susan G. Komen Breast Cancer Foundation. She is an elected member of Sigma Xi, has been elected to fellowship in the American Academy of Microbiology and is a Fellow of the AAAS. Also, included in her honors are the Geraldine P. Woods Sciences Award and the 1999 ONI Award from the International Congress of Black Women, among others. She was awarded the 2003 Thurgood Marshall Alumni Award from the Thurgood Marshall Scholarship Fund.

Wallace O. Johnston, PE
Mechanical Engineering

Is a Mechanical Engineer holding the degree, Bachelor of Mechanical Engineering, May 1968. He and classmate Fred Hannaham opened the firm Hannaham and Johnston, consulting electrical and mechanical engineers. Johnston served as a Board Director for two years with New York Association of Consulting Engineers and was selected by NYCACE Board of Directors to be the moderator for their Mechanical Engineering Design Competition. He designed an engineering solution to the large quantity of jet aircraft exhaust fumes entering the baggage areas of American Airlines, LaGuardia Airport. His paper: "Unique Air Curtain Installation Solves Difficult Airport Problem" was featured in a national engineering journal in 1976. He became sole proprietor of Wallace Johnston Engineers in 1976. Some of his engineering designs include a 650,000 gallons swimming pool, New York City College; new Neo-Natal Suite 4th floor NYC Metropolitan Hospital; new 14-story 450,000 sq. ft. NYC Transit Authority Office Building. He holds a Library of Congress copyright for a multi-lamp design. Johnston received the Certificate of Merit for Excellence in Design, Riverside Convention Center, Rochester, NY. He was listed in WHO'S WHO IN ENGINEERING, 1982 edition. Life Member, National Society of Professional Engineers.

Albert Jose Jones, Ph.D.
Marine Biologist, Enviromental Science

Dr. Jones is very unique. He is an academician, earning his Ph.D. in Marine Biology. He has been a Professor of Marine Science. As an Administrator, he served as the Acting Dean of the College of Life Sciences, Chairman of the Environmental Science Department, and Acting Provost and Vice President of Academic Affairs. Dr. Jones also studied marine science for nearly two years at the University of Queensland, Australia as a Fulbright Scholar. He has written many publications in his field and holds over a dozen copyrights on his underwater slide and video series. He has produced several underwater videos, including one entitled "Dive and Tour Morocco" which was shown at the Paris Scuba Show. Because of their similarities in experiences and training in the military, oceanographic research, exploration, underwater photography and videography, scuba diving, and education. Dr. Jones is often referred to as The Black Jacques Cousteau. He has logged over 6000 dives in 50 different countries and certified over 2000 divers. In addition to his scuba interests, Dr. Jones is a 7th Degree Black Belt in Tae Kwon Do and the former U.S. Heavyweight Tae Kwon Do Champion. Through his efforts and those of his friend, Ric Powell, in Miami, the National Association of Black Scuba Divers (NABS) became a reality in January of 1991.

Gregory P. Jones, PE
Civil Engineering

Mr. Jones has over 25 years of experience as a practicing civil engineer. He is a seasoned engineer, well versed in the design and construction of civil and structural engineering projects varying in sizes and complexities. Prior to working as an independent engineer for 20 years, he operated Hammurabi Construction Company, a general contracting firm. Earlier, Mr. Jones was a project engineer for Harris Consulting Group, Bechtel Corporation, Lawrence Berkeley Laboratory and EG&G. He is a Registered Professional Civil Engineer, a Registered Professional Mechanical Engineer and General Contractor.

Lovell A. Jones, Ph.D.
Biochemistry & Molecular Biology

As a scientist, Dr. Jones has done extensive research into the relationship between hormones, diet and endocrine responsive tumors. He earned his Ph.D. 1977 in the field of zoology with an emphasis in endocrinology and tumor biology from the U.C., Berkeley. In 1979 he was appointed to the faculty in the departments of Physiology and Obstetrics, Gynecology & Reproductive Sciences at UCSF. In 1980, he accepted a position as assistant professor in the department of Gynecologic Oncology at University of Texas M.D. Anderson Cancer Center (UTMDACC). Dr. Jones is presently a full professor in the departments of Gynecologic Oncology and Biochemistry and Molecular Biology. Since 1988, he has served as Director of the Endocrine Research Laboratory. In January 2000, Dr. Jones was named as the first director of the congressionally mandated center for research on minority health. In addition to publishing over 100 scientific articles ranging from hormonal carcinogenesis to health policy, he has received research support from several funding institutions. In 2000, he was honored on the floor of the U.S. House of Representatives for his work addressing health disparities in the underserved. Dr. Jones has devoted extensive time to the subject of minorities and cancer. He has edited one of the few comprehensive textbooks on this subject entitled "Minorities & Cancer".

Marshall G. Jones, Ph.D.
Laser Technology Through Optical Fiber Research, Physicist

Growing up in the small farming village of Aquebogue on the eastern tip of Long Island, New York, it was not clear to young Marshall Jones what an engineer did. Today, as a senior research engineer and project leader, Dr. Jones is one of the world's foremost authorities in the field of laser technology. His research work has been in the mechanics of laser material processing concerning material removal, welding, and heat treating, and heat transfer as related to laser beam material interaction. He has directed research aimed at high power laser beam transmission through optical fibers. Dr. Jones is currently involved in the research of laser-fiber optic integration for factory automation, processing for electronic packaging, and laser processing underwater. in 1985, his research work on laser/fiber optic/robot systems was voted one of the nation's top 100 innovations of the year by Science Digest magazine. Dr. Jones' research in the laser and robot area has been cited in over 120 newspapers and 25 trade magazines around the world. He has authored or co-authored over 35 publications, received 29 patents, and presented numerous talks at national and international technical conferences.

Rena T. Jones, Ph.D.
Microbiologist

Professor of biology for thirty-four year at Spelman College. In her first year, she was appointed the first director of the Health Careers Program, a position she held for 14 years. In this role, she raised the profile of the College among health professions schools, which placed Spelman, as early as the early 1980s, in the top 5 of all colleges and universities in the United States in getting minorities admitted to medical schools. Dr. Jones became chair of the biology department in her second term at the College, and served in this capacity for 15 years. She and the faculty brought about major changes in the department which resulted, in a very short time, in a three-fold increase in the number of majors graduating from the College. In addition, she recruited faculty who developed a full and strong research program which involves the majors. She is most proud that she was honored for her teaching skills by the United Nego College Fund with the 1989-1990 "Tenneco Excellence in Teaching Award." Dr. Jones has several publications, including three laboratory manuals. Dr. Jones was a post-doctoral fellow on two separate occasions at Georgia State University in the laboratory of Dr. Ahmed Abdelal, where she was a member of his research team for a number of years.

Venita A. Jones, RN, MPH
Nursing

Frederick E. Jordan, P.E.
President, Consulting Engineering Co.

Mr. Jordan is President of F. E. Jordan Associates, Inc. (FEJA), which provides professional civil and structural engineering, planning, architecture, environmental, and construction management services to a variety of public and private clients. As the first African American-owned civil engineering and construction management firm in California, the firm has planned, designed and managed the construction of over a 1,000 projects throughout the Western U.S., Africa and Central America. FEJA has received over 45 awards for business and engineering excellence, including Best Minority Contractor for the State of California (presented by the Governor), and was noted as one of the Top Ten Outstanding Minority Businesses in the United States (presented by FOX-TV and the US Department of Commerce). FEJA also received awards for the construction management on the $242 million San Francisco International Airport's Elevated Roadways and the Chas. P. Howard Container Terminal, Port of Oakland, CA, which was rated the most outstanding container terminal design in the world. The firm, in joint venture, is the construction program manager of the $1.3 billion Oakland International Airport Expansion and development of the 42-story St. Regis Hotel/Condominium complex in San Francisco, CA.

Soodursun Jugessur, Ph.D.
Chairman, University of Mauritius; Chairman, Mauritius Research Council; President of the Mauritius Academy of science and Technology; Physics, Electrical Engrg.

As a scientist and engineer with an M.Sc in Physics and a D.Sc in Electrical Engineering (Quantum Electronics), Dr. Jugessur has worked for over three decades promoting social and economic development through a better development and application of science and technology, while ensuring the needs of the economic operators and the community at large. He served the United Nations from 1982 to 2000 as the Chief of the Science and Technology Section of the Economic Commission for Africa (UNECA). Presently he is the Chairman of the Mauritius Research Council, and Chairman and Pro-Chancellor of the University of Mauritius. He has published widely, and his latest book "Science-Based Development, Policy Issues" has laid the basis for a proper national science and technology policy. He is a Fellow of the African Academy of Sciences, past Chairman of the African Regional Accreditation Committee on Standards, and present Fellow and President of the Mauritius Academy of Science and Technology (MAST). As a Professor of Industrial Technology, Dr. Jugessur engaged in research in harnessing new and renewable energies, engineering education, bio-feedback effects, and technology and society.

Calestous Juma, Ph.D.
Science and Technology Policy

Dr. Juma is Professor of the Practice of International Development and Director of the Science, Technology, and Globalization Project at Harvard university. He also directs the Agricultural Innovation in Africa Project and a high-level executive course on Innovation for Economic Development. He is a former Executive Secretary of the UN Convention on Biological Diversity and Founding Director of the African Centre for Technology Studies in Nairobi. He also served as Chancellor of the University of Guyana. Dr. Juma has been elected to several scientific academies including the Royal Society of London, the US National Academy of Sciences, the Academy of Sciences for the Developing World, the UK Royal Academy of Engineering and the African Academy of Sciences. He has won several international awards for his work on sustainable development. He is lead author *of Innovation: Applying Knowledge in Development* and editor of the peer-reviewed *International Journal of Technology and Globalisation* and *International Journal of Biotechnology*. His next book, *The New Harvest: Agricultural Innovation in Africa*, will be published in 2011. He teaches graduate courses on "Innovation, Development and Globalization" and "Technology and Sustainability" and an undergraduate seminar on "Biotechnology, Environment and Public Policy".

Jackie Kakembo
Nursing

Ms. Kakembo is a nurse with a passion for Africa. As an African American female, she possessed a deep burning desire to travel to Africa and be a part of the life and people there. This passion was answered when in 1965; she was selected by Operation Crossroads Africa (OCA) and assigned to a project in Sierra Leone, West Africa. Upon her return to America, she worked towards sharing her love for Africa, by sharing with others the opportunity to travel to Africa as volunteers for humanitarian programs and fact-finding missions as their travel coordinator and guide. "The bridge of friendship that I crossed going into Africa over forty years ago, in an effort "to make a difference for others" also resulted in me seeing a difference in myself. That very difference continues to lead me back to Africa on different missions to different countries." Ms. Kakembo always She has worked for the past 10 years as a member and now second term President of the African and American Women's Association Inc., organizing cultural, educational, and charitable activities to improve relations between women of Africa and America. For several years she worked closely with the African Ambassadors' Spouses Association, (AASA) on their annual fundraiser, which provides funding to charitable organizations for the betterment of Africa's children.

Alafuele Mbuyi Kalala, D.Sc.
Chemistry, Biochemistry, Biophysics

Dr. Kalala holds a Doctor of Science Degree with a specialization in biochemistry and biophysics. Dr. Kalala worked as a scientist (Biomedical Research/ Biophysics/ Biochemistry) at the National Institute of Health (NIH) from 1990 – 1997 in Bethesda, Maryland. He also holds advanced degrees in philosophy, pedagogy and applied economics. He is a member of numerous professional and cultural societies, ranging from the New York Academy of Sciences to the World Federation of Scientists. Dr. Kalala served as a member of parliament in the Democratic Republic of the Congo (DRC) from 2003 to the present. He also serves, since 2002, as the chairman of the "Africa Friendship and Renaissance Association, AFRAS" the aim of which is the promotion of collaboration, understanding, and integration between Africans at the grass-root level. Since 1996 Dr. Kalala chairs the "Rally for a New Society, RNS", a DRC's political party. He was a presidential candidate in the 2006 DRC's presidential elections.

Abu Bakarr Kamara, P.E.
Civil Engineering

Mr. Kamara has been practicing civil engineering, project management, and construction management for 30+ years.

Jane-Frances Kengeya Kayondo, D.Ph.
Epidemiology; Tropical Diseases

Dr. Kengeya works in World Health Organization's (WHO) Special Programme for Research and Training for Tropical Diseases (TDR). Earlier (2005-2007), she was the Coordinator of the Implementation Research and Methods (IRM) unit of TDR as well as Coordinator of the Multilateral Initiative on Malaria in TDR (MIM/TDR). She was Manager of a Task Force on Malaria Home Management (1997-2002), which initiated and coordinated large multi-country studies of strategies to improve home management of malaria and demonstrated the impact of improving ome management on the burden of disease. Based on this evidence, home management of malaria has become accepted as a key strategy by WHO and RBM (Roll Back Malaria partnership) and African countries have incorporated it in their strategic and implementation plans. Dr. Kengeya was a Senior Research Scientist and National Team Leader, Medical Research Council (UK) Programme on AIDS, Entebbe, Uganda (1988-1997). Under her co-leadership, this rural-based programme was developed and became the largest AIDS Research Programme in Africa.

Larry D. Keith
Biology, Anatomy, Medical Education Development

(1946 - 2010) Larry Keith, who worked at UNC-CH for more than years, held five titles with the School of Medicine: associate director of the Office of Educational Development; assistant dean for admissions; director of special programs; director of recruitment and clinical assistant professor in the Department of Allied Health Sciences. In his roles, he was a tireless mentor and advocate, helping recruit and guide students through the challenging program. As assistant dean of admissions, Keith worked specifically with minority and disadvantaged applicants. His work in the Office of Educational Development includes directing the Medical Education Development program. The program, known as M.E.D., is an intense nine-week course that helps minority and disadvantaged students prepare for medical and dental school though work in such topics as biochemistry, microbiology and physiology. He earned bachelor's and master's degrees in biology from North Carolina A&T State University and Virginia State University, respectively. Attending UNC-CH for his second master's degree gave Keith a taste of what he called "the other side of the coin". UNC-CH School of Medicine Dean William L. Roper credited Keith with helping UNC-CH's medical school rank ninth and fifth, respectively, in the graduation of African-American and Native American students.

Harmon W. Kelley, M.D.
Obstetrics & Gynecology, Physician

Dr. Harmon W. Kelley practices medicine with his daughter Dr. Margaret A. Kelley, both certified in Obstetrics and Gynecology. Dr. Kelley and his wife Harriet (who is a biologist) In the past two decades, have acquired more than three hundred pieces by black artists in the past two decades. Their artwork is sought by many museums throughout the country. His other daughter, Jennifer Kelley works as a licensed Social Worker. Dr. Harmon Kelley has been appreciated in his community and has a school named in his honor, *Dr Harmon W Kelley Elementary School*, San Antonio, TX.

Howard E. Kennedy
President, H.K. Enterprises, Inc.

Howard E. Kennedy is a renown perfumer who creates fragrances and flavors for the beauty, food/beverage and household products industries. Of the 300 or so perfumers working internationally (for major companies), only about 10 are African Americans. He was the only minority individual, while employed by Pfizer, to lead a company to five prestigious awards from the Fragrance Foundation for "Fragrance of the Year": IRON; LADY STETSON; STETSON (for men); SOPHIA (Sophia Loren) and NUANCE. He also created and developed UNDENIABLE FOR MEN and WOMEN, marketed by Avon and endorsed by Billy Dee Williams. His additional successes include GINGER WITH A TWIST marketed by Estee Lauder and the very popular maple flavor in Log Cabin's Country Kitchen Syrup marketed by Pinnacle Foods Group. His firm also developed the fruity flavors for Seagram's "Extra" and "Sunfrost Tea" wine coolers. Other clients include, but are not limited to, Kraft Foods, Ulta, Carol's Daughter, Pantresse and Revlon.

James M. Kennedy
President, Pyramid Business Systems, Inc. IT Services

James Kennedy demonstrated ability to research, develop, present and negotiate economic development, trade, infrastructure improvement and Good Governance policies for developing countries. He applied knowledge of U.S. policies and resources for developing nations through research on the Millennium Challenge Account, Africa Growth Opportunity Act II, Foreign Service Act, USAID and other organizations resulting in several published articles. Mr. Kennedy has outlined how to make practical use of the IMF, World Bank, United Nation and World Trade Organization whose mission is to assist developing countries. Received BSEE and MSEE in Computer Science and MBA in Finance degrees from the University of California, Berkeley and attended the University of Ghana. He taught Computer Programming, "Computer Literacy", Data Networking, Communication and Management Information Systems at various colleges and universities. Mr. Kennedy managed a Pacific Bell/AT&T PC product and services contract for over 10 years, supplying thousands of PC and networking systems. Most recently, as a Kaiser Permanente (KP) Sr. Business Application Coordinator, became and Epic Systems certified, performed enterprise wide KP HealthConnect (Epic Systems) Lab order and hospital operations workflow Build, Development and implementation.

Stranger Kgamphe, Ph.D.
Biology and Anthropometry

Dr. Stranger is involved with the development and implementation of the SA's national HIV/AIDS clinical trials alternative treatment program. He is a Business Consultant and participated in the Project Management Standards at PMI, Pennsylvania in 2000/1. He is a Deputy Director at SA National Department of Basic Education (Dbe) and was appointed by cabinet to be The Secretary General/Director of the SA national Commission For UNESCO, and helped in the establishment of some of the SA's UNESCO chairs, selection of L'OREAL PhD awardees and partnerships with NGO's. His academic focus is Human Biology and Anthropometry of individual and population growth and development of rural children. He was involved during the establishment of the ABSA Bank restructuring process leading up to the new ABSA logo and was a senior Manager at Standard bank in Customer Focused Quality. He is a founder Member of SA Business Excellence Foundation and Chaired the SA Quality Institute for five years post Apartheid.

James King, Jr., Ph.D.
Ret'd Director, Tech Divs, NASA-JPL; Chemistry

Past " Mr. JPL", he was Asst. Director for the Technical Divisions of: (1) the Systems, (2) Earth and Space Science, (3) Telecommunications Science and Engineering, (4) Electronics and Control, (5) Mechanical Systems Engineering and Research, (6) Information Systems, (7) the Institutional Computing and Missions Operations, and (8) Observational Systems. Previosly, he served as Technical Manager for Space Science and Applications, as program manager for Astronomy, Astrophysics and Atmospheric Sciences. Dr. King worked directly for NASA, first as the Director of the Shuttle Environmental Effects in the Space Shuttle Program, where he was responsible for managing the overall program on the potential effects of Space Shuttle operations on the Earth's environment, including sonic boom, ecological effects around the launch sites, and the interactions of the Shuttle engine exhaust products with the Earth's atmospere. He has also performed research on the interaction of gases with solid surfaces, effects of ionizing radiation of gases, and the use of ion cyclotron resonance to study the reactions between ions and molecules. His research on gas-solid interactions led to an internationally recognized theory of anesthesiology.

Sandra A. Knight, M.D., MPH
Physician, U.S. CDC, Jamaica; Medical Officer at the Ministry of Health

Dr. Knight is a Public Health Specialist with the Center for Disease Control and prevention; focusing on the HIV/AIDS focusing on the epidemiology and Strategic Information as it relates to the twelve Caribbean countries funded under the Presidents Emergency Plan for Aids Relief (PEPFAR). The focus is primarily to quantify the extent of the epidemic, prevent new infections and for those who are infected, treat to prevent advanced HIV disease and deaths. She has a Honors medical degree from Santa Clara University in Cuba, a Masters in Public Health from the University of the West Indies and was a Fulbright Fellow at the Rollins School of Public Health/ Emory University where she focused on epidemiology and Global health. Dr Knight is very interested in evidence based public Health practice and participates in many research projects to achieve that. She has a passion for Medicine and still practices at local Hospitals when time permits.

Wade M. Kornegay, Ph.D.
Retired Division Head, MIT Lincoln Laboratory

Dr. Kornegay is a recognized expert on ballistic Missile defense. He has worked in the area of ballistic missile defense technology for 45 years. He conducted research and led efforts in remote sensing, detection and identification of objects at long distances throughout his career in technical staff and management positions. He served as head of Radar Measurements Division from 1993-2000. Dr. Kornegay is currently a Division Fellow at Lincoln Laboratory and is a member of the U.S. Army Science Board. He graduated Summa Cum Laude from North Carolina Central University. He later earned his Ph.D. in physical Chemistry from the University of California, Berkeley. He also studied at Bonn University, Germany, as a Fulbright Fellow, and at the Sloan School of Management at MIT.

Pierre M. Labossiere
Agriculture Science

Pierre is a Feed, Fertilizer and Livestock Drugs Investigator for the California Department of Food and Agriculture. He is also Co-Founder of the Haiti Action Committee, a San Francisco based Haiti solidarity group which has supported the grassroots democracy movement in Haiti since 1991. As an inspector, Pierre conducts routine sampling and inspections; conduct quality assurance inspections of the manufacturing facilities; respond to consumer complaints; and enforce the laws and regulations that govern the manufacturing and distribution of livestock feed.

Elaine LaLanne, Ph.D.
Physics

Dr. Lalanne is an assistant research scientist at the Center for Advanced Studies in Photonics Research (CASPR) at the University of Maryland. She earned her BA degree in physics from Wellesley College in 1994 and her a Ph.D. from the joint department of Applied Physics from New Jersey Institute of Technology/Rutgers University-Newark in May 2003. Dr. Lalanne conducted research investigating the ultrafast photophysics and nonlinear optical properties of Silicon nanostructured materials and single-walled carbon nanotubes. Her dissertation work focused on the nonlinear refractive index and time resolved measurements. She has extensive experience in the use of ultrafast laser systems such as Ti:sapphire oscillator , Ti:sapphire regenerative amplifier, Ti:sapphire pumped optical parametric oscillator and the Nd:YAG laser. At CASPR, she is responsible for helping Dr. Johnson to develop and run the Ultrafast Optics and Optoelectronics Laboratory. She has extended her research to investigate ultrashort pulse propagation in fibers and optical limiting. She is a member of Optical Society of America (OSA), American Physical Society (APS) and National Society of Black Physicists (NSBP). She is a current member of the OSA Member and Education Services Council (MES).

Michael LeNoir, M.D.
Allergist, Physician

Dr. LeNoir is a practicing allergist and pediatrician in the San Francisco Bay Area and the CEO of the Ethnic Health America Network. He is also the director of the Bay Area Multicultural Clinical Research and Prevention Center and the president of the Ethnic Health Institute at Summit Medical Center. He has been the chairperson of the Allergy & Asthma initiative as a member of the National Medical Association. Dr. LeNoir's specialty is asthma in urban inner city children. He has won the distinguished honor of being selected as one of the 50 most positive physicians in America and was named one of the Nations Top 100 Black Physicians in the August 2001 edition of Black Enterprise magazine.

Carl N. Lester
Former Alameda County Health Director

Carl N. Lester's public health career has been has had a challenging and distinguished for nearly 40 years of service. This includes top policy administration of a major health agency, teaching, planning medical and health services, providing extensive volunteer community service, and establishing new and innovative ethnic-relevant health services and programs, all through which he has received numerous honors and awards. He has also been appointed by California governors to serve on state medical and health advisory boards and committees. In the years before his retirement, Mr. Lester was Director of the Alameda County Health Care Services Agency, one of the largest public health agencies in California. His responsibilities included administration of Alcohol and Drug Abuse Services, Environmental Health Services, Public Health Services, the Highland General Hospital and Fairmont Hospital. At Highland General Hospital, he started the *Licensed Vocational Nurse Upgrade Project,* which enabled licensed vocational nurses and nursing assistants to pursue a Registered Nurse Degree while remaining employed at Highland Hospital. Since his retirement in 1987, he has developed culturally relevant educational strategies and programs that help high-risk urban youth get into collegiate health-related and biotechnology programs.

William A. Lester, Jr., Ph.D.
Professor, Chemistry Research

His more recent research is focused on theoretical studies of the electronic structure of molecules. Efforts in this area are directed at extending the quantum Monte Carlo method to the range of chemical problems that form the traditional domain of quantum chemistry, and beyond because of the capability of not imposing the Born-Oppenheimer approximation. Research by the Lester group has confirmed that highly accurate ground state and excited state energies are attainable by the method. Properties other than the energy including dipole and quadrupole moments as well as matrix elements connecting different electronic states have been determined following algorithms developed by his group. Dr. Lester's professional experience includes senior staff positions at the University of Wisconsin, Madison, and the IBM Research Division. During the period 1978-81, he was Director of the U.S. National Resource for Computation in Chemistry at Lawrence Berkeley National Laboratory and concurrently an Associate Director of the Laboratory. He is a Fellow of the American Physical Society, the American Association for the Advancement of Science, and of the California Academy of Science. He is a past member of the Department of Energy Advanced Scientific Computing Advisory Committee (2000-2004) and the Committee on the National Medal of Science (2000-2002) among others.

James C. Letton, Ph.D.
Chemistry

Inventor or co-inventor on 23 patents, assigned to his employer with other patents pending. His inventions include an enzyme stabilization system which allowed his company to market the first liquid detergent, containing stain removing enzymes, technology which is licensed outside the company and several key inventions in the food area of fat substitutes. Early in his career, Dr. Letton spent several years working with the late Dr. Percy L. Julian,one of the most famous chemist of the twentieth century". Dr. Letton also spent five years as professor and Chemistry Department Chairman at Kentucky State University where he had earned his BS degree. Dr. Letton continued to be active in the laboratory while at KSU, functioning as Director, Principle Investigator or Co-Investigator on several funded research projects. Dr. Letton returned to industry and was eventually inducted into the compays Victor Mills society. This is the highest level of recognition that is given to company scientists worldwide and is the top level of the technical career ladder. There are currently less than 20 members at the Victor Mills level from more than four thousand scientists and engineers worldwide in his company.

Mwananyanda M. Lewanika, Ph.D.
Biochemistry and Microbiology

Dr. Lewanika is Founder and Chief Operating Officer of the STEM Education Centre (STEM-Z), established to implement the African Union's Declaration on Science, Technology and Scientific Research for Development of January 2007. He was the Founding President of the Zambia Academy of Sciences. He has served as a Vice-chairperson of the Intergovernmental Committee of Intellectual Property and Genetic Resources, Traditional Knowledge and Folklore of the World Intellectual Property Organisation (WIPO) and a former Chairperson of the National Health Research Advisory Committee and the National Steering Committee on Intellectual Property and Genetic Resources, Traditional Knowledge and Folklore; and Chairperson of the Southern African Development Community (SADC) Advisory Committee on Biotechnology and Biosafety. From 1990 - 2003, he was Executive Director, National institute of Scientific and Industrial Research (NISIR). *He has represented Zambia in consultations that lead to the development of the United Nations Environment Programme (UNEP) International Technical Guideli*nes for Safety in Biotechnology. *He was in Zambian Delegations to Ministerial Meetings of the* WTO, *to the Commission on Investment, Technology and Enterprise Development of UNCTAD.*

Ronald W. Lindsey, M.D.
Trauma and Spine Surgery

Dr. Lindsey is Chair of the Department of Orthopaedic Surgery and Rehabilitation at University of Texas Medical Branch and Professor in the Department of Orthopedic Surgery at Baylor College of Medicine in Houston, where he has served since 1988, and has served as the Associate Chief of Orthopedic Trauma Surgery Service at Ben Taub General Hospital, as well as Chief of Orthopedic Services. He was Acting Chair of the Department at Baylor from 2000-2002. Dr. Lindsey earned his M.D. degree from Columbia University in 1977, and completed his residency in Orthopedic Surgery at Yale in 1982. From 1982 to 1988, he completed fellowships in trauma and spine surgery, hand and microvascular surgery at the University of Basel in Switzerland, the University of Marseille in France, the Stoke Mandeville Hospital in Aylesbury England, and the University of Innsbruck in Austria. Dr. Lindsey has received numerous teaching awards and scientific awards, including the President Award, The 11th Annual Scientific Meeting of ASAMI – North America; The Limb Lengthening and Reconstitution in 2001. He is also a member of multiple Orthopedic, Trauma, Neurologic and Spine surgery societies, as well as an editor the textbook, *Orthopaedic Implants: Application, Complications, and Management.*

Janice Lord-Walker
Science Education

Ms. Lord-Walker is a graduate of McGill University (Montreal, Canada) in Microbiology and Immunology with a minor in Chemistry. She worked as a research assistant at McGill University in the field of Parathyroid hormone and Calcitonin hormone research. She earned a Master Degree in Science Curriculum and Instruction from Hayward State University. She has four years experience in administration and is presently the Assistant Principal for Life Academy of Health and Bioscience. She is dedicated to the academic success of all students. She was awarded the Outstanding Student for Education from Hayward State University. The city of Oakland presented her with the Oakland Civic Pride Award for her work with mathematic students, science students and Developmental Delayed students. She earned the Kingsley W. Wrightman, Science Education Award for secondary science teaching. She has taught for over 20 years as a chemistry teacher, biology teacher, TSA coordinated k-12 science and science mentor teacher. She loves to read about science and education, swim and workout. She is married and has two sons.

William Lucy
Ret'd Sec-Treasurer of AFSCME; Civil Engineer

Bill was the International Secretary-Treasurer of the 1.4 million-member American Federation of State, County and Municipal Employees (AFSCME), AFL-CIO. He was first elected AFSCME Secretary-Treasurer in May 1972. He joined the AFSCME International staff in 1966 as the Associate Director of the Legislation and Community Affairs departments. Bill is a member of the AFL-CIO Executive Council and a Vice President of the Maritime Trades Department and Department of Professional Employees. For more than three decades, he has been involved in international affairs. He is the highest-ranking African American in the Labor movement. Bill was one of the founders of the Free South Africa Movement that launched the successful anti-apartheid campaign in the United States in the mid 1980s. He led an AFL-CIO delegation to South Africa to monitor the first democratic election. Bill serves as vice-president of Public Services International, the world's largest union federation. He is a founder and the president of the Coalition of Black Trade Unionists (CBTU), an organization of union leaders and rank-and-file members dedicated to the unique needs of African Americans and minority group workers. A civil engineer by trade, Bill Lucy attended the University of California at Berkeley.

Phindile E. Lukhele-Olorunju, Ph.D.
Plant Breeding and Virology

Dr. Lukhele-Olorunju is Director of Research – Africa Institute of South Africa. She is a Representative for the Minister of Agriculture, Forestry and Fisheries in the Winter Cereal Trust and a Board Member of Bioversity International (CGIAR Centre). She was Director of Research and Innovation at the University of Venda (2009-10). From July 2002-2008, Dr. Lukhele-Olorunju was Group Executive: Grain and Industrial Crops Business Division of the Agricultural Research Council of South Africa (ARC), where she managed three Research Institutes: ARC-Grain Crops Institute-Potchefstroom, ARC-Small Grains Institute – Bethlehem and ARC-Institute for Industrial crops – Rustenburg. She was Professor and Head of her Department, University of the North (2001-02), South Africa and Lectured at Ahmadu Bello University, Nigeria (1991-2000). Dr. Lukhele-Olorunju was responsible for Groundnut Breeding at the Institute for Agricultural Research, Nigeria (1983-2000).

John L. Mack
Telecommunications

John's activities encompass assisting firms interested in doing business in the Information and Communication sector in Africa and the Middle East. Additionally, he engages in short-term consulting assignments under the auspices of his own firm, or in collaboration with other firms, in the policy, operational and business areas of information and communication technologies (ICTs). He has been an invited speaker or workshop participant at several events including those of the Africa Communications Conference, the World Bank, the American & African Business Women's Alliance (AABWA), the African Business Roundtable, etc. Most recently, he traveled to Senegal to complete a USAID-funded study, with recommendations for improvement, of the U.S. Presidential "The Digital Freedom Initiative". He was the Managing Director, based in Nairobi, of WorldSpace Africa (WSA), one of three subsidiaries of the billion-dollar WorldSpace Corporation based in Washington, D.C., with responsibility for overall P&L. Mr. Mack has a long history in the area of ICTs having been a founder of the African Internet Forum and the Partnership for Information and Communication Technologies in Africa (PICTA). Both organizations are public-private partnerships to improve the status of Internet connectivity and overall telecommunication modernization and expansion in Africa.

John W. Macklin, Ph.D.
Chemistry

Current research in the Macklin laboratory involves spectrometric studies to obtain structural information about intermolecularly associated molecules and ions in solution and adsorbed, self-assembled interfacial aggregates. Micro-Raman spectrometry is the primary tool used for structural characterization of dissolved and adsorbed substances. The micro-Raman measurements are generally complemented or corroborated by ultra-violet visible (uv-vis), Fourier transform infrared (FTIR) and/or nuclear magnetic resonance (NMR) spectrometric measurements. In one such effort, uv-vis and Raman spectrometry are used to study aggregation of various dyes in solution. The dyes of interest are the photo-active cyanine dyes and others that are useful in photographic, photovoltaic and other photochemical and electrical applications. Another example of ongoing research activity involves the development of ultra-sensitive chemical sensing capabilities based on micro-Raman spectroelectrochemical indications. The approach chosen in this case is to begin with chromophores that adsorb strongly from solution onto a silver surface and by resonance and surface enhancement show extremely high Raman intensities. The goal is to discover changes that are capable of indicating chosen biochemical interactions and/or the presence of small concentrations of environmental contaminants.

Bereneice McClentton Madison, Ph.D.
Clinical and Public Health; Pathogenic Microbiology/Immunology

Dr. Madison is Associate Chief for Program Integration in the Centers for Disease Control and Prevention's International Laboratory Branch/Division of Global AIDS Program. Her work focuses primarily on system strengthening of Africa's national public health laboratory networks through linkages with Field Epidemiology Laboratory Training Programs. Madison served as Chief of Laboratory Infrastructure and Support for CDC Zambia from 2005- 2008. She is currently the Chair of the International Education Committee for the American Society for Microbiology and is a member World Health Organization's (WHO) STOP TB REACH program review committee. She works extensively in implementing and managing tuberculosis (TB) diagnostic quality assessment programs for smear microscopy and drug susceptibility test proficiency programs. She has published several book chapters, TB training and reference laboratory publications based on her work in TB laboratory activities and microbial pathogenesis. Madison received her undergraduate degree in biology from Jackson State University (MS); Master's degree in Education, Administration and Supervision from the University of Memphis (TN); and Ph.D. in Microbiology and Immunology from the University of Tennessee, Memphis.

Elizabeth J. Maeda, Ph.D.
Agriculture Research

Dr. Maeda is a Principal Agricultural Research Officer, assigned to the Farming System Research/Socioeconomics unit, where she coordinates national farming systems programs and develops and oversees the implementation of client-oriented research program with special emphasis on the socioeconomics aspects. She is an expert in Low external input farming and livelihood systems research and development; Agronomy, Varietal development; soil fertility management; agroforestry; technology development; livelihoods and gender analysis; Social Learning facilitation and project proposal writing. Dr. Maeda has been awarded *The African Women Leaders in Agriculture and the Environment (AWLAE)* under Winrock International and *The Margaret McNamara Memorial Fund* for women in developing countries.

Eiman A. Mahmoud, M.D., MPH
Pathologist, Infectious Diseases

She is an expert in Pathology of Tropical Diseases, with special emphasis on Leishmaniasis and Schistosomiasis. Dr. Mamoud is former director of Women & Health Office of the Sudan - Natural Human Resource Protection Group. Dr. Mahmoud is Associate professor of Pathology and Director of Global Health program – Touro University. She is also Program Director –Global Physician Corps. She has Worked as resident pathologist for Medicine San Frontier and as a Member of Drug and Safety Monitoring Board, Leishmania Clinical Trail – Behar-India sponsored by the Institute of One World Health and World Health Organization. Dr. Mahmoud Served as president of Women and Health office of Natural and Human Resource Protection Group in Sudan and Country representative in African Women Medical Association. She was nominated for Success Story: The Global assembly of women and Environment in Florida and WOAFA (Women of Africa) Recognition Award nominees. Her Major interest in pathogenesis and epidemiology Tropical diseases and global health.

Dominic W. Makawiti, Ph.D.
Biochemistry

Since 2007, Prof. Makawiti is Deputy Vice-Chancellor (Academic Affairs), Maseno University, Kenya. Earlier, he instructed Biochemistry from 1985 – 1998 at the University of Nairobi. During this time period, he was Head of Laboratory, Reproductive Biology Unit, College of Biological Sciences at the University of Nairobi. From 1992 – 2002, he was Chairman of the Department of Biochemistry. Prof. Makawiti served as this university's Dean, School of Medicine (2002 – 2006). Prof. Makawiti's research interests include -- *Academic:* Biochemical Endocrinology with emphasis on: (a) Steroid hormones, their metabolites, techniques of identification and quantification, and use in prediction and detection of ovulation and prediction of parturition. (b) Natural products of plant origin involved in fertility regulation; The effect of trypanosomosis on host endocrine function; Nutritional bioenergetics. *Industrial:* Production of antisera to hormones; Production of haemoagglutination pregnancy testing kits; Production of insulin. *Consultancy:* Assessment of the activity of papain (an industrial enzyme) in local papaya with the potential for industrial exploitation; Evaluation of anti-snake venom potency having been subjected to ambient conditions in transit; Hormonal measurements for clinical diagnosis in humans.

Sello T. Makoa
Water Distribution Technology and Construction

Tindale currently works as a Site Engineer in Lesotho, overseeing the construction of pump house with pipe connection to the existing 13ML reservoir; laying of pipeline-pumping main of DN250(MPVC, Class 16) from 13ML reservoir to the new 5ML reservoir; providing telemetry and electro mechanical works; and laying of pipeline, gravity main DN200 from 5ML reservoir to designated point at Tikoe Industrial Estate site. From 1997-2003, he was Project Supervisor for the Microprojects Management Unit, responsible for 'Muela Infrastructure Enhancement Programme by providing supervision of all site activities for issuing site instructions to contractors on foot bridges, roads and buildings. From 1989-1996 Tindale was the Chief Technical Officer (Head of Technical Section) in the Urban Sanitation Improvement Project; his duties included design of on-site-sanitation facilities, training of local latrine builders, liasing with water and sanitation co-ordination sectors both local and international, supervision of pit-emptying pilot programme, implementation of 13 towns water and sanitation projects and monitoring of sludge lagoon disposal units.

Mosibudi Mangena
Former Minister of Science and Technology, Republic of South Africa, 2004 – 2008

Hon. Mangena was the Minister of Science and Technology from 2004 to 2008. He was Deputy Minister of Education of the Republic of South Africa from 2001 – 2004. Earlier, he was elected Member of the Parliament in 1999. He was the first Patron of Sowetan-Telkom Mathematics and Science Teacher of the Year awards, and the founding chairperson of the South African National Literacy Initiative (SANLI) and Masifundesonke Reading Campaign in 2001. He earned an MSc degree in Applied Mathematics from the University of South Africa (called the *University of Azania* on the AZAPO website). He joined the South African Students' Organisation (SASO) and was elected onto the Students Representative Council at the University of Zululand in 1971. Moving back to Pretoria, he became chairperson of the SASO Pretoria branch in 1972. He chaired the Botswana region of the Black Consciousness Movement of Azania (BCMA) in 1981 and the BCMA central committee from 1982 to 1994. Mosibudi returned from exile in 1994 and became President of the Azanian People's Organisation (AZAPO).

Samwel V. Manyele, Ph.D.
Chemical and Process Engineering

Dr. Manyele is Assoc. Professor and Head of the Department of Chemical & Process Engineering, University of Dar es Salaam. He established the Undergraduate degree at this university in Food Processing and Biochemical Engineering. Earlier, he has worked in research in Canada for the Fluidization Research Laboratory, The University of Western Ontario. Dr. Manyele is a Principal Researcher for Oil seed Processing/Edible Oil Extraction Parameters for Major Agricultural/Oilseed Products in Tanzania: Sunflower and Ground nuts, using Solvent Extraction Process. He even works with Tanzania Meteorological Agency (TMA) by providing Time Series Analysis to Predict Climate Clusters in Tanzania. He works in analyzing Environmental and Climate Stressors and their Major Categories associated with Biomass Power Production and the corresponding areas impacted: Toxicants, Particulates, Air Pollutants, Solid Waste, Physical Trauma, Climate Change, Acidification Precursors, and Resource Depletion. Dr. Manyele designed a CFB Reactor for Medical Waste Incineration Facility and he designed, constructed and commissioned a Three-Phase Bioreactor for Treatment of Industrial Wastewater (CPE Department Laboratory, currently used for research and student laboratory).

Benjamin Siyowi Mapani, Ph.D.
Geology

Dr. Mapani is a university Lecturer of Structural Geology, Tectonics, Environmental geology and Remote Sensing, Metamorphic Petrology, Economic Geology and Geostatistics and Mapping in Namibia. He also served as as a Senior lecturer and Head of the Department of Geology in Zimbabwe, where he taught courses in Environmental Geology, Mine dumps research, Economic/Exploration, Metamorphic Petrology, Mineralogy and Structural Geology. Prior to joining academia, Dr. Mapani work for various mining companies and served as a Geologist at the Geological Survey of Zambia, where he was involved in Regional mapping in the Irumide mobile belt, structural and petrological studies in Igneous, Metamorphic and sedimentary rocks. He has published several papers about geosciences and provided consultancy to various countries.

Phillip J. Marion, M.D.
Physician

Is a specialist in Physical Medicine, Rehabilitation and Pain Management. Currently, he serves as Associate Clinical Professor; Director of Physical Medicine & Rehabilitation at The George Washington University. He earned his M.D. from New York University School of Medicine (1985), his M.S. from New York University Wagner School of Public Service (1989), and his M.P.H. from The George Washington University (1993). Dr. Marion was one of the Washingtonian Magazine's Top Doctor (2005).

Wayne J. Martin, Ph.D.
Environmental Scientist

Dr. Martin is an environmental scientist managing a group of scientists and support staff dealing with projects in Geology, Geochemistry, Waste Disposal, and Contaminant Fate and Transport. His 30 year career includes positions as a researcher, principal investigator, and project manager of a variety of projects related to hazardous, toxic, and radioactive wastes. He has managed multi-million dollar programs for developing environmental technologies related to environmental restoration and waste management. Also, he works with the Army Corps of Engineers for deploying innovative environmental technologies. Dr. Martin has also worked internationally with the International Atomic Energy Association, developing procedures for radioactive tracer techniques and studying containment-migration mechanisms and problems. Presently, he manages a group of 45 scientists and support staff who work on projects related to applied geology and geochemistry. Dr. Martin earned his B.S. degree in Wildlife Management with a minor in Chemistry in 1978. Later in 1990 he earned his M.S. degree in Radiological Sciences, with an emphasis in environmental transport. Within three years, between 1993 – 1996, he earned his Ph.D. in Environmental and Natural Resources Sciences.

Judy Martin-Holland, Ph.D., RN
Nursing

She is a Family Nurse Practitioner and Assistant Dean at UCSF School of Nursing. Her research interests include health disparities, currently with a specific focus on asthma and asthma care, perceptions of health services by persons of color, patient-focused healthcare decision-making, patient-provider relationships, and access to health care for marginalized populations. Related areas of interest include: culturally sensitive nursing practice, nursing workforce issues and health care policy. Dr. Martin-Holland's administrative and teaching responsibilities include: diversity and social responsibility of the health care professions; recruitment, retention and graduation of diverse students in nursing, and courses on Leadership, Theory in Advanced Practice, Socio-Cultural Issues in Health and Illness, Pulmonary Advanced Practice Nursing.

Tshilidzi Marwala, Ph.D.
Executive Dean of the Faculty of Engineering and the Built Environment at the University of Johannesburg, South Africa; Electrical Engineering

Dr. Marwala is the Dean of the Faculty of Engineering and the Built Environment at the University of Johannesburg. He was a full Professor of Electrical Engineering, the DST/NRF South Africa Research and Chair of Systems Engineering at the University of the Witwatersrand. He has received more than 40 awards including being the youngest recipient of the Order of Mapungubwe (other recipients include Nobel Prize Winners Sydney Brenner, Allan Cormack, JM Coetzee, FW de Klerk and Nelson Mandela). His research interests include the application of computational intelligence to engineering, computer science, finance, social science and medicine. Dr. Marwala co-invented and internationally patented: 1) a computational method for radiation imaging; 2) coded apertures masks that are used in computer based radiation-based medical imaging; and 3) the artificial larynx that uses neural networks. He developed the neuro-rough model and Bayesian based genetic programming method and applied these to modeling complex systems such as HIV, interstate conflict and biomedical processes. He has received over 41 awards; has published over 170 articles in refereed international journals, conference proceedings and book chapters.

Verdiana Grace Masanja, Ph.D.
Applied Mathematics

Dr. Masanja is Professor of Mathematics at the National University of Rwanda and Vice President, Africa Mathematical Union (AMU), Eastern Africa Region. From 1996- 2001, she coordinated the Female Education in Mathematics and Science in Africa (FEMSA) Tanzania project; FEMSA operated in 12 sub- Saharan Africa countries. FEMSA was a project of the Association of Development in Education in Africa (ADEA). FEMSA Tanzania was hosted by the Ministry of Education and Culture, the University of Dar es Salaam and the Forum for Women Educationalist, Tanzania Chapter. She has authored and co-authored several books and book chapters, as well as many papers which were published in refereed journals. Her publishings has covered a wide range of mathematical topics, including *"Pollution models in Lake Victoria: The case of Re-suspension and Normal Flow at Mkuyuni area"*; *"Mathematical Modelling and Simulation of Transport of Dust Particles in Dar es Salaam City"*; *"A Numerical Method for Solving two-dimensional Non-Newtonian Fluid Flow Problems"*. An example of her talents includes providing a book chapter on *"The Impact of Modern Mathematics in Other Disciplines"*, in the book *"Importance of Mathematical Modelling of Biological Processes"*.

Jonathan I. Matondo, Ph.D.
Civil Engineering; Hydrology

Dr. Matondo obtained his first and second degree in applied hydrology and surface hydrology (1976 and 1978) respectively from the University of Dar es Salaam, Tanzania. he was recruited as one of the staff members of the department of hydrology after the completion of his first degree. He obtained his Ph.D. degree from Colorado State University in the area of water resources planning and management in spring 1983. While at the University of Dar Es Salaam he lectured undergraduate and masters civil engineering students. He joined the University of Swaziland in August 1995. While at the University of Swaziland He am engaged in the lecturing of undergraduate and postgraduate students, conducting research and consultancy activities. Dr. Matondo's research interest are in the areas of hydrology, water resources planning and management, computer applications in hydrology, hydraulics and water resources related problems.

Robert A. Matthews, Ph.D.
Professor Emeritus, Geologist

(1926 – 2006) His interests and experiences included Environmental geology; engineering and economic geology; hydrogeologic studies in alpine areas; mine reclamation studies in the western U.S. Recent projects include environmental geologic and land use study of the Lake Tahoe Basin and the application of geology to solving the liquid and solid waste problem of the north Lake Tahoe area, hydrogeologic studies in the rift zone of East Africa, fog drip in groundwater recharge and hydrogeologic characterization of waste disposal sites.

James A. Mays, M.D.
Physician, Hypertension, Cardiology

A prominent Los Angeles physician who maintains offices in the inner city. The Pine Bluff, Arkansas native continues to be a social conscience in the "hood", despite his medical achievements and professional accomplishments both in and out the medical arena.

Wilfred Mbacham, Ph.D.
Biochemistry; Molecular Parasitology; Tropical Public Health

Dr. Mbacham is a associate professor and researcher who has asserted himself in the field of molecular parasitology in the past 16 years amid difficult circumstances in Cameroon, Africa. His work started off in the biochemistry and immunochemistry of filariasis and extended into molecular biology of Plasmodium sp with which he graduated from the Harvard School of Public Health in 1997, with a Science Doctor in tropical public health. He founded the laboratory for public health research biotechnologies (LAPHER Biotech) at the biotechnology centre of the University of Yaounde, Cameroon and has contributed scientifically in the profiling of the molecular epidemiology of drug resistance in Cameroon and Africa. His laboratory is a reference centre for the International Atomic Energy Agency (IAEA) in the training of other Africans for the use of radioisotopes in the surveillance of drug resistant TB and Malaria. He has set up two laboratories in Sudan and Burkina Faso in this light for the IAEA. He coordinated the Anti-malaria Drug resistance network of the Multilateral Initiative on Malaria at TDR, WHO that grouped 5 countries in Africa. He principal of an EU funded project - the Poverty Related Diseases College (PRD College). His laboratory has recently been involved in other regional initiatives in molecular epidemiology, cloning and enzyme discovery.

Alphonse Mboussa
Director General, Civil Engineering

Lphonse Mboussa is Director General of Civil Engineering in the Republic of Congo. He earned his MS in Civil Engineering in France. He worked with the African Scientific Institute in 2002 when investigating the physical condition of Dolisie General Hospital.

Victor R. McCrary, Ph.D.
Chemistry

Dr. McCrary is his organization's Business Area Executive for Science, where he is responsible for the management and business planning for the science and technology business area's strategic investments for long-term research and development support of its mission to provide critical contributions to critical challenges in the areas of national security, homeland defense, and space. Earlier, Dr. McCrary was the Chief of the Convergent Information Systems Div. at the National Institute of Standards and Technology (NIST), where he led research and development efforts and standards development activities in areas of biometrics, digital preservation, DVD reliability and standards, digital TV standards, quantum communications, and electronic books. Dr. McCrary also served as a program manager for the Advanced Technology Program, where he was responsible for directing the high-risk technology programs in the areas of photonics and electronics. In 1985, he earned his Ph.D. from Howard University in Physical Chemistry. From 1985 to 1995, he was a Member of Technical Staff at AT&T Bell Laboratories in Murray Hill, NJ, where he conducted research efforts in crystal growth for semiconductor lasers. Dr. McCrary has received several awards and is a member of the IEEE, the NOBCChE, and Sigma Xi. He has authored or coauthored over 60 publications and edited two conference books.

Gene McGowen, RN
Resource RN, Flight Nurse

Gene is a Resource R.N. and Flight for a Pediatric Burn Intensive care Unit. He is a charge nurse, Nurse mentor, and preceptor. His flight nursing duties include the stabilization and air medical transport of acutely burned pediatric patients via helicopter and fixed wing aircraft. His flight team does domestic and international transports of critically burned children. He is a member of Sigma Theta Tau International honor society of nursing, The American Burn Association, and the Air surface transport nurses association. Gene lectures at Prairie View University School of Nursing. He is a Burn Nurse consultant, and serves on outreach programs to introduce students to careers in air medical nursing.

Alston B. Meade, Sr., Ph.D.
Entomologist

A native of Jamaica, W.I., Dr. Meade earned his B.A. in Zoology at Fisk University, and his M.S. and Ph.D. in Entomology at the University of Minnesota. He spent the next 30 years as a research scientist at Du Pont de Nemours & Co, primarily involved in the research and development of crop protection chemicals. He has served as President of the International Society of African Scientists, and is currently engaged by the Government of Jamaica as Honorary Consul, based in Philadelphia, PA.

Linda C. Meade-Tollin, Ph.D.
Biochemistry

Dr. Meade-Tollin is a member of the Surgery faculty and of the Comprehensive Cancer Center at the University of Arizona. She has established a novel angiogenesis assay with human microendothelial cells that allows rapid screening of pure compounds and crude extracts for factors that modulate angiogenesis. The assay has been used to screen and identify extracts of desert fungi and herbs present in an alternative therapy for prostate cancer. which are effective at sub-cytotoxic concentrations. Other research interests include the role of stem cells in invasion and metastasis and of of matrix metalloproteinases in human angiogenesis, and development of in vitro models for the early stages of human angiogenesis. She is a recipient of the National Organization for the Professional Advancement of Black Chemists and Chemical Engineers Henry Hill Award in 1998. She teaches a course, Strategies For Success for minority doctoral students in biomedical disciplines, and lectures on invasion and metastasis in a graduate Tumor Immunology course. The Wild Butterfly Foundation has been established by Dr. Jacqueline Bell-Jones and Will Jones, to support and further the cancer research of Dr. Linda Meade-Tollin, to encourage the development and education of future research scientists, and to disseminate information about cancer to minority populations.

C. Ralph Melton, M.D.
Urologist

For more than 25 years, Dr. Melton has been thriving and privately practicing adult and pediatric urology. He is well known throughout the San Francisco - Oakland, CA Bay Area as one of the best urologists. He not only practices his specialty, he also engages in community activities to make African American men aware of the necessity to to check the condition of their prostate. Prior to his pursuit in medicine, Dr. Melton served as a Staff Microbiologist in Alameda County Public Health Department. Not only is he a member of various professional medical societies, Dr. Melton also served as a Past President (3 yrs) and Treasurer (3 yrs) of the Sinkler-Miller Medical Association.

Francis Mensah, Ph.D.
Theoretical and Mathematical Physics / Applied Laser Physics

Francis Mensah was born in Porto-Novo in Benin. He obtained successively a B.Sc. and a M.Sc. from the National University of Benin, after which Professor L. Olatunji, former chairman of the Physics Department, encouraged him in pursuing a Doctoral Degree in the new Doctoral Program "Material Sciences". Dr. Mensah obtained a DEA degree or Degree of Advanced Study in theoretical physics having done research on the mathematical integrodifferential equations of Volterra in population dynamics. He also obtained a Doctorate in Sciences (D.Sc.) in Theoretical Physics from the National University of Benin with honors and congratulations. In his dissertation he developed a Unified Theory to describe the stationary rheological properties of the aggregation of deoxy-HbS molecules in a simple shear flow. Francis Mensah later transferred to the department of Physics and Astronomy at Howard University where he earned a Ph.D. in Laser/ Lidar Physics having worked on the Calibration of Lidar Systems for the determination of water vapor and other aerosols in the atmosphere with Professor Arthur Thorpe. Francis Mensah's present research interests include theoretical physics, mathematical physics, biophysics, biomathematics, molecular dynamics, stochastic processes, bifurcation theory and simulation of biological processes, mathematical models in medicine, laser, lidar, and atmospheric physics.

Debra Meyer, Ph.D.
Biochemistry

Debra has experience in Biochemistry, Molecular Biology, Immunology and Virology techniques. Her interests lie in viral and bacterial infections and their effect on immune system function. Prof Meyer has contributed to research in the chemistry of HIV/AIDS in particular developing synthetic vaccine components based on the viral envelope, factors augmenting concurrent HIV/Mtb infection as well as studying extracts from South African plants for activity against HIV. In one strategy, her research makes an attempt at directly addressing hypervariability of envelope proteins of HIV. She has successfully demonstrated how the immune system responds to hypervariable immunogens and identified plant extracts with the ability to inhibit HIV-1 reverse transcriptase. She still studies novel viral inhibitory compounds, synthetic vaccine components and AIDS pathogenesis.

Carolyn W. Meyers, Ph.D.
University President

Was named the fourth president of Norfolk State University in February 2006. She officially assumed her new duties on July 1, 2006. Meyers previously served as provost and vice chancellor for Academic Affairs and as a tenured professor in the College of Engineering at North Carolina Agricultural & Technical State University. She holds a bachelor's degree in mechanical engineering from Howard University, a master's in mechanical engineering from the Georgia Institute of Technology (Georgia Tech), and a Ph.D. in chemical engineering, also from Georgia Tech. She has done post doctoral work at Harvard University's Institute for Educational Management. Highlights from her 30-plus years in education include serving as the first chair of the Board of Directors of the National Institute of Aerospace; serving a second term as a member-at-large of the ASME Committee on Honors; serving as a member of the State Council of Higher Education for Virginia's 2007 Assessment Task Force; holding membership on the Board of Trustees of Norwich University, the Center for Advancement of Engineering Education, Board of Governors for RTI International, the Advisory Board for the Journal of Engineering Education Board of Directors of Riverside Health Foundation, Hampton Roads Partnership, and the Historically Black Colleges and Universities Capital Financing Advisory Board.

Ronald E. Mickens, Ph.D.
Physics, Mathematics and Modeling

In 1970, Dr. Mickens was appointed Professor of Physics at Fisk University, where he remained until 1982, when he became Professor of Physics at Atlanta University (now, Clark Atlanta University). In 1985, he was named Distinguished Fuller E. Callaway Professor at CAU. His research areas include physics, mathematics, modeling, and the history/philosophy of science. He has participated in efforts to open careers in science and mathematics to African Americans, and for twenty-five years, served as Historian for the National Society of Black Physicists. In 1999, Dr. Mickens was honored with election to Fellowship in the American Physical Society, a position limited to 0.5% of the society's membership. His publications include more than 15 authored or edited books, and 300 refereed journal articles. Two of his history-based books are *The African American Presence in Physics* (1999) and *Edward Bouchet: The First African American Doctorate* (2002).

Gregory Miller, R.N.
Registered Nurse, Health Educator and Consultant

Mr. Miller has been a nurse and advocate for the health of the African American Community for over twenty five years. He has worked in Emergency Rooms and Intensive Care Units in numerous hospitals. He has also worked as a community nurse visiting patients that were too sick or unable to travel to local health centers or clinics. Mr. Miller was the nurse assigned to care for the first HIV/AIDS patient admitted to the Intensive Care Unit at Kaiser Hospital, Oakland, CA in 1981. Since then he has worked throughout the San Francisco Bay Area on AIDS wards and have seen the changing faces of HIV/AIDS go from White to Black, from gay to straight and from adults to teens. In more recent years, Mr. Miller, a certified HIV tester, has been working with the AIDS Minority Health Initiative (AMHI), a community-based non-profit organization that provides educational classes, support groups, mental and physical health assessments, HIV testing, referrals for housing, legal issues, transportation (to medical appointments) and food to a largely African American, urban population in Oakland, CA. Mr. Miller has traveled to Zimbabwe to support, educate and assist with the devastation caused by HIV and AIDS.

Atty. John W. Milton
Engineer and Attorney

John has served as an engineer and attorney with over 20 years experience. He has found several companies doing business in West Africa and the Caribbean Islands. He is a professor and author of international business courses, certified on- line instructor; have taught a range of MBA and business courses: Business Management, Marketing, Business Law and Finance at several University and Colleges in the Washington, DC metropolitan area since 1995; an International Business Consultant and holds a B.S., Electrical Eng. /Computer Science, New York Institute of Technology , graduate work in Physics, MBA, Global Enterprise Management, Jones International University, 2003 ; JD, Doctor of Law, Rutgers University School of Law, 1975 ; Ph.D Philosophy of Religion, Bible Believers College and Seminary, June 2008. He is a recipient of numerous awards and citations; experience in intellectual property rights, patents and products liability issues.

Robert B. Mims, M.D.
Physician, Enocrinology

Dr. Mims has been a specialist in Endocrinology for 40+ years. He founded the Endocrine Society of the Redwoods. He has extensive experience in research and has participated in many clinical trials of new drugs for the pharmaceutical industry and recently has added Neutraceuticals to his research. Prior to becoming the director of a private clinic in Santa Rosa, CA in 1984, he served as an Associate Clinical Professor in the University of Southern California's School of Medicine for 8 years. Earlier at this same institution, he served as an academic professor for 13 years. Besides belonging to several professional organizations, Dr. Mims has received numerous awards, including an award for dedicated service to Med-Cor Affairs at USC's School of Medicine.

James W. Mitchell, Ph.D.
Chemistry and Chemical Engineering

Dr James (Jim) Mitchell, a National Academy of Engineering Member and Bell Labs Research Fellow, retired in 2001 as Vice President of Materials Research at Lucent Bell Labs, Murray hill, NJ. Mitchell is recognized for developing high reliability quantitative characterization methods which laid the foundation for the analytical chemistry of optical waveguide technology. His x-ray fluorescence techniques first extended the use of this method for the analysis of ppb levels of elements. He received with collaborators the IR-100 Award in 1982 for developing the first laser intracavity spectrometer for practical quantitative analysis. He and collaborators conceptualized and constructed the first on-demand electrochemical generator for producing hazardous CVD reagents used in the manufacture of electronic devices. This R&D 100 Award winning invention was produced commercially. In 1989, he was inducted into the materials engineering section of the National Academy of Engineering. Dr Mitchell's second career involves academia, where he is the David and Lucille Packard Professor of Materials Science at Howard University .At Howard, he also is the Director of the CREST Nanomaterials Characterization Science Center, where his group innovates methods for the synthesis and characterization of ultra pure biocompatible nanomaterials for research and technological applications.

Willie Mitchell

In 1989, Willie Mitchell received degrees in Petroleum Engineering, Industrial Safety Technology, and Chemical Science from Nicholls State University in Thibodaux, Louisiana. He is a certified Technical Training Specialist (Langevin Learning Systems), with certifications in Technical Management (UCLA - Department of Engineering), Occupational and Environmental Radiation Protection (Harvard University), Management Theory and Principles (University of the Pacific), and Hazardous Materials Management (UC, Berkeley). For 5 years he served as the Environmental Editor of *SCITECH NEWS*, a quarterly informational newsletter that highlights minorities working with new developments in science and technology. Currently, Mr. Mitchell develops and instructs advanced engineering and scientific principal training courses for different project operations to professionals requiring Nuclear Science Certification, Authorization Basis and Integrated Safety Management needed to satisfy the Department of Energy regulatory requirements. Earlier in his career, he was matrix to the LLNL Laser Program Department where he received a Directorate Award for his independent research, specialized contribution and outstanding performance working with Laser Plasma Fusion. In 1992, he married Kathryn L. Mitchell; they now have two sons.

Raphael Mmasi, Ph.D.
Engineering Science

Dr. Mmasi has a strong commitment to promote efficient and sustainable utilization of ICT for sustainable economic growth and wealth creation, started as an executive engineer (MEM), senior scientific officer (COSTECH), Part time lecturer (DIT), Senior Lecturer (KIST), Director of ICT Center at KIST, Interim Executive Director for Rwanda Information Technology Authority (RITA), Director of National Computing Centre, ICT Infrastructure Coordinator in the Ministry of Infrastructure under the communication sector (Government of Rwanda), Senior Lecturer and Director of Planning and Investment at the University of Dodoma, and currently Director of Information and Documentation at Tanzania Commission for Science and Technology. He has knowledge, skills and experience in ICT policy & projects implementation, Electronics and Electrical Engineering. His major interest is to develop capacity in putting human and sustainable development into practice in ICT projects design (last mile solutions), development, implementation, monitoring and evaluation.

Aberra Mogessie, Ph.D.
Metamorphic, Igneous Petrology, Geochemistry and Economic Geology

Prof. Mogessie's main field of research is mineralogy, petrology, geochemistry and mineral deposits. His research field areas are located in Austria, Argentina, Egypt, Ethiopia, Tanzania, North America (Minnesota) and Bulgaria. Though born Ethiopian, Dr. Mogessie is an Austrian citizen, working as a professor of mineralogy and petrology at the University of Graz, Austria. Since November 2008 he is elected President of the Geological Society of Africa(GSAf) which represents all the 53 African countries and territories. Apart from being a leader of several scientific research projects mainly in the field of Platinum mineralization with international cooperation, Dr. Mogessie is serving as editorial board member and reviewer of several earth science journals. His research has resulted in understanding of the Platinum and gold deposits of the Yubdo area, Ethiopia and their future economic significance. He is a member of the Executive Board of the Austrian Mineralogical Society and its representative in the Commission for Ore Mineralogy of the International Mineralogical Association. Due to his scientific achievements which resulted in over 180 scientific publications as well as authorship of books and proceedings, Dr. Mogessie is a Fellow of the Society of Economic Geologists (SEG) and the African Scientific Institute (ASI).

Michel F. Molaire
Research Chemist

Michel, MSE MBA, is a former Senior Research Associate chemist at Eastman Kodak Company (1974 – 2010). His research experience includes project leadership, polymeric materials, materials compatibility, free-volume effects in polymeric systems, photoreceptor formulation and development, infrared sensitive pigment for electrophotography, dip coating technology, UV curing systems, electrophotographic transfer materials, molecular glasses (organic monomeric glasses), sol-gel overcoats, robustness testing of electrophotographic printers, Taguchi methods, business analysis and database design. Mr. Molaire is a prolific inventor holding 53 US patents, more than 100 foreign patents, and author of several scientific publications. In 1994, he was inducted into the Eastman Kodak Distinguished Inventor's Gallery (Inventor Hall of Fame) for reaching the milestone of 20 or more patents. Mr. Molaire is the author of three collections of poems; in 1998, he wrote and published in *African American Who's Who, Past & Present, Greater Rochester Area*, and *African American Who Was First, Greater Rochester Area*. Michel is listed in *Who's Who Among African Americans* (2008, 2010), Marquis *Who's Who in America* (2000, 2001, 2006), Marquis *Who's Who in America Science and Engineering* 5th Edition (1999).

Stanislas Ebata Mongo, M.D.
Director, Disease Control

He has served as the Head of the Poliomyelitis Control Department at the Congolese Ministry of Health. Dr. Mongo duties has also served as the Director of the National Malaria Control Program, Director of his country's fight against Ebola. He has also been his country's Director of the struggle against buruli ulcers.

Ulysses J. Montgomery, P.E.
Civil Engineering

He has over 50 years experience as a project engineer, developer and manager of major projects, hig-density and single family housing, civil engineering, agricultural, mining, petroleum and industrial projects in the U.S., Asia, Africa and the Middle East. Mr. Montgomery specializes in the systems approach of providing financial, engineering, construction and management services for the creation of viable projects pursuant to specifications, on schedule, and within authorized budgets. He graduated from MIT in 1952. After graduation, he traveled to Africa developing projects in Angola, Nigeria, Ghana, and Liberia. There he met W.E.B. DuBois, Malcolm X, Congo's Patrice Lumumba, Zimbabwe's Nkomo, and Kenyatta in Kenya. "All of these were friends," he said. He was with Nelson Mandella's group the day the great revolutionary leader was sentenced to prison.

John P. Moon
Corp. Vice President, Computer Imaging Products

The possibility of working on computers never crossed Mr. Moon's mind until 1962, when he was hired by International Business Machines (IBM). He found the 'new' ferrite technology heads used to store and retrieve data fascinating. He eagerly worked with others to manufacture and apply these heads. In 1970, Mr. Moon took a bold step and joined with others who had founded a new company, National Micronetics Corporation. They were working on ways to use ferrite in devices that stored data as a permanent part of the computer's memory. In 1976, Mr. Moon joined Tandon Magnetics Corp. where a double-sided disk head was invented that could store and retrieve on both sides of a floppy disk. In 1980, Mr. Moon joined Apple to to work on the company's new 'Macintosh' disk drive (a joint venture with Japan's Sony Corp.). Eventually,as with other companies, Mr. Moon career soared. He became Apple's Vice President for peripherals engineering. Though Mr. Moon modestly says his inventions has not made major changes in the computer industry, he believes he has always been around things that have significantly changed the industry, including Jugi Tandon's two-sided disk head and Sony's 3-1/2 inch disk drive. Mr. Moon says his engineering skills helped make these historical inventions "better" and easier to manufacture.

Gregory B. Morrison
Corp. Vice President and CIO

Greg Morrison is vice president and chief information officer for Cox Enterprises, Inc., one of the nation's leading media companies and providers of automotive services. He is responsible for technology planning for all corporate headquarters operations. He previously served as vice president of information systems at Prudential Financial, Inc., where he progressed through the ranks from 1989 to 2000. He briefly left Prudential to become chief operating officer and chief information officer for RealEstate.com in 2000, then rejoined the company later that year as vice president of information systems. Mr. Morrison received a Bachelor of Science in Mathematics from SC State University and a Masters of Science in Industrial Engineering/Operations Research from Northwestern University. Greg serves on the board of trustees of Clark-Atlanta University and on the board of directors of TechBridge and Georgia CIO Leadership Association. He was named one the top 50 Most Important Blacks in Technology by U.S. Black Engineer (USBE) magazine in 2005.

Edmond Moukala
Civil Engineering; Personal Assistant to the Chairman of the Executive Board, UNESCO Paris

Edmond is a civil engineer who specializes in hydro-power station work. He has worked as a consultant for the Chinese Three Gorges Dam project before joining UNESCO (1998)in the preservation of cultural sites threatened by flooded rivers. During 1993-1999, Edmond work for the International Hydrological Program of UNESCO and later he coordinated post-disaster activities (i.e.: every year in summer, major rivers of China overflow and flood most of the cities along the banks, causing severe damages to schools, heritage sites and other irrigations systems). As a civil engineer, he participated in the UN Disaster Management Team and coordinated UNESCO's contribution to most of the UN disaster response's activities in China. Presently, he is employed in Paris at the Office of UNESCO Executive Board.

Hassina Mouri, Ph.D.
Metamorphic Petrologist

Dr. Mouri has studied and worked in different institutions on three continents (Africa, Europe and America). Here core interest focuses on "*Ultra-high temperature granulites*" rare rock suites in nature that record still unexplained events when regions of the Earth's crust reached temperatures approaching, even excess 1000°C. These rocks preserve in their textures and minerals, "*snapshots*" of the Earth's past geological history, which are necessary to understand how mountain belts form and how the Earth's crust evolved during early times. She has worked at several different institutions (University of Algiers; University of Paris; University of Helsinki; Geological Survey of Finland; Swedish Museum of Natural History; University of Minnesota and University of Pretoria). She has published many papers in refereed international journals, and presented about 26 contributions at international conferences. In 2008, she was elected Secretary General (2008-2012) of the Geological Society of Africa. She is currently leading the organization of the 23rd Colloquium of African Geology (CAG23) organized under the auspices of the Geological Society of Africa. Prof. Mouri received a number of recognitions including the AU-EU Regional Award for women in science, 2010 Edition, the first African female geologist to achieve this distinction in Earth and Life science.

Sospeter M. Muhongo, Ph.D.
Tectonics, Structural geology, Petrology, Geochronology and Economic Geology

Professor Muhongo was the first and founding Regional Director of the International Council for Science Regional Office for Africa (ICSU ROA). He is Vice President of the Commission of the Geological Map of the World (CGMW); Immediate Past Chair of the UNESCO/IUGS/IGCP Scientific Board; and member of the Southern African Regional Universities Association (SARUA) Science and Technology Advisory Group. He has been recently elected to Chair the Steering Committee of the EU-funded project, "African-European geo-resources observation system (AEGOS)." Prof Muhongo is co-Editor-in-Chief of the Journal of African Earth Sciences (Elsevier), Associate Editor of the Precambrian Research Journal (Elsevier) and also co-Editor of a book (2009, in press) entitled "Science, Technology and Innovation for Socio-Economic Development: Success Stories from Africa." He is author or co-author of over 200 scientific articles and technical papers. Prof Muhongo is a Professor and was Head of the Department of Geology at the University of Dar Es Salaam (1997 – 2000) and is currently Honorary Professor of Geology at the University of Pretoria in South Africa. In the 1990s he was instrumental in raising the profile of the Geological Society of Africa (GSAf) and served as its President from 1995 to 2001. He is a Member of the International Experts Group (Global Science Forum) of OECD.

Kassim S. Mwitondi, Ph.D
Data Mining and Business Intelligence

Dr. Mwitondi specialises in Data Mining – a fast growing field focusing on the extraction of knowledge from data. He has maintained a well-balanced ratio between teaching, consulting and research with clients and colleagues from all continents. He has taught data mining, computing, mathematics and applied statistics on numerous undergraduate and postgraduate programmes both in Africa and Europe. His consulting outputs include developing an index for particulate emission for a large engineering firm in northern England and developing a customer satisfaction index for a British high street bank. His research interests involve the application of data mining techniques in uncovering naturally arising structures in large dimensional biomedical, environmental and business data in which he has published extensively. He has actively taken part in a number of EU-funded projects using predictive methods in preventing chronic diseases and improving patients' care through enhancements in information management. A keen supporter of STI for development in Africa, he works closely with African biomedical and environmental research institutions in transforming raw data into knowledge. He is a member of an international consortium of inter-disciplinary researchers investigating African clays for the purpose of characterizing and documenting their chemical and distributional properties across the continent.

M. Paul Nampala, Ph.D.
Executive Secretary, Uganda National Academy of Sciences (UNAS); Entomology; Crop Science

Dr. Nampala is a practising scientist in areas of Pest Ecology & Entomology and Science for Evidence-based Policy decision-making. Since 2005, he has been the Executive Secretary of the Uganda National Academy of Sciences (UNAS). He also lectures part-time in Crop Protection, Insect Pest Ecology, Biometry, Biosafety, Biopolicy, Bioethics and Environmental Impact Assessment at the Faculty of Agriculture in Makerere University. Since 2003, Dr. Nampala serves as Scientific Editor of the *African Crop Science Journal* and Reviewer of several other high impact journals. He is a member of UNAS, African Crop Science Society, International Biometrics Society, African Association of Insect Scientists, etc. Since 2001, Dr. Nampala has undertaken more than 20 consultancies in various fields, including Project Development and Monitoring and Evaluation, Participatory Training and Learning, Farmer-Field School training, Integrated Pest Management, Assessment of Prospects for Improved Crop Productivity and the Role of evidence-based approaches and models in policy formulation. Among the main clients to whom I have rendered consultancy services are ASARECA, FAO, USAID, CGIAR (e.g. CIP, ILRI, INIBAP), Rockefeller Foundation, World Bank, Universities and the Government of Uganda, etc.

Edith Eliakim Ndemanisho, Ph.D.
Agriculture Science

Dr. Ndemanisho is an Associate Professor of Agricuture, where she teaches students about animal health and production and small ruminants production (ruminant - a mammal of the order artiodactyla that digests plant-based food by initially softening it within the animal's first stomach, then regurgitating the semi-digested mass, now known as cud, and chewing it again). Her research activities/ supervision of research/consultancy/other related activities have included studying the effects of feeding *Leucaena leucocephala* forage and cotton seed cake as sources of protein to late gestation dairy goats; researching the potential of mulberry (*Morus alba*) for rabbit production; Potential of selected Tropical Multipurpose Trees (MPTS) as feed for growing goats and soil improvement; assessing the processing and preservation of fish at market places.

Ahmadou Lamine Ndiaye, DVM
Veterinary Science

Dr. Ndiaye was Director of Ecole Inter-Etats de Sciences et Médecine Vétérinaires (E.I.S.M.V.) of Dakar from 1976 to 1986. He was full Professor of the Tenure of Animal Science and Food at the E.I.S.M.V. from 1977 to 1988. On January 1990, he was appointed Vice-Chancellor of the Second Public University of Senegal – the University of Saint-Louis. He has been a Member of the Executive Board of African Universities Association from 1997 to 2005, where he has been Vice President and then President ad interim of this Association. Dr. Ndiaye is a Founding Member of the Academy of Sciences and Techniques of Senegal, of which he is the Vice-President and Chairman of the Agricultural Sciences Section. He is a Member of the Administrative board and Vice President of the Université Senghor (Alexandria). He is Secretary General of the Network of African Science Academies (NASAC).

Lucy Mande Ayamba Ndip, Ph.D.
Director, Laboratory for Emerging Infectious Diseases; Biochemistry and Microbiology

Dr. Ndip is an ardent scientist in Emerging Infectious Diseases and has been in academia for 12 years as a Lecturer of Microbiology at the University of Buea, where she also serves as the Head of Service of Teaching and Research at the Faculty of Science and as the Director of the Laboratory for Emerging Infectious Diseases. This laboratory, affiliated to the US Army Medical Research Unit, Nairobi, Kenya is funded by the Global Emerging Infections Surveillance Program of the US Armed Forces Health Surveillance Center with a vision to track the emergence of new pathogens. Dr. Ndip is well trained with classic diagnostic and research skills obtained as a Fogarty International Center fellow at the University of Texas Medical Branch at Galveston which includes diagnosis of emerging infectious diseases, knowledge of GLP (international standard) including working in BSL 3 facility, development of SOPs, PCR and Real-time PCR, tissue culture and isolation techniques, immunological techniques such IFA and Western blotting, RFLP, proteomic techniques and basic genomic analysis tools. As a scientist in tropical medicine, she pioneered the first demonstration that African tick bite fever caused by *Rickettsia africae* has a high incidence among the indigenous population of Cameroon and also for the first time that infections with *Ehrlichia chaffeensis* and *E. ewingii* occur in a tropical country.

Roland Ndip, Ph.D.
Medical Microbiology

Prof. Ndip has been in the academia for 18years. Before joining the services of the University of Fort Hare, South Africa, he lectured at the University of Buea, Cameroon where he also served as Head of Department of Life Sciences, and Vice-Dean for Students' Affairs in the Faculty of Science. He currently serves as the Vice President of the Pan African Environmental Mutagen Society and as reviewer to several international journals. He also belongs to several National and International professional societies. Historically, Prof. Ndip's research has concentrated in Microbiology, Immunology, Molecular biology, Environmental biotechnology and drug discovery. His central theme lies in the diagnosis, epidemiology and control of enteric bacterial pathogens, intracellular bacteria as well as bacteria implicated in sexually transmitted disease. Emphasis has been laid on some members of the Enterobacteriaceae and intracellular bacteria, including *Salmonella, Klebsiella, Vibrio, Rickettsia* and *Ehrlichia.* He has generated enormous and significant data published in reputable journals, which highlights the importance of these pathogens as important causes of different infectious diseases. With an apparent indication of a high morbidity rate of gastritis, he is now focusing his interest on the gastric pathogen, *Helicobacter pylori*, which has been implicated as a significant cause of gastritis and gastric cancer.

Eddie Neal, Ph.D.
President, Engineering Research Firm

Throughout his career, Dr. Neal, an outstanding scientist and successful entrepreneur, has concentrated on the application of advanced mathematical and engineering analysis technology to solve practical problems, particularly those related to the national defense, the environment, and transportation. Dr. Neal's research has included use of statistical techniques to design U.S. and NATO ships with improved speed and maneuverability, the development of mathematical models to predict water pollution concentrations resulting from urban watershed runoff, and computational analyses to ameliorate traffic congestion and upgrade highway safety. Dr. Neal has authored over thirty technical reports and has published in national and international journals, including Water Resources Research, Proceedings of International Symposia on Naval Hydrodynamics, and publications of the American Society of Civil Engineers. Dr. Neal is the founder and CEO of The Scientex Corporation. The company is a leading provider of Intelligent Transportation Systems (ITS) for automated real-time control of motor vehicle traffic.

Claire A. Nelson, Ph.D.
Futurist; Industrial Engineering; Founder and President of the Institute of Caribbean Studies

Dr. Nelson has been actively engaged in the business of international development for over twenty five years, working in the area of project development and management, with a particular focus on private sector development. A renaissance woman, she has been alternately described as a Social Entrepreneur, Futurist and Change Leader. The first Jamaican woman to hold a Doctorate degree in an engineering discipline and only Black in her graduating class, Dr. Nelson holds Industrial Engineering Degrees from the State University of New York at Buffalo, Purdue University, and a Doctorate in Engineering Management from the George Washington University. She has served on numerous Boards and Committees including: US Department of Commerce US/Caribbean Business Development Council; Advisory Board; DC Caribbean Carnival Association; International Think Tank, Commission on Pan-African Affairs, Office of the Prime Minister of Barbados; African-American Unity Caucus; National Democratic Institute/Carter Center Election Observer Mission to the Dominican Republic; Black Professionals in International Affairs; and the International Committee, National Society of Black Engineers-Alumni Extension.

Mbangiseni P. Nepfumbada, M.Sc., Pr. Sci. Nat
Soil Scientist and Manager in Water Resources Monitoring and Information

Mr. Nepfumbada has been a senior manager in the Department of Water Affairs (DWA) in South Africa since 1999, holding positions of Director: Institute for Water Quality Studies (1999–2002), Chief Director: Scientific Services/Water Resources Information Management (2002- to date) and recently Acting Deputy Director-General of Water Policy and Regulation (2010-11). He has been leading managers, scientists and other professionals responsible for, among others, the development and maintenance of national information and monitoring systems for the water resources management, Review of National Water Resources Strategy, as well as development of Water Policies and Guidelines. He has served in various governing boards of scientific organizations such as Council for Geosciences (CGS) board member. He is also the current Chair of the South African National Committee for UNESCO International Hydrological Programme (IHP) and in 2008-10 represented the sub-Saharan region in the Bureau of the UNESCO IHP. Prior to joining Water Affairs, Mr. Nepfumbada was at the University of Pretoria (1996-99) as a scientist and in the academic environment doing research and lecturing both at undergraduate and postgraduate levels. He has presented in various meetings and seminars on a wide range of topics, mainly on water issues.

Mortimer H. Neufville, Ph.D.
Agriculture Scientist

Mortimer H. Neufville assumed his position as Executive Vice President on January 3, 2000 and Director, Federal Relations Food, Environment and International Affairs at NASULGC on January 2, 1997. At NASULGC, Dr. Neufville provides leadership for Federal Relations activities and is responsible for internal management operations. More specifically, Dr. Neufville also coordinates the activities in food, agriculture, natural resources, environmental affairs, human sciences, forestry and international affairs for the Land-Grant and affiliate member institutions. Prior to joining NASULGC, Dr. Neufville held a number of positions at the University of Maryland Eastern Shore (UMES), (1983-96) including Vice President for Academic Affairs (1994-1996), Associate Director of the Maryland Agricultural Experiment Station (1989-1994), Acting Vice President for Academic Affairs (1993-94); Associate Vice President for Academic Affairs (1991-93); 1890 Research Director (1983-95) and Dean of Agricultural Sciences (1983-91). During his tenure at UMES Dr. Neufville, was the project manager for the Cameroon Root and Tuber Food Crops Research Project (1986-94), funded by USAID and the Government of the Republic of Cameroon, where UMES served as lead institution.

Jane Catherine Ngila, Ph.D.
Analytical and Environmental Chemistry

Dr. Ngila's research interests the development of solid-state and chemically-modified electrodes, biosensors and gas sensors in flow injection & chromatographic analyses for environmental, biological and gas monitoring applications; adsorption studies using polymer membranes and biomass for removal of pollutants in contaminated water; studies of chemical speciation of heavy metals in water systems; method development for sampling and sample preparation to improve sensitivity of analytical techniques in trace level analysis of pollutants in freshwater bodies. Dr. Ngila has authored and co-authored books in her areas of research and published in many refereed scientific journals.

Magnus Ngoile, Ph.D.
Large Marine Ecosystems; fisheries; coastal management; marine protected areas

Dr. Ngoile is the Policy and Governance Coordinator of the Agulhas Somali Currents Large Marine Ecosystems Project, servicing ten countries of the western Indian Ocean. He has extensive research and management experience in fisheries, marine ecology, population biology, marine protected areas and environmental management as well as advancing the concept of large marine ecosystem approach to managing marine resources globally. He specializes in national and regional processes related to the establishment of integrated coastal management. At the regional level, he has been integral to the development of marine sciences in East Africa. He was Director of the Institute of Marine Sciences (IMS) of the University of Dar es Salaam in Tanzania for 10 years where he enhanced curriculum and advocated implementations. Internationally, Dr. Ngoile has actively fostered networks and partnerships that facilitate improved coastal management initiatives through his position as coordinator of the International Union for Conservation of Nature (IUCN) Global Marine and Coastal Program, where he worked for three years until his appointment as Director General of Tanzania's National Environmental Management Council. He also helped launch the Western Indian Ocean Marine Science Association and has served as its President and board member of the organization over ten years.

Victor Anomah Ngu, M.D.
Retired surgeon; Former Public Health Minister and researcher on HIV/AIDS, inventor of VANHIVAX vaccine; former President of the Cameroon Academy of Sciences

Though a retired physician, Prof. Ngu has an amzinging history as a medical doctor. He was Pro-Chancellor, University of Buea (1993 – 2005); President, Cameroon Academy of Sciences (2001); Professor of Surgery and Director of the Cancer Research Laboratory C.U.S.S. (1984 – 1991); Professor of Surgery and Director of the Cancer Research Laboratory C.U.S.S. - 1984 – 199;. Minister of Public Health Cameroon (1984.-1988); Vice-Chancellor, University of Yaoundé, Cameroon (1974-1982); Professor and Head of Surgery of both, University Centre for Health Sciences, University of Yaoundé, Cameroon (1971-1974) and University of Ibadan, Nigeria (1965-1971); Founder member 1960 and President of the Association now College of Surgery of West Africa (1972-1974); President of the Association of African Universities -1980-1982. He has authored 16 publications on general surgery and 43 publications on cancer and HIV.

Obed Norman, Ph.D.
Science Education

Dr. Norman is Principal Investigator and Director: Performance Enhancement for African American Students in Science (PEASS) Research Project and Associate Professor of Science Education, Graduate Programs in Science and Mathematics Education at Morgan State University. He was an Associate Professor in Science Education, San Jose State University, CA (2001 - 2005). From 1994 - 2001, he was Assistant Professor in Science Education, Washington State University, Vancouver. In 1999, Obed was Awarded Early Career NSF Research award for $500,000, which recognized and supported the early career development activities of those teacher-scholars who were most likely to become the academic leaders of the 21st century. He has written "Do Black Adolescents Equate Getting Good Grades with 'Acting White? : A Historical and Empirical Exploration", "Voices from the Classroom: African American Students' Perceptions of their Science Classroom and Science Learning Experiences", "The Black-White Achievement Gap in Science: Trends, Questions, and Implications for Research and Practice", and "Science, Race, and Education: A Symposium", presented At the Annual Meeting of the National Association for Research in Science Teaching. Dr. Norman has always excelled in school. In 1983, he was listed among top ten High School Graduates in South Africa.

Godfrey O. Nunoo, DDC
Medicine, Chiopractor

Dr. Nunoo is past president of the Alameda County Chiropractic Society, where he served as president for two terms and vice president for one term. He is also active in numerous community organizations, including the American Heart Association, the American Cancer Association, the American Red Cross, and the Kiwanis Club of Oakland, and serves as a volunteer for the Oakland Mayor Summer Jobs Program. He also serves on the board of directors for Continental Resource Institute, a humanitarian relief nonprofit organization. A native of Accra, Ghana, West Africa, Dr. Nunoo is a member of the on-call staff in the radiology department at Kaiser Hospital in Hayward, and in the radiology department at ReadiCare Industrial Medical Clinics.

Emmanuel Andrew Chukwuedo Nwanze, Ph.D.
Recent University Vice-Chancellor; BioChemistry

Prof. Nwanze has been Vice Chancellor, University of Benin (2/ 2004-2/2009). He has been a Professor of Biochemistry since 1987 and head of the department from 1987-1994. He was Dean, Faculty of Science from 1994-1998. His interests in research span a wide spectrum of lipid biochemistry with special reference to (i) lipid methodology, (ii) biochemistry and disease as well as (iii) neuro-biochemistry. He has authored/co-authored over 60 publications in various international journals of science. Since 1976, as a University Lecturer and Professor, he has been involved in the design, preparation and teaching of Biochemistry to Science, Medical, Dental and Pharmacy students. His lectures to undergraduate students span the areas of lipid biochemistry and membrane biophysics. At the post-graduate level, his lectures cover the areas of biochemical methodology, neurobiochemistry and clinical biochemistry.

Bertram Ekejiuba B. Nwoke, Ph.D.
Public Health Parasitology & Entomology

Prof. Nwoke interests and areas of lecturing and research include Medical & Public Health Parasitology & Entomology, Ecology and Epidemiology of Infectious Diseases, Pest and Disease Management, Medical Entomology, Impact Assessment of Parasitic Disease's Control and Environmental Impact Assessment. He has served as Deputy Vice Chancellor (Academic) and is now Dean of the Faculty of Science. He was a Pioneer Board Member, Imo State University Teaching Hospital. Prof Nwoke also provides technical service to outside bodies such as being consultant to Nigerian River Blindness and Lymphatic` Filariasis Control Programmes, Global 2000 River Blindness Programme (GRBP) USA, and WHO African Consultant for WHO African Programme for Onchocerciasis Control (APOC) in Africa; serving as Facilitator, National Orientation Agency; on the Editorial Board *Medicare Journal*; Member, Editorial Board *Science Research Journal*.

Rudo Nyachoto
Chemical Engineering

From 1994 - 1997 she worked in the Environmental Services industry as a Project Manager for ChromaLab. In this capacity Ms. Nyachoto provided quality controls for the laboratory to assure accurate chemical analysis data was provided to customers. Afterwards, she worked in the automotive industry for 12 years as a chemical engineer at NUMMI, where she managed multiple projects efficiently and professionally.

Ntahondi Nyandwi, Ph.D.
Marine Sciences

He is Associate Director of the Institute of Marine Sciences (IMS), University of Dar-es-Salaam, mandated to conduct research and offer postgraduate and undergraduate training and consultancy services in all aspects of marine sciences. His main area of research includes marine geology, coastal erosion, sediment transport and hydrodynamics. In 1995 during his PhD study he managed to bring to light the mechanism by which sediment in the German Wadden Sea fines up seawards.

Tebello Nyokong, Ph.D.
Medicinal Chemistry and Nanotechnology; 2009 L'Oreal-UNESCO Women in Science Awardee

Professor Nyokong has become the first South African scientist to win the L'ORÉAL-UNESCO award for women in science for research in physical sciences. Each year one laureate is selected from five world regions. She is the Laureate for Africa and the Arab states for 2009. She earned her MS and Ph.D. (1987) in Chemistry from the University of Western Ontario. As Chair of NRF/DST in Medicinal Chemistry and Nanotechnology at her university, she has led the field in ground-breaking research on a new cancer diagnosis and treatment methodology called "photo-dynamic therapy" which is intended as an alternative to chemotherapy. Nyokong's researches compounds known as porphyrins, which have been used as potent therapies for cancer and have been used in developing highly sensitive sensors for detecting pathogens. Owing to their broad catalytic nature and optical properties, porphyrins have also been used in cleaning of polluted water. The only woman in her department and the mother of two grown children, Dr. Nyokong is familiar with the academic loneliness female scientists often experience as well as the challenges of combining a career in science with the demands of raising a family. "Female scientists act as role models for young women. They also create a scientifically literate community since they bring up children and can encourage scientific thinking quite early in life."

Joseph Oakley, Jr., P.E.
Civil and Structural Engineering

He heads Oakley & Oakley, a civil and structural engineering company established in 1976, headquartered in Oakland, California, with affiliate offices in San Francisco, Big Bear Lake, and Los Angeles, California. His company has performed special studies, and evaluations for pre-earthquake and post-earthquake building safety, and performed investigations for the County of Los Angeles on more than 500 public buildings after the Northridge Earthquake of January 1994. In 1996, our outstanding engineering of the Fox Studios facilities in Rosarito, Mexico, which included the world's largest inland tank, enabled Director, James Cameron to complete the enormously successful movie, "Titanic". We are currently Consulting Structural Engineers for the 200,000 square foot Air Cargo Facilities for the San Francisco International Airport as part of the F. E. Jordan Associates design team.

Theresa Nkechi Obiekezie, Ph.D.
Research Physics

Dr. Obiekezie is a Lecturer in the Department of Physics and Industrial Physics. She has authored and co-authored several articles such as "Possibility of a correlation between the cloud factor and the flux of galactic cosmic rays: A Review"; "Upper mantle conductivity determined from the solar quiet day ionospheric currents in the dip equatorial latitudes of West Africa". She made the Best Ph.D in the Faculty of Physical Sciences in the University Of Nigeria Nsukka in 208/2009 Academic year and got the Vice Chancellor's Prize. This year, Dr. Nkechi has emerged winner of African Union (AU) co-sponsored African Union-Third World Academy of Science (AU-TWAS) Young Scientist National Award. Several African nations like Nigeria, Benin, Cameroun, Egypt, Guinea, Lesotho, Malawi, Senegal and Zimbabwe have the awards in their respective countries. In Nigeria, the award is being administered by the Federal Ministry of Science and Technology and the Nigerian Academy of Science (NAS). Dr. Obiekezie is the Managing Editor *Journal of Basic Physical Research*.

Chuma Obiudu, Ph.D.
Pomology; Agriculture Education

Dr. Obiudu is the founder of Sustainable Management Consulting-SMC. He is a pomologist. He promotes social and economic well-being of children, families, and communities through an outdoor garden learning setting. He fosters the development of urban agriculture, community and school gardens as portals for nutrition, environment and health education. His greatest challenge today at local level is controlling child obesity, aggression, short attention span, asthma and food allergies resulting from poor food habits. At a global level he strives for the establishment of proactive and active action programs for the sustainable management, monitoring and evaluation of non-renewable natural resources. He states, "Man is never independent until he attains food security and safety status."

Eric O. Odada, Ph.D.
Palaeoclimatology; Palaelimnology

Eric O. Odada holds a PhD degree in geochemistry from Imperial College, London University. He is the Director of the African Collaborative Centre for Earth System Sciences (ACCESS), and is a Professor of Geology at the University of Nairobi and Director of UNU Regional Centre for IWRM. His current research interests included climate change adaptation, water quality monitoring, waste water treatment, studies of lakes and dams as archives of climatic and environmental dynamics, coastal and marine processes, sedimentary processes in large lakes and oceans and integrated water resource management. He is currently undertaking a strategic assessment of water resources vulnerability to environmental change in Africa for UNEP-DEWA, and working with UNFAO on a study of water-related environmental impacts in agriculture. He is also leading a research consortium of African, European and North American scientists involved in promoting the investigations of African Great Lakes as archives of climatic and environmental dynamics. He has published over one hundred papers in peer reviewed international journals and many books on Ecology, hydrology, climatology and biodiversity of African Great Lakes and their Basins. Professor Odada is a Member of the United Nations Secretary General's Advisory Board on Water and Sanitation.

Tolu Odugbemi, M.D., Ph.D.
Medical Microbiology and Parasitology

Dr. Odugbemi is Vice-Chancellor, Ondo State University of Science and Technology (OSUSTECH), Okitipupa. He has been Professor and Head, Department of Medical Microbiology and Parasitology, College of Medicine, University of Lagos intermittently since 1983. In 2000, he was appointed Provost of this university. Dr. Odugbemi extensive research experiences include: *Streptococcus* and its major non-suppurative sequelae in Nigeria Urban population; Prevalence and behaviour of *Vibrio cholerae* in Lagos environment; *Neisseria gonorrhoeae*: *Yersinia enterocolitica* and other bacterial diarrhoeagenic agents Isolation, transportation and antibiotic susceptibility testing. His awards have been too numerous to list, but includes the Nigerian National Order of Merit (NNOM), conferred by the President of the Federal Republic of Nigeria in December 2007 and the Officer of the Order of the Niger (OON) conferred by the President of the Federal Republic of Nigeria in 2008. He is also Editorial Adviser, the *Nigerian Medical Journal* and Coordinating Editor/ Co-founder of the *Nigerian Journal of Health and Biomedical Sciences*, April 2002.

Ferdinand A. Ofodile, M.D., FACS
Plastic & Reconstructive Surgery

Dr. Ofodile is a board certified Plastic Surgeon and a Clinical Professor. He is a Fellow of the American College of Surgeons (FACS), and a Fellow of the American Association of Plastic Surgeons. He is also board certified in general surgery. He earned his BS and MD degrees at Northwestern University, Illinois. Dr. Ofodile designed a nasal implant for rhinoplasty in Blacks and Hispanics, named the *"Ofodile Implant"* after his name. The Implants are designed to produce more natural results that fit the black and Hispanic features. Dr. Ofodile has published numerous scientific articles in plastic surgery and presented scientific plastic surgery papers in many international conferences. Not only is he an active member of several societies, he has received several awards and has been named one of "America's Top Physicians" by the Consumers' Research Council of America and "Top African American Doctor" by the Network Journal. Dr. Ofodile has led volunteer medical missions to several parts of the world, including the Dominican Republic, Haiti, Nigeria and Mozambique.

Olugbenga Okunlola, Ph.D.
Geology

Dr. Okunlola has been teaching Geology since 2002 at the University of Ibadan. Prior to this appointment, he has worked for the Geological Survey of Nigeria, first as a Senior Mining Geologist (1989 – 1994), then as Principal Mining Geologist (1994 – 1998), Assistant Chief Geologist (1998 – 2001), Chief Geologist (2001 – 2002). Dr. Okunlola's research interests include has been on the understanding of compositional features, ,petrogenesis of basement complex and sedimentary hosted ore deposits and industrial minerals and their lithological associations. The rocks and minerals which outcrop within the Precambrian of Nigeria comprising associated gneisses, migmatites, quartzites, schists, older granites, pegmatites and secondary rocks such as amphibolites, banded iron formation are foci of the research. This has led to evaluation of ores of rare metals -tantalite, tin, columbite and wolframite within the pegmatite, and gold in the late quartz veins, often associated with meta volcanics. Industrial minerals which are as a result of hydrothermal, epigenetic or residual weathering such as Kaolin, Gypsum, and Phosphate brine salts have also been studied. Recent research efforts are also geared towards using inorganic geochemical methods to characterize Nigeria's sedimentary basin and evaluate their lithologic successions as industrial raw materials.

Ken Olden, Ph.D.
Cell biology and Biochemistry

From 1991-2005, Dr. Olden was Director of the National Institute of Environmental Health Sciences (NIEHS) and the Nation Toxicology Program (NTP). He was the first African American to become director of one of the NIH institutes. In 2005, he returned full time to his research position as Chief of The Metastasis Group in the Laboratory of Molecular Carcinogenesis at the NIEHS, which he also held while director. He is now Founding Dean of the School of Public Health at the City University of New York. From 1979-1991, Dr. Olden held several positions at the Howard University Cancer Center, including Director, Professor and Chairman of the Department of Oncology. Most recently, he served on the IOM Panel on the Health Effects of the Oil Spill in the Gulf of Mexico and was appointed by the Administrator of EPA to membership on the Board of Directors of the National Environmental Education Foundation, and by the Deputy Administrator to membership on the Board of Scientific Counselors Advisory Committee of the EPA. His honors and awards are numerous to list and include President George H.W. Bush appointing him to membership on the National Cancer Advisory Board (1991), and President William J. Clinton selecting him to receive the Presidential Distinguished Executive Rank Award (1996), and Presidential Meritorious Executive Rank Award (1997).

Abiodun Francis Oluwole, Ph.D.
Nuclear Physic; Environmental Science

Professor Oluwole, a nuclear physicist whose pioneering research in nuclear energy and techniques and leadership of multidisciplinary teams had contributed to the application of nuclear analytical techniques in providing answers to a variety of problems of national relevance in geology, the environment and human health.

Soji F. Oluwole, M.D.
Medical Surgery

Dr. Oluwole is Professor of Surgery at Columbia University College of Physicians & Surgeons at Harlem Hospital Center, where he also serves as General Surgery Residency Program Director. Before joining Columbia University, he was a Professor of Surgery at Obafemi Awolowo University Ile-Ife, Nigeria for five years. He has been awarded several times; he was the Recipient of 2003 New York State Innovation in Breast Cancer Early Detection and Research Award and Recipient of the 2004 Nigerian National Order of Merit in Medicine bestowed by the President of the Federal Republic of Nigeria for the highest national prize for academic and intellectual attainment in Medicine. At the Harlem Hospital Center, he serves as Medical Director, Cancer Control Center of Harlem, Associate Director of Surgery Harlem Hospital Center, and Attending in Surgery and Surgical Intensive Care. Dr. Oluwole has authored and co-authored about 200 publishings and has authored chapters in several books.

Josiah Ouma Omolo, Ph.D.
Chemistry

Dr. Omolo is a senior lecturer at Egerton University, Kenya and has extensive research interests in natural products chemistry and fungal biotechnology. He is investigating biologically active compounds from biotechnological cultures of higher fungi from different habitats in Kenya. He earned his BS and MS degrees from Kenyatta University, Kenya (1991-1994 in Chemistry and his Ph.D. in Chemistry from Kenyatta University/University of Kaiserslautern, Germany (1996-2000). Not only has he authored several papers, but Dr. Omolo is a member of The International Council for Science (ICSU) Regional Office for Africa Project Development Team, Natural Products Research Network for Eastern and Central Africa Kenya Branch (NAPRECA-K), German Society for Microbiology, Kenya DAAD Scholars Association, and the Kenya Chemical Society, KCS

Peter Azikiwe Onwualu, Ph.D.
CEO, Raw Materials R & D Council; Agricultural Engineering

Dr. Onwualu's areas of research, development and professional interests are quite extensive: some include Processing of Agro-based and Mineral Raw Materials; Science and Technology for Sustainable Development, Agricultural Power and Machinery, Soil-Machine Dynamics, Post Harvest Systems and Agro-Industrial Management, Technology Policy, Gender Issues in Technology, Information and Communication Technology in Agriculture and Rural Development, Science and Engineering Infrastructure, and Renewable Energy Systems. Currently, he is the Director-General/CEO, Raw Materials Research and Development Council, Nigeria Federal Ministry of Science and Technology. Earlier, he was the Director, Engineering Infrastructure, National Agency for Science and Engineering Infrastructure, Federal Ministry of Science and Technology. Some of his achievements include Funding a list of R&Ds on raw materials development in Research Institutes and Universities across the nation, Upgrade of laboratory facilities in Research Institutions and Secondary Schools, Production of pharmaceutical grade talc from local mineral and Surveying 10 selected agro raw materials such as Cassava, Maize, Soyabeans, and Cocoa, and survey of 5 additional fruit crops. His authored papers and awards are too numerous to count; yet he still has time and interest to further new R&D to move Africa forward.

C.O.E. Onwuliri, FAS, Ph.D.
Vice-Chancellor of Federal University of at Owerri and Professor of Zoology (Parasitology)

Not only does Prof. Onwuliri serve as Vice-Chancellor of a prominent university, is an erudite scholar and distinguished Professor of Zoology (Parasitology). Earlier, at the University of Jos, where he spent 26 years of his career, he served the University as a three-time former Dean, Faculty of Natural Sciences, Deputy Vice-Chancellor (Academic) and Acting Vice-Chancellor. Prof. Onwuliri has over 30 years of University Teaching and Administrative experience spread over Five Universities in Nigeria within which period he supervised over 100 research projects at B.Sc., M.Sc. & Ph.D., levels. Professor Onwuliri is very active in research in Experimental Parasitology, Physiology and Biochemistry of Parasitic Nematodes; in Ecology and Epidemiology of Parasitic helminths with emphasis on Communicable Diseases such as Dracunculiasis (Guinea worm disease), Onchocerciasis (River Blindness disease), Filariasis, UrinuryIIntestinal Schistosomiasis and other intestinal helminthiu.sis and their impact on the environment in the Central, North Eastern, and South Eastern Nigeria. Prof. Onwuliri published more than 126 high quality Scientific Articles spread in over 52 different peer-reviewed reputable national and international Scientific. He is very actively involved at the National and International levels in Service to Community, Science, Technology and Education.

John O. Onyatta, Ph.D.
Environmental Soil Chemist

Dr. Onyatta areas of specialization are environmental soil chemistry, applications of X-ray diffraction analysis in mineralogy and chemical Speciation. While he is a professor of soil chemistry and analysis, his experiences include serving as Assistant National Liaison Officer (ANLO) and coordinator of International Atomic Energy Agency (IAEA) funded projects in Kenya in the area of Agriculture and food security, Human health, Livestock production, Water resources management, Energy planning, Radioactive waste management, Industrial applications and Environmental degradation as well as coordination of the programs and activities of the Comprehensive Nuclear Test-Ban Treaty Organization (CTBTO) in Kenya. Dr. also serves as a lead consultant on project management, planning & development, technology and innovation dissemination, scientific advice and application of new technologies.

Theophilus A. Ossei-Anto, Ph.D.
Science Education

Dr. Ossei-Anto has taught Science Education for 31 years (including Principles and Practices of Science Curriculum Design, Development, Implementation and Evaluation), Physics, Chemistry, Mathematics, General Science, and Integrated Science at the University and secondary school levels. His areas of expertise and research interest include: Open, Distance, and Flexible Education; Science Performance Assessment; Curriculum Development, Implementation, Practices, Principles and Innovation. Dr. Ossei-Anto is Co-author/Advisor on five Science/Physics textbooks for Secondary Schools and Adviser and Instructional Format Designer of thirty (30) distance learning modules/Course books for upgrading Ghana's untrained teachers to the Diploma in Basic Education status.

Kwadwo Osseo-Asare, Ph.D.
Material Science, Metallurgy

Distinguished Professor of Metallurgy and Energy and Geo-environmental Engineering, Kwadwo's research interests include: Particle design in order to create environments that systematically constrain particle nucleation, growth, and aggregation; Microemulsion-mediated synthesis; (Electro)chemical behavior of metallic, semiconductor, and insulator materials: thermodynamic modeling, solution equilibria, surface complexation, and semiconductor electrochemistry; Surfactant aggregation phenomena.

Chidi Gideon Osuagwu, Ph.D.
Biochemistry

Dr. Osuagwu is a Senior Lecturer (Biochemistry), Department of Biochemistry, School of Science and Biomedical Technology; School of Health Technology, Federal University of Technology, Owerri, Nigeria. Since 1978, he has taught in different universities (United States: Youngstown State University, Ohio and University of Houston, Texas) and (Nigeria: Alvan Ikoku College of Education of Research and, Imo State University and Federal University of Technology, Owerri, Imo State). A standing Resource Person (1990 to date) to the Federal Ministry of Environment on Environmental Impact Assessment (with special Interest I Waste Management). Dr. Osuagwu's research interest includes Investigation into the Bioenergetics/Redox aspects of Diseases, including Sickle Cell, Diabetes, Redoxive stress, Malaria, HIV/AIDS, etc.; studies on the Chemistry of African traditional herbs/foods; studies on African Cosmology/indigenous knowledge system in relation to Science. He has published sizable journal articles/books in Chemistry/Biochemistry/Systems' Modeling, and African Cosmology.

Rose Uzuma Osuji, Ph.D.
Solar Energy Physics

Dr. Osuji is a professor of Physics and Astronomy at the University of Niegeria at Nsukka, where she has taught Solar Radiation and its Availability; Solar Energy Collection and Storage; Solid State Physics, *Mathematical Methods in Physics; Science of Materials and Introduction to Industrial Processing. She has served is the Acting head of this department from 2006-2008. Her research interests include Fabrication and Characterisation and applications of Thin Films and nanostructures; Photoconductivity Studies; Comparative Performance Studies of Various Photovoltaics Modules; Solar radiation characteristics and measurement; PV for Electricity Generation in Rural Areas; Energy Policy Studies. While Dr. Osuji is very busy authoring publications, lecturing, attending professional functions, she still finds time to help in her community. She is an Executive member (i/c Curriculum) of AYEDEF NGO that caters for the literacy program for the destitute in Aku town, Nigeria.

Alfred Oteng-Yeboah, Ph.D.
Environmentalist

Prof. Oteng-Yeboah is the Deputy Director General for the Council of Scientific and Industrial Research. He has served as a Chair to both the Bureau of the Subsidiary body for Science and Technical Advice as well as the Committee on Communication, Education, and Public Awareness to the United Nations Convention of Biodiversity. While he says he is retired, he remains an active academician and environmentalist. His extensive international experiences include: Chair, 9th and 10th meeting of the Subsidiary Body on Scientific Technical and Technological Advice (SBSTTA) of the UN Convention on Biological Diversity (CBD). During his tenure, specific targets and goals running along the UN Millennium Development Goals were introduced into the CBD to achieve a substantial reduction in the loss of global biodiversity by 2010. Not only is Dr. Oteng-Yeboah the alternate and now the full Council member for coastal West Africa to the Global Environment Facility (GEF), he also serves as Co-chair of International Mechanism of Scientific Expertise on Biodiversity (IMoSEB), an initiative started by the President of France to charge and encourage nations to protect and use their biological resources in a manner that will ensure sustainability. Recently, the committee published an article in Nature calling on mankind to ensure the halt in the loss of biological diversity.

Neville A. Parker, Ph.D., PE
Transportation Systems, Civil Engineering

He has extensive experience in the use of systems engineering and analysis in the solution of transportation problems. Professor Parker also directed a NSF-funded Research Careers for Minority Scholars (RCMS) program in academia. As director, Professor Parker coordinated researchers and students on research projects. He serves as an academic advisor to these students, and as a mentor in its Fellows Program. Professor Parker currently teaches courses on construction project management, airport design and planning, highway engineering, and pavement management systems, and is involved in research. Dr. Parker also serves as Principal Investigator of the NASA funded Institute on Climate and Planets and Global Climate Variability Project. As Director of the university's Institute for Transportation Systems, Dr. Parker is responsible for leading a comprehensive multidisciplinary inter-college effort, which addresses transportation issues affecting the economic and social life of the city, state, and region. Institute activities include pure and applied research, the coordination and development of curriculum, policy analysis, urban and transportation systems analysis, modeling, forecasting, and professional training and development.

Paul E. Parker
Mechanical Engineering

Paul Parker, recently retired assistant dean in the UI College of Engineering and the director of the minority engineering program. Since Parker became director of the UI's minority engineering program in 1973, the number of minority undergraduate engineering students at the university has grown from 92 in 1969 to 400 in 2000. Over the years Parker has garnered numerous honors and awards for his professional accomplishments and his commitment to minority student education. Among Parker's many honors are being included in the "International Who's Who of Information Technology (2000)," being named outstanding faculty member for 1992 by the UIUC Dad's Association and being named black engineer of the year in 1991 by U.S. Black Engineer magazine.

Richard Patterson
Nuclear Waste Management

Is President of a nuclear waste management company, specializing in high level and low level radioactive waste processing His company was the first minority owned and operated company of its kind. Mr. Patterson began his career in the nuclear power industry in 1974 at Duke Power's Oconee Nuclear Station, South Carolina. In 1979 a highlight in his career came just after the "Three-Mile Island Nuclear Accident". Mr. Patterson was selected and sent to lead the first "Recovery Team" given the responsibility for engineering efforts to gather the first radioactive gas and water samples and perform cleanup tasks. The reactor on Three-Mile Island in Harrisburg, Pennsylvania became America's first crippled nuclear reactor that caused worldwide attention. Mr. Patterson managed this task as the Unit 2 Radiological Controls Supervisor for eighteen months after the accident. In 1982 Mr. Patterson was employed by Southern California Edison to work at its San Onofre Nuclear Generating Station to develop its Emergency Response Training Program. He later became a Refueling Engineer and was given credit for managing the movement of 142 Highly Radioactive Spent Fuel Assemblies.

Anthony R. Pegram, P.E.
Civil and Structural Engineering, Transportation and Contract Administration

Anthony has practiced engineering in the San Francisco Bay Area through four decades. He has worked as a design engineer for oil refineries, nuclear power plants, industrial and residential buildings and rail and marine transportation facilities. He is a member and past president of the Northern California Council of Black Professional Engineers. He served as Vice President for the consulting engineering firm of F.E. Jordan Associates, establishing the firm as a major contributor to projects with the Port of Oakland. His experience includes more than 15 years as a Principal Contract Specialist with the San Francisco Bay Area Rapid Transit District. He was a member of the City of Oakland Planning Commission, serving as Chairman and participated in the development of updates to the City's General Plan. He is President of the Universal Development Company, one of the Universal Group of firms established to address development opportunities throughout the United States and abroad.

Arnold Perkins
Public Health

Arnold X. C. Perkins served as Director of the Alameda County Public Health Department (serving a population of 1.4 million people) in Oakland, California from 1994 through 2006, providing leadership and management of the administrative, program and policy activities of the department, which has a budget of $105 million and over 500 employees. During his tenure, Mr. Perkins led the Department through a major organizational shift that reflects a broad vision of Public Health with a community development orientation. He believes that public health is a social change organization that must be integrated into the community and responsive to its needs. His diverse background includes positions as a high school teacher and principal; non-profit organization executive director; family counselor and advocate; foundation program officer; college teacher and administrator; and restaurant owner and operator. Mr. Perkins is an experienced speaker, planner, and facilitator, especially in the areas of youth development, organizational change, team building, creative leadership, executive coaching, community development, and group dynamics. Over the years he has worked with incarcerated youth and adults.

Waverly J. Person, Ph.D.
Seismologist, Geophysicist

Waverly Person, Mr. Earthquake, retired on February 3, 2006, after 51 years of tracking earthquakes around the world for the National Earthquake Information Center in Golden, Colorado. In 1977, Dr. Person was named director of the Colorado National Earthquake Information Center and was often sought out by national and international media as an earthquake spokesperson. As chief of the NEIC, Dr. Person was responsible for locating earthquakes, computing their magnitudes, and disseminating this information quickly and efficiently to emergency crews, government officials, and news media throughout the world. Satellites and a host of sophisticated measuring devices record the quakes—as many as 50 a day worldwide. Though it is estimated that millions of earthquakes occur throughout the world each year, the NEIC staff annually tracks approximately 20,000 events. Since the early 1970s, the NEIC has located and reported on more than a quarter million earthquakes. A veteran seismologist and geophysicist, Dr. Person was the first African American to hold such a prominent position in the U.S. Department of the Interior and believed to be the first African American earthquake seismologist.

Linda Phaire-Washington, Ph.D.
Cell Biology, Immunology, Molecular Biologist

Dr. Linda Phaire-Washington has done extensive research on monoclonal antibodies, macrophage cells and the role of the cytoskeleton in the cell membrane function. She earned a BS degree in Biology at Boston University in 1970. She immediately began graduate work in immunochemistry and cellular immunology at CUNY, Mt Sinai Medical School and completed her Ph.D. in 1975. She then pursued a postdoctoral research fellowship at Rockefeller University (1976-1977), then two years in the Department of Anatomy at Howard University College of Medicine (1977-1979). Dr. Phaire-Washington later worked as Associate Professor of Immunology and Cell Biology at Tuskegee University. She recalls that she always had a curiosity about the workings of the cell and was always excited about looking at cells under the microscope. As she grew older her curiosity grew with her. Later in Medical School, two very stimulating immunologists fueled her interest in science. She states that she became overwhelmed by the manner the body defends itself against disease and the remarkable way the body can heal itself. Dr. Phaire-Washington continues her work toward instilling this same awe and passion for scientific research in students, particularly minority students. In addition to her research and teaching, Dr. Phaire-Washington has ardently supported the participation of minority women in science.

Denis Sekoja Phakisi
Mechanical Engineering

Sekoja is a manufacturing manager, where he is Responsible for planning, managing, coordinating and directing all aspects of the manufacturing operation of Loti Brick to ensure the efficient and timely production of around 15 million of clay bricks of the correct quality within the agreed budgetary limits. He leads a manufacturing team consisting of around 100 employees (production, mining and support personnel, technicians and attached students of various South African universities and Lesotho's institutions of higher learning). Sekoja experiences include manufacturing, mentorship, entrepreneurship, benchmarking, innovation, product development, appropriate technology, research and development, project management, design and repairs of mechanical systems, environment, energy, computer applications, farming and tendering. Previously, he worked for Appropriate Technology Services (ATS), Lesotho, implementing research and development projects.

Barry Pierce, PLS
Chief Surveyor, Software Developer

Barry is a chief surveyor for a design firm, where he manages all survey aspects of the company, including but not limited to preparing final maps (ROS, Parcel Maps, Subdivision Maps, etc.), writing legal descriptions and performing calculations for construction staking, control surveys, and boundary resolution. He established Bik Wah International in 1995 to enter into software usage of the civil engineering and construction industry. This company established a JV company in the People's Republic of China. This company had national distribution rights for products related to design and construction, products such as Autodesk, Softdesk, etc.. Local work included consulting for CAD services, database customization and development. Not only has Mr. Pierce performed several domestic and international projects, he is well versed in the use of several software products and speaks Mandarin.

Karl Pierce, AICP
Urban Planning, GIS Mgmt.

Mr. Pierce has over twenty-five years experience in the Engineering/Design fields. He holds a BA Degree in Urban Planning, with practical hands on knowledge of engineering, architecture, urban planning and information technology. He acts in both the capacities of project manager or principal-in-charge of engineering production drawings, construction management, Surveying/Mapping, and GIS projects. Mr. Pierce has served as project manager on global mapping effort for Geotopo as a subcontractor to a prime firm on a DOD project let by NIMA (The National Imagery and Mapping Agency). He was responsible for a team of GIS technicians who are performing detailed map finishing for NIMA. He was the Richmond, CA GIS - Principal-in-Charge, leading the Geotopo GIS team in the solution of a parcel based GIS for the city planning dept. This team prepared a base map from Contra Costa County Microstation files, and created linkages through FMS ADE software. Mr. Pierce was Principal- in-charge for Geotopo on the San Francisco Water Department Gate Book. They teamed with CH2M Hill to convert a specific section of the department=s paper maps into electronic files. They migrated these maps to GIS converting AUTOCAD design files into ARCVIEW shape files. Later these drawings were used to build a comprehensive GIS adding intelligence to all pipe runs, valves etc.

Lasha Kim Pierce, M.D.
OBGYN, Surgeon

Dr. Lasha Pierce is a Board Certified Obstetrician Gynecologist, specializing in high risk pregnancies in underserved populations. She received her Bachelors degree from California State University at San Francisco, her medical degree from the University of California at Irvine, and her specialty training in Obstetrics and Gynecology from Kaiser Permanente Hospital in San Francisco. Her experience spans the rural villages of East Africa to the inner city urban populations in Alameda and San Francisco Counties, and she also offers consultative health services to incarcerated women in the East bay. She currently serves as a volunteer Clinical Instructor at the University of California at San Francisco, College of Medicine in the division of Obstetrics, Gynecology and Reproductive Sciences. She has recently accepted a fellowship with the African Scientific Institute, and is a married mother of three teenage children.

Wiley Pierce, PLS
Urban Planning, Land Surveying, Construction Mgmt.

Mr. Pierce has over 45 years of experience in the construction industry, including more than 40 years as a licensed Professional Land Surveyor on a wide variety of surveying projects, and 20 years as a Licensed Contractor. As Principal-in-Charge of the Universal Group of firms, he has the overall responsibility for all projects, working directly with the Operations Manager and professional staff to maintain constant oversight of all surveying, engineering, land development and construction matters - reviews survey procedures, checks and signs survey plats, and prepares property descriptions. Mr. Pierce's experience includes conducting control, cadastral, topographic, hydrographic, route surveys, and right-of-way engineering throughout California. In addition to his experience in field of surveying, Mr. Pierce also has experience in site planning and engineering for various land development projects. He has organized a wall panel manufacturing section - Universal Structures - that will provide wall panels as a job generator and for the construction of affordable homes for the United States and Africa. In Alaska he was part of a team of six professional surveyors that surveyed over a million acres of land for the U.S. government to return to Native Americans. He has also performed land surveys and development projects in Nigeria, Ethiopia, Angola, and South Africa.

Derrick H. Pitts, Ph.D.
Astronomy

Dr. Pitts, who as chief astronomer and planetarium program director at Philadelphia's Franklin Institute, reaches millions with edutainment programs when he steps away from his official duties in the observatory. He has been named as one of the 50 most important African-Americans in research science. Dr. Pitts is a scientific consultant to many organizations. He has written numerous astronomy columns for newspapers and national magazines. He appears regularly on all the major television networks as a science content expert. He has made numerous television appearances, including shows such as *The Colbert Report* and *Late Late Show* with Craig Ferguson, and *Countdown* with Keith Olbermann. He has been the resident "Science Guy" for WXPN's award-winning radio program 'Kids' Corner' for 18 years. He is one of less than a handful of astronomers with a gift for simplifying the grand scheme of the cosmos. Dr. Pitts is active in the community. He finds time to visit school classes and is President of Tuskegeee Airmen Inc., Philadelphia chapter. His career has been recognized with one of Philadelphia's highest honors, the Liberty Bell Award. He is also a recipient of the George Washington Carver Scientist of the Year Award and is a 2004 inductee into the Germantown Historical Society's Hall of Fame.

Brent D. Pogue
Nuclear Engineering, Engineering/regulatory affairs

Brings over 20 years of experience in engineering and regulatory affairs expertise in the electric power industry. He has worked for Bechtel Power Corporation on various engineering projects, Pacific Gas and Electric Company in nuclear regulatory affairs and as a system engineer. He has been involved in several regulatory audits of power plants for PG&E and preparation of cost benefit analysis reports for an electric rate case task force for Southern California Edison. Mr. Pogue has worked as a consultant on a contract basis for various utilities such as Xcel Energy Corporation, American Electric Power Company, and Exelon Corporation; managed projects for electric utilities, which included verifying corporate regulatory commitments, safety analysis reporting, and power plant system design document development. In 2007 Mr. Pogue assisted in the project for the successful submittal of the License Application of the Yucca Mountain Nuclear Repository, sponsored by the Department of Energy. He is currently involved in consulting activities regarding Independent Spent Fuel Storage Installations and Power Plant Risk Assessments. Mr. Pogue earned his Bachelor of Science (Mechanical Engineering) and a Master of Engineering (Mechanical) from Cornell University, Ithaca, New York.

Richard H. Pointer, Ph.D.
Biochemistry

Dr. Pointer has a deep interest in Hormonal Regulation of Intermediary Metabolism, including diabetes research and hormonal regulation of carbohydrate and lipid metabolism. Over the years, he has been a Research Technician, Teaching Assistant, Research Associate, Department of Molecular Physiology, Assistant, Associate Professor, and now Full Professor, Department of Biochemistry and Molecular Biology. Dr. Pointer has also been a Visiting Scientist, Section on Membrane Regulation, Laboratory of Cellular and Developmental Biology. He has served on the Medical Student Applicant Interview Committee, College of Medicine (1981 - 1990) and Appointments, Promotion and Tenure Committee, College of Medicine and Graduate School. He has been Director of the Graduate Program, Department of Biochemistry and Molecular Biology, Preliminary Academic Reeinforcement Coordinator (PARP), College of Medicine, 1988 - , Chair, Appointments, Promotion and Tenure Committee, Department of Biochemistry and Molecular Biology, 1995 - , Chair, Curriculum Committee, Graduate School. Dr. Pointer has also served on several national technical grant review panels such as the National Research Council; American Institute of Biological Science, TMM; NASA, Endocrinology and Regulatory Physiology Panel; etc.

Anthony J. (Tony) Polk, MT (ASCP) SBB
Immunohematology and Blood Banking; Medical Laboratory Management

Colonel (Ret) Polk has over 45 years in the medical laboratory field. As one of the first African American medical laboratorians in the military, he began his career supporting medical care for the wounded during the Viet Nam war. He later served six years in Europe, where he directed all US military blood bank operations. He became internationally known when he conducted a study of the blood programs of all the countries that belong to NATO and devised a process for the sharing of blood products among the NATO countries. He was selected by the Assistant Secretary of Defense to be director over the worldwide Armed Services Blood Program (ASBP). In this capacity he modernized the ASBP to have the capacity to deliver blood products by military air to anywhere in the world within 72 hours. COL Polk oversaw an innovation that is unique to the military in the prepositioning of frozen Red Blood Cells in military blood depots in select locations around the world. COL Polk ended his military career with the highly successful provision of blood products to Operation Desert Storm. He became the first African American executive in the American National Red Cross blood program. In this capacity he served as Chief of Staff of Biomedical Services, overseeing blood operations throughout the United States. He is current CEO of Tony Polk & Associates consulting firm.

Clarence A. Porter, Ph.D.
Retired V.P. and Provost, Parasitology

Dr. Clarence A. Porter has served Montgomery College with dedication and distinction for 20 years and retired from the College as of December 31, 2004. During those years, he served as Instructional Dean at Takoma Park Campus from 1985 to 2000 and also served as Vice President and Provost from 2000 to 2004. During this time, he played a pivotal role in the growth of the health sciences programs, in part, resulting in the creation of a new state-of-the-art Health Sciences Center which officially opened in January 2004; and when serving as an instructional dean, Dr. Porter was the first convener of the deans collegewide, developing a model of collaborative work among the deans that continues to this day. Dr. Porter was a strong advocate for student academic support centers, fostering the development of the Math/Science Center at Takoma Park and working toward the expansion of such centers, including the opening of an 80-seat open computer laboratory for students without access to technology, all with the goal of providing more out-of-class academic assistance to students. Dr. Porter served as a member of the American Red Cross Life Board; and was extremely active in the National Council of Black American Affairs (of the American Association of Community Colleges), for which he was president of the Northeast Region.

James Pringle
Electrical Engineering

Nathaniel R. Quick, Ph.D.
Materials Science and Engineering

Dr. Quick is President, CTO and founder of AppliCote Associates, LLC, a green materials and process technology development company using lasers to synthesize energy conversion materials and devices. He co-founded InflectSOL, LLC, to commercialize these technologies. He is a Fellow, Past-President, and Board member of the Laser Institute of America and a member of MRS and ASM International. He reorganized and aligned R&D programs (metallic membranes and other advanced alloy fiber products) with marketing to accelerate new product implementation for Memtec. Dr. Quick was co-founder of AT&T Coatings; Supervisor, Technology Applications; Supervisor, Keypads and Interconnect Technology; and Resident Metallurgist while with Bell Labs. He was VP of R&D at Washburn Wire Products, a minority owned steel wire processor, and co-founder of a Pan African agricultural-technical organization. He holds 44 United States patents, was a NIST guest researcher and served on the Army Science Board and the Florida Photonics Center of Excellence Board.

Clyde T. Raby, DVM
Veterinarian

Dr. Raby has practiced Veterinarian Medicine for more than 40 years. After earning his DVM from Tuskegee Institute in 1964, he served as an Assistant Professor at Southern University for 6 years. Afterwards, he became the owner of his own veterinary hospital in Louisiana, which he still owns today. During 1980 – 96, he served with the Louisiana Department of Agriculture as an Assistant Commissioner of Agriculture and Forestry, Office of Animal Health Services – Assistant Director of Emergency Preparedness. He was responsible for the overall administration of the Animal Health Services Programs for the State of Louisiana. He is a member of professional associations, including the American Veterinary Medical Association (AVMA) and has written several articles that were published in the Journal of Dairy Science, Journal of Animal Science, and the American Journal of Veterinary Science. Dr. Raby has received several awards, including being chosen as the Louisiana Veterinarian of the year in 1981. He is a Member of the Board of Directors of Tuskegee Veterinary Alumni.

Melvin R. Ramey, Ph.D., P.E.
Civil and Environmental Engineering

Dr. Ramey is Professor Emeritus of Civil and Environmental Engineering at the University of California at Davis, where he has been a member of the faculty since 1967. He has served UC Davis in several capacities including Associate Dean of Graduate Studies, Faculty Athletics Representative to the National Collegiate Athletic Association (NCAA), Chairperson of the Department of Civil and Environmental Engineering (1991-97), Vice Chairperson of the Exercise Science Department (1999), Assistant Track Coach (1967-1992) and Faculty Assistant to the Vice Chancellor-Academic Affairs (1989-90). Dr. Ramey has performed research in the areas of structural design, structural testing, fiber reinforced concrete and biomechanics (including human jumping and rehabilitation). He has received numerous awards, including the Black Engineer of the Year Award (1993), Magnar Ronning Award for Teaching Excellence, ASCE Outstanding Teacher Award, College of Engineering Outstanding Teacher Award, UC Davis 2002 Engineering Alumni Distinguished Teaching Award and the Inspiration Award from the UC Davis Black Students. In addition, an anonymous alumnus donated funds at UC Davis to establish the Melvin R. Ramey and Karl M. Romstad Conference Center and Library Complex, and the Ramey and Romstad Endowed Scholarship.

Gen. Bernard Randolph
Four Star General, Engineer

Only the third African-American to reach the rank of four-star general in any branch of the U.S. Armed Forces, serving as head of the USAF Space and Defense Systems Command. General Bernard P. Randolph, USAF, retired is currently a consultant to Spectrum Astro, TRW Space and Electronics and other companies on a series of major development programs.

Cordell Reed
Ret'd Vice Pres., Utility Co., Fossil & Nuclear Fuel

Mr. Reed was responsible for the Fuel Department which which purchases fuel for the company and spends $800 million dollars annually on coal, natural gas, oil and nuclear fuel. He was also the Ethics Officer with overall responsibility for the Corporate Ethics Program. Additionally, he is the Chief Diversity Officer responsible for the Corporate Diversity Management activities. Earlier, he had the opportunity to work as a mechanical engineer on the start-up of the Dresden nuclear power plant, which was the largest nuclear plant in the world at the time. In this position, he first learned nuclear physics, health physics and reactor operations and the taught the personnel who operated the units. Mr. Reed went on to head the Company's Nuclear Engineering Department where he managed a group of over one hundred Engineers who were responsible for the engineering activities for the nuclear generating units. In 1987 he was appointed Senior Vice President for Nuclear Operations which included the overall corporate responsibility for the operation, maintenance, engineering and technical support for the Company's twelve nuclear generating units. Of the six thousand employees that worked in his area, 1500 were Engineers or had other technical related degrees.

Kennedy Reed, Ph.D.
Theoretical Physicist

Kennedy Reed is a theoretical physicist in the Physical Sciences Directorate at Lawrence Livermore National Laboratory (LLNL). He also is director of the LLNL Research Collaborations Program for HBCUs & MIs - connecting LLNL scientists with professors and students at HBCUs and other Minority Serving Universities. He has over 100 publications on his research on atomic collisions in high temperature plasmas, and is a Fellow of the American Physical Society (APS). He has worked with several international organizations to promote science in Africa, and in 2003 he was awarded the prestigious APS John Wheatley Award for his contributions to Physics Research and Education in Africa. He was also a co-founder of the National Physical Science Consortium (NPSC) - a national coalition of corporations, national laboratories and universities organized to provide fellowships for graduate studies in the physical sciences for women and minority students. Prior to starting his work at LLNL, Dr. Reed was a Professor of Physics at Morehouse College in Atlanta, GA. In 2005 the California Section of the American Physical Society honored Dr. Reed by the establishment of the "Kennedy Reed Award" which is presented annually to recognize "Best Theoretical Research" performed by graduate students and postdoctoral researchers.

Madison F. Richardson, M.D.
Chief head and neck surgeon

Dr. Madison Richardson is a Board Certified Specialist in Otolaryngology, Head and Neck Surgery. He is an expert in the management of diseases of the ear, nose, and throat. He treats disorders of hearing and balance disturbances, nasal/sinus problems, snoring, sleep apnea, voice disorders, and also has subspecialty training in Head and Neck Reconstructive Surgery. Dr. Richardson has maintained one of the largest and most distinguished otolaryngology practices in Los Angeles. He was named one of America's Top Doctors by the Center for the Study of Services. In addition, he has been featured in the Los Angeles Times, Essence Television, Health Matters, and many other print and news media.

Lee Riley, M.D.
BioResearch; Infectious Diseases

Dr. Riley is a university Professor and Head of the Division of Infectious Disease and Vaccinology. He is a physician who has been trained in both epidemiology and molecular biology research. After residency, he joined the Epidemic Intelligence Service at the Centers for Disease Control and Prevention, and then became an infectious disease fellow at Stanford University School of Medicine. Later he joined the World Health Organization to work as a project manager for a program called India Biomedical Support Project in New Delhi, India, for two years. He has published more than 180 peer-reviewed papers and book chapters. In 2004, he published a textbook, *Molecular Epidemiology of Infectious Diseases: Principles and Practices,* by ASM Press. He served as the program director for Fogarty's International Training and Research in Emerging Infectious Diseases at UC Berkeley (1997-2003), Tuberculosis Training and Research (1998-2003), and Global Infectious Diseases (since 2003). He has been elected as a fellow to the American Association of Advancement of Science (1998), Infectious Disease Society of America (2002), and American Academy of Microbiology (2004). He was a member of the NIH's Fogarty International Center's Advisory Committee from 2003 to 2007. He currently has collaborators in Brazil, India and Japan.

Shelly W. Riley, II
Fighter Aircraft Mission Simulations

Retired Director of Mission Simulation and Support Systems Programs for Loral Vought Systems Corporation where he had total cost, schedule and technical performance responsibilities for developing weapon system system simulators, support equipment and logistic for Loral Vought's Line-of-Sight Anti-Tank Program. Mr. Riley joined Loral Vought Systems Corporation in 1980 as Chief Engineer for the A-7 Tactical Fighter Support Systems Program. Prior to joining his present company, he was Unit Chief for Avionics Software Development for McDonnell Douglas for the F-18 Quadruplex Digital Control-By-Wire Flight Control System. His responsibilities included developing complex detailed computer program specifications, developing the software and critical documentation, subcontractor management, integration of the Quad Redundant System into the flight simulator for technical evaluation and verification of safety of flight parameters prior to flight test. Additionally, he was Chief Engineer for avionics laboratory integration for the F-4 Advanced Wild Weasel Program for software simulation. Mr. Riley also served as a McDonnell Douglas consultant to the U.S. Air Force for retrofit of Loran Navigation Systems for the F-4D aircraft.

Stephen S. Robinson, M.D., M.P.H.
Physician

Dr. Robinson has had a long interest in health workforce development and the provision of care to underserved populations. With an MD from the University of Washington and an MPH in international health from the Johns Hopkins School of Hygiene and Public Health, he completed an internal medicine residency at Harlem Hospital Center. He was an associate administrator at the City University of New York, working on the development of a new medical school, and later, director of the Physician Assistant Program at Harlem Hospital Center. He has worked in Tanzania, East Africa, with Morehouse College's Public Health Sciences Institute, as senior associate for international programs, and as resident HIV/AIDS advisor for Columbia University's Mailman School of Public Health. In New York City he was the chair of the Community Advisory Board of the CDC-sponsored Columbia University-Harlem Hospital Prevention Research Center. Currently, he is a member of the Oakland Task Force on Health and Workforce development. He is also the Director of the San Francisco Welcome Back Center. Dr. Robinson is proud of several recreational accomplishments: becoming a certified SCUBA diver, climbing Mt. Kilimanjaro in 2003, and completing his first marathon in Florence, 2006.

Joan Robinson-Berry
Aerospace Engineering

Joan Robinson-Berry, Boeing Director of Supplier Diversity for its Integrated Defense Systems business. She has recently been appointed the company's Small Business Liaison Officer (SBLO) which involves integrating the over $5 billion dollar Small Business program across Boeing Commercial Airplanes, Phantom Works, Shared Services and Integrated Defense Systems Business Units. In addition, Joan is responsible for maintaining and improving Boeing relationships with the federal government on matters related to small business subcontracting and supplier diversity. Joan is responsible for developing strategies and integration plans to enhance Boeing relationship with HBCU's, Industry Affiliations, and Minority Institutions; specifically focusing on innovative research partnerships which are key to IDS' future business objectives. Ms. Robinson-Berry has an M.S. in Engineering Management & Business Administration and a B.S. in Manufacturing Engineering. Her honors include The President's Quality Award, the AES Women of Achievement, Women making a difference in technology and a Congressional Black Caucus – "Women Opening the Pipeline Award in 2005, Top Blacks in Technology 2003, Black Engineer of the Year- Career Achievement 2007. She also lent her talent overseas to create one of Africa's first aerospace curriculums in Ghana.

Christopher Rose, Ph.D.
Electrical & Computer Engineering

Dr. Rose received the S.B. (1979), S.M. (1981) and Ph.D.(1985) degrees all from the Massachusetts Institute of Technology in Cambridge, Massachusetts. Following graduate school, he joined AT&T Bell Laboratories in Holmdel, N.J. as a member of the Network Systems Research Department. Chris is currently a Professor of Electrical & Computer Engineering at Rutgers University in New Jersey and an IEEE Fellow cited "for contributions to wireless communication systems theory." He won the *2003 IEEE Marconi Prize Paper Award in Wireless Communications* for work on "interference avoidance" for cognitive radios, He is also a three time winner of the Engineering Governing Council's Teaching Excellence Award in E&CE. In September, 2004 his work on communication efficiency over interstellar distances appeared on the cover of Nature resulting in his 15 minutes of fame through an astounding amount of press coverage.

Wallace Russell, P.E.
Mechanical Engineering, Co-Founder LACBPE

(1932 - 2006) Before recently retiring from Los Angeles Department of Water and Power (LADWP), Mr. Russell's 35 years of experience as a mechanical engineer included: 2 years with the U.S. Army Corps of Engineers; one year as an Air Force Plant representative at Lockheed aircraft Company; and a member of the LADWP technical staff for 31 and 1/2 years, where his responsibilities included managing an engineering organization's construction scheduling for capital projects. Other experiences at the LADWP included the contract administration for mechanical systems for the intermountain power project, for solar and geothermal power plant demonstration projects. Mr. Russell was an active and founding member of the Los Angeles Council of Black Professional Engineers (LACBPE) for more than 30 years. In 1973, he designed, developed, implemented and managed LACBPE'S 6th grade engineering classroom program (EOCP), and also assisted in developing and implementing LACBPE'S EXCELL Saturday morning program, which develops the skills of 2nd - 12th grade students in mathematics, physical and computer sciences instruction. He also managed LACBPE's (MESA) for a few years. He assisted LACBPE and local colleges in developing the Minority Engineering Program (MEP) in 1970.

Rashid Saeed, Ph.D.
Communications and Network Engineering

Dr. Saeed is an Assistant Professor – International University Malaysia, Kuala Lumpur, Selangor, Malaysia, where he has taught Signals and Systems; Statistics & Stochastic; Modern Electronics Communications; Computer Networks; Antennae Propagation; Digital Signal & Image Processing; and RF Devices and Circuits. In 2008, he was a contributor to the "National Wireless Communications Technology Roadmap" for Ministry of Science, Technology and Innovation (MOSTI), Malaysia, Kuala Lumpur. He was a Senior Researcher at Telekom Malaysia R&D Innovation Centre (2009 - 2010) and the Malaysian Institute of Microelectronic Systems (MIMOS), Wireless Networks and Protocol (WNP) Lab (2007 – 2009). Dr. Saeed worked as a Lecturer - Sudan University for Science and Technology (SUST) - Engineering Faculty– Electronics Dept. (1999-2003) and Head of the IT Unit - Sudan University for Science and Technology (SUST) –Engineering Faculty. He is the co-holder of 13 patents and has authored and co-authored more than 80 publishings.

Gilles Sagodira, Ph.D.
Technology of information and communication in Education

Dr. Sagodira is a Professor-Researcher at the University of La Reunion. He is also Chairman of the Organization for Diaspora Initiatives (ODI) is working to understand the status and role of diasporic communities across the globe, both in domestic and international context. His thesis research work on andragogy covered areas of concepts as cognition, praxiology and guidance. In the 90's, he developed teaching methods with the use of the technology of information and communication in education. In the first decade of the 2000's his research work in education were oriented towards open archives and data bases of the universal library. His methods of teaching were experienced in the network of the CNAM (Conservatoire National des Arts et Metiers) for long distance teaching and tutoring. He is currently working on a sub-african educational ring, linking the universities of the island countries in the indian ocean (Magagascar - Comoros - Scheychelles - Mauritius and Reunion).

Papa Ibra Samb, Ph.D.
Plant Pathology

Prof. Samb is a member de la CRUFAOCI (Conference of the Rectors of the French-speaking Universities of Western Africa and Indian Ocean). In 2002, as Professor of Plant Biology, he was appointed Director of Upper National School of Agriculture (ENSA) of Thies. In 2007, he became Rector of the University of Thies and served in this position until October, 2010.

Bernard Sammons, Ph.D.
Regulatory Scientist

His academic training is in the area of plant pathology, with a specialty in the epidemiology of viruses infecting yellow summer squash. Afterwards, he started his career with Monsanto Company, working in field product development, followed by transition to research involving the development of transgenic (genetically modified) plants; then by serving as the Team Lead for Cotton Improvement in Trait Development to his current role in Regulatory Sciences. Dr. Sammons' current area of research is focused ecological risk assessment and characterization of genetically enhanced crops. Highlights of his scientific accomplishments include: the first report of Tobacco Ringspot Virus in squash in South Carolina and the first report of seed transmission of this virus in smooth pigweed (a common weed species found in many areas of the U.S.); development of transgenic potatoes resistant to Potato Leafroll Virus; Potato Virus X; and Potato Virus Y; development of transgenic tomatoes with extended shelf-life; and development of tomatoes with genes that confer resistance to Tobacco Mosaic Virus, Tomato Mosaic Virus and Cucumber Mosaic Virus. He led a team that delivered new and improved Roundup Ready Cotton to market. Dr. Sammons' effort is presently focused on gaining approval of 2nd generation improvements in corn that will provide benefits to U.S. agriculture and third world countries.

Henry T. Sampson, Ph.D.
Aerospace Engineer, Black Film Expert

Dr. Sampson is the Director of Planning and Operations Directorate, Space Test Program. Also, he is one of the foremost experts on the history of African Americans in show business. In 1967, he joined his current employer as a Project Engineer, when he co-invented and co- patented the Gamma-Electric Cell in 1968, which produced stable high-voltage outputs and current. He also holds three patents concerning solid rocket motors and one on the direct conversion of nuclear energy into electricity. Dr. Sampson's expertise includes Nuclear and Aeronautical Engineering, Space Vehicle Systems design, Satellite Electrical Power Systems design, and Direct Energy Conversion Radiation Effects on Polymers. He has written technical papers in rocket propulsion, direct conversion of nuclear energy to electricity, and computer simulation of electrical systems. After hours, Dr. Sampson serves as an expert on Black history in show business. He has written three books in this area: "Blacks In Black and White", Blacks in film from 1910-1950 (Scarecrow Press, 1995), "Blacks In Black Face", early Black musical shows (Scarecrow Press, 1980), and "The Ghost Walks: A Chronological history of Blacks in Show Business, 1860-1910" (Scarecrow Press, 1988). He has helped produce documentary films and lectures on early Black film-makers and films.

John B. Sampson, M.D.
Neuroanesthesia and Critical Care Medicine

Dr. John B. Sampson is a faculty member and neuroanesthesiologist at the Johns Hopkins Hospital department of Anesthesiology & Critical Care Medicine. He earned his BS degree from Jackson State University and Medical degree from the University of California, San Francisco. Dr. Sampson has extensive expertise in facilitating the improvement of health care opportunities for people in Africa and the Caribbean. He is the Founder/President of Doctors for United Medical Missions Inc. (DrUMM), through which he has been instrumental in leading and organizing the journey of numerous American volunteers into Africa, who have touched the lives of thousands of Africans in need of medical care. In addition to his international work with Doctors for United Medical Missions, Physicians for Peace, The Society of Critical Care Medicine and the Korle-bu Neuroscience Center, Dr. Sampson has served on the board of directors for The Greater Washington Society of Anesthesiology, Pro-Health International, Doctors for United Medical Missions, The Havre de Grace Rotary and Village Education Development Foundation, Inc. Dr. Sampson is dedicated to promoting excellence in patient care in anesthesiology and critical care medicine, and to improving standards of perioperative care in Africa, while also increasing the awareness of health care problems in Africa.

Barbara A. Sanders, Ph.D.
Advanced Automotive Engineer

She is rhe Director of Engineering, Advanced Development Group, for a major automobile company, responsible for all research and development activities in diverse areas as automotive door systems, lighting systems, seat systems, instrument panels, airbags and steering wheels. She oversees the work of engineers, scientists, technicians, and other support groups. Since 1972, Dr. Sanders has spent most of her professional career in Automotive Manufacturing Research and Development activities, working in areas as: Director, Assembly Systems; Director, Artificial Intelligence (AI); Manager, CAD/CAM Tooling Systems Development; and Manager, Composite Materials Processing and Experimental Physicist, Laser Processing. She was responsible for two major components of AI: knowledge engineering or expert systems, and natural language processing. In the materials lab, Dr. Sanders moved from lasers to computers. She was assigned to find, order and program a computer that could perform real-time calculations, or analyze information during a test instead of afterward, so researchers and machines could react immediately rather than wait hours or days for the data to be run. She later moved into reinforced plastics, the program that eventually led to a plastic-bodied sports coupe.

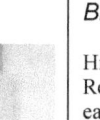

Robert B. Sanders, Ph.D.
Biochemistry

His research includes the biochemistry of hormone action, the biochemistry of reproduction, and uterine biochemistry. Research projects have included the study of the properties of uterine adenylate cyclase (AC) in the rat. Among the earliest biochemical events associated with the decidual cell reaction in the uterus of the mouse or rat is an increase in the concentration of cyclic adenosine 3',5'-monophosphate (cAMP). Thus several workers have suggested that cAMP is a major factor in initiating decidualization and implantation in rats and mice. Previous work in our laboratory has shown that adenylate cyclase (AC), the enzyme which catalyzes the formation of cAMP, was activated after a decidual stimulus was applied to the uterus only on Day 4, the day of maximal sensitivity to decidual induction. These studies supported the concept that the AC system might play a central role in transducing the stimulus for decidualization.

Yacouba Sankare, Ph.D.
Marine Biology

Dr. Yacouba earned his Master of Sciences (USA - NCSU, North Carolina) and a PhD from University of Cocody (Abidjan, Côte d'Ivoire). He is a Researcher working at Center for Ocean Research, "Chevalier du Mérite National de la Recherche Scientifique, Chevalier du Mérite National de l'Education Nationale". He is a member of the National Ramsar (Wetlands), Board member of the Ivorian Association for Agricultural Sciences (AISA), and has led several research efforts, particularly in the areas of wetlands and mangrove forests, wildlife associated with the roots and the biological control of invasive floating plants, estuary, lagoon and marine invertebrates (crustaceans and molluscs). The results of his efforts (those involving biological control) have contributed to the decline of invasive floating plant on lakes, rivers and lagoons of the country and those on the management and operation of swimming crabs. These efforts have also led to better management of living resources of marine costal and estuaries and have improved lives of local riverine residents. Dr. Yacouba has also served as AISA's Vice-President, responsible for scientific affairs in the framework for the implementation of Participatory Study Projects (PEP) and the creation of the National Center of Agronomic Research (NCAR).

Cheryl L. Scott, M.D., MPH
Former U.S. CDC Director in Tanzania

Dr. Scott was the former director of the Centers for Disease Control in Tanzania, and currently on CDC assignment with the California Department of Public Health's TB Center. Under her leadership, CDC–Tanzania has supported improving blood-transfusion safety, strengthening laboratory services, developing a national HIV/AIDS surveillance system, and preventing mother-to-child HIV transmission. Battling HIV/AIDS in Tanzania is the latest step in an international career that has taken Scott to the Ivory Coast, Kenya, India, and the Caribbean. An investigator in the elite Epidemic Intelligence Service at the CDC, Scott has also worked in maternal and child health and disaster epidemiology in California, New York, and New Jersey, where she was the state's maternal and child health epidemiologist. While at CDC headquarters, Dr. Scott led an update of postneonatal mortality surveillance and developed an evaluation strategy for the Guide to Community Preventive Services. Prior to joining CDC, Dr. Scott provided clinical services to underserved populations in New York City and the U.S. Virgin Islands and worked on global health projects in Africa and India.

Michael Seals, P.E.
Civil Engineering

As owner of his own business since 1984, Michael Seals has provided civil engineering design, construction and construction management services. Since graduating from college, Mr. Seals has acquired diverse experience in the civil engineering and construction phases of various small and large public works projects. His civil engineering experience includes geotechnical investigations, land development grading, sanitary and storm sewers design, roadway alignments and pavement design, reinforced concrete, structural steel and wood design. He has been a design engineer, project engineer, resident construction engineer and project manager. His duties have consisted of preparing design calculations, preparing plans and specifications (including field investigations and surveys), monitoring contractor compliance with plans and specifications, preparation of construction progress reports, preparation of change order cost estimates and preparation of construction schedules. His construction projects include sanitary and storm sewers, street paving, excavation, site grading, rip-rap erosion control, reinforced concrete foundations and concrete retaining walls. His responsibilities have included estimating the costs of the projects and managing the construction. Mr. Seals has supervised drafting, design, engineering and construction personnel.

Mesgun Sebhatu, Ph.D.
Physics

His research is on theoretical particle and nuclear physics. He specializes on the derivation and an investigation of one of the four fundamental forces of nature: The Strong Nuclear Force-A force that binds nuclei and is important in numcelar fission. He heavily uses computers and scientific databases in his research.

William A. Shanks, R.N.
Oncology Clinical Nurse Specialist

After graduating as a nurse and earning specialized education to become an OCNS, Mr. Shanks went on to be employed designing and implementing non-standard interventions in patient health care and nursing practices. He recently retired as a Clinical Nurse Specialist in an ambulatory hematology/oncology setting at the Alameda County Medical Center in Oakland, CA. He directed ongoing care of cancer therapy patients, and assisted in chemotherapy and ensures optimal nursing care to all cancer patients and provide a smooth transition upon discharge. He continues to participate and assist with the patient support groups and the cancer research programs at the medical center. The focus of his role is on the implementation and development of clinical practice standards and care delivery innovations to improve outcomes and assure the quality, relevance and integrity of the research data gathered at the medical center. Mr. Shanks goal is to find/develop a vehicle to relieve obstacles to these patients receiving care and screening in a timely manner. He is also an Assistant Clinical Professor in a University School of Physiological Nursing. Besides his extensive education and recipient of numerous awards, Mr. Shanks experiences include teaching marshal arts, an area in which he possesses Black belts in two forms of marshal arts.

Earl D. Shaw, Ph.D.
Physics, Laser Optics

Dr. Shaw is a pioneer in laser technology and is recognized by some history books as one of the early developers in his field. He worked 19 years as a Research Scientist for Bell Laboratories in Murray Hill, New Jersey, where he was the co-inventor of the spin-flip Raman tunable laser, "an important demonstration of lightwave turnability used for air pollution and other molecular measurements." He joined Rutgers in 1991 and moved to the Newark campus a new laser technology - the far-infrared free electron - that he developed at Bell Labs. The laser generates short tunable far-infrared light pulses that permit the analog or pulsed magnetic resonance techniques in the optical wavelength regime.

Umaru Shehu, M.D., D.P.H.
Medicine; Public Health

Since 1991, Dr. Umaru Shehu has been Hon. Consultant Physician, University of Maiduguri Teaching Hospital. He was WHO programme Coordinator/Representative in Nigeria (1980-1985); Director, WHO sub-regional health development office (1985 – 1989); WHO representative to Ethiopia, 1990. From 1991-1993, he served as Provost, College of Medical Science, University of Maiduguri and Prof. Emeritus of Community Medicine at this university in 2000. From 1996-1999, he was Pro-Chancellor and Chairman Governing Council, Bayero University; Pro-Chancellor and Chairman Governing Council, University of Lagos. Dr. Shehu has received too many awards to list and has published many, many papers; he has just about chaired every national health care organization since the early 1970s. He was President of Medical Schools in Africa 1973-1975; and External Examiner in Public Health at the University of Ghana Medical School. He is the current Chairman Board of Governors of the STOPAIDS organization; Chairman Governing Board of the National Agency for the Control of AIDS (NACA); Member Board of Trustees, Nigerian Tuberculosis and Leprosy Assoc.; Member Editorial Board, *West African Medical Journal*; Consulting Editor, the *Nigerian Medical Practitioner*; Joint Editor-in-Chief, *British Medical Journal (West Africa) Edition*.

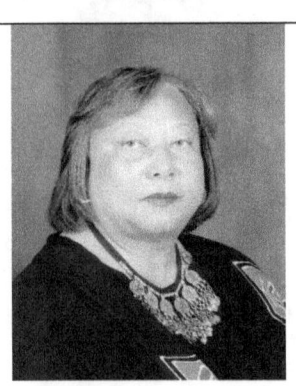

Hazle Jeffries Shorter, M.D.
Pediatrician and Pharmaceutical Research Physician

Dr. Shorter is most proud of joining the Peace Corps and becoming Chief of Pediatrics at Zomba Central Hospital in Zomba, Malawi, Africa for two long years. Earlier, she served as Director of Medical Services, Medical Products Div. of E.I. Du Pont de Nemours & Co., as a Research Physician in the Dept. of Clinical Pharmacology, responsible for R&D of medical and pharmacological products and testing of new drugs on humans. Previously, she was a Research Physician in the Dept. of Clinical Pharmacology of Hoffmann-La Roche, Inc., NJ, then this company's Asst. Dir. of Professional Services, responsible for Phase III and IV trials for products such as Dalmane (sedative-hypnotic), Bumex (loop diuretic), Rimadyl (non-steroidal anti-inflammatory), and Cipralan (anti-arrhythmic). Dr. Shorter went on to become Assoc. Dir. of Clinical Research at Abbott Laboratories, IL where she designed and initiated Phase III and IV studies with 20 investigators for Hypertension in the Geriatric Population. She also became a specialist in Child Development and became the Dir. of Children's Evaluation Rehabilitation Clinic in Bronx, NY, while simultaneously serving as an Instructor in Pediatrics at Albert Einstein College of Medicine. She is the daughter of the famous Dr. Jasper Jeffries, Ph.D., one of two African American physicists who worked on the "Manhattan Project".

Omega C. Logan Silva, M.D., MACP
Physician

Dr. Silva is professor emeritus of medicine. She is a long-standing advocate for universal health care and a committed supporter of the advancement of women in medicine. In 2000 Dr. Silva was elected President of the American Medical Women's Association. After graduating from Howard university, she spent the next five years working as a chemist as the National Institutes of Health, and in 1963 returned to Howard University to train as a physician. She was always interested in science and research. As a chemist at the NIH she decided an M.D. degree offered more flexibility - clinical, administrative, research, and teaching. Dr. Silva has made numerous media appearances to highlight issues in women's health including smoking, cervical cancer, and thyroid disease. She has published over 200 articles in peer-reviewed journals, abstracts, and book chapters in endocrinology. In 1984, Dr. Silva received a Letter of Commendation from the President Reagan and in 1995 she was given a Letter of Thanks from President Clinton for her participation in health care reform. In 2003 Dr. Silva was elected to a Mastership at the American College of Physicians. In1997 she received the Distinguished Alumni Award from the College of Medicine, Howard University. Dr. Silva was the first AA woman Research Associate and the first AA Clinical Investigator in the VA nationally.

Benito A. Sinclair, P.E.
Civil Engineering Co. Exec., Structural Engineering

Benito Sinclair was the first African American to complete the Program at the School of Architecture and Environmental Design at the California Polytechnic State University at San Luis Obispo in 1957, and a few years later, the first graduate from this school to be designated as a Distinguished Alumnus. He thereafter launched into his career as a structural engineer with a couple of private engineering firms before initiating his own professional practice in 1965: Benito Sinclair-Darshville & Associates. In 1968, Mr. Sinclair became the first African American to pass the California Structural Engineers Examination. Initially his firm worked on small projects, but later became a major designer in large projects such as a Los Angeles Subway System. Later, his firm designed 13+ stations along the Los Angeles-Long beach Light Rail System. His firm joint ventured to design the Tom bradley International Terminal at LAX. Mr. Sinclair co-founded the Los Angeles Council of black Professional Engineers (LACBPE), served on the Committee on Minorities at The National Academy of Engineering of the National Academy of Science and has been a Board Member of MESA.

Todd Singleton, Ph.D.
Software Architect

Todd received an undergraduate degree in Electrical Engineering from Duke University, where he played four years of division I basketball. He then attended Stanford University on a fellowship to continue his studies of Electrical Engineering and Software Systems. While at Stanford, he was active in the entrepreneurial community. In 2002, he took first place in Stanford's first annual Social Entrepreneurship Challenge amongst a field of 32 teams from North America and Europe. His winning entry was for a program to support the recreational inclusion of special needs children through the sport of soccer. Today, this program still operates throughout the California Bay Area, and has just launched a sister program in Africa. There are over 100 children that actively participate in this program. Upon completing his masters at Stanford, Todd worked at various startups throughout Silicon Valley. Currently, Todd works as an architect for IBM Tivoli - a systems management software group. He serves as a technical lead for an open source storage management project called Aperi. Todd has worked for IBM for 5 years, specializing in middleware and OSGi technologies.

Norma M. Sklarek, FAIA
Architect Fellow

The first African American woman registered as an architect in the U.S. She is one of only 43 female architects in over a century to have been named FELLOW by the American Institute of Architects and the only African American female so honored. Projects to her credit include a 360,000 sq.ft. passenger terminal at Los Angeles International Airport; Oakdale Shopping Mall in Minneapolis, MN; Park Center Commercial Complex, San Jose, CA; Financial Plaza of the Pacific, Honolulu, HI; and the U.S. Embassy in Tokyo, Japan. Has taught for several years at UCLA on the graduate architectural staff. Served as Commissioner to the Calif. Board of Architectural Examiners and as Master Juror for NCARB, grading architectural design and site planning exams.

John B. Slade, Jr., M.D.
Physician

Dr. Slade is Physician of Hyperbaric Medicine, board certified in Family Practice and Undersea and Hyperbaric Medicine. Prior to his private practice, Dr. Slade graduated from the U.S. Air Force Academy, and served in the U.S. Air Force medical service from 1978 - 1997 as a Chief Resident Family Practice, Medical Director of Hyperbaric Medicine and Wound Care, and Chief of the Medical Staff at Travis Air Force Base. In his capacity, he uses hyperbaric oxygen as an adjunct in the treatment of multiple medical and surgical problems including acute thermal injury, radiation tissue injury, necrotizing infections, carbon monoxide poisoning and decompression illness. He has been involved in multiple research studies concerning the use of hyperbaric oxygen. He has studied and uses transcutaneous oxygen measurements to predict healing of diabetic leg wounds with hyperbaric therapy. Dr. Slade has served as a Guest Faculty member for countless universities and military healthcare institutions, and has multiple publications.

Patricia C. Sluby
Author, Chemistry, Registered Patent Agent

Patricia Sluby is a registered patent agent, author, and a professional genealogist, previously certified. She is a retired primary patent examiner and Special Patent Cooperation Treaty Examiner from the U.S. Patent and Trademark Office. Also, she is a free-lance writer, historian, and lecturer on local history, genealogy, and inventions, often appearing on radio and television. Ms. Sluby earned her BS Degree in Chemistry from Virginia Union University and pursued graduate studies at Fisk and American Universities. Afterwards, she accepted a chemist position at the Radiocarbon Dating Laboratory of the U.S. Geological Survey, before transferring to this agency's patent office to its chemical division to examine patent applications in the fields of chemistry and chemical engineering.

Howard Smith
Computer Science, Mathematics

Howard is President of Vasona Technology, the leader in providing the delivery of targeted, critical emergency information, instructions, and procedures in 2 seconds through its automated disaster planning and response management software system. Howard is on several for-profit and non-profit boards of directors. He is co-founder of Clarity Software, Conference Objects, and Vyou, Inc. Howard was the first Vice President of Engineering for Silicon Graphics and has been a senior officer of high technology computer companies for the last 25 years which included 15 years of leading Product Development. He was the recipient of Engineer of the year by four USA national organizations. Howard received a BS in Mathematics from California State University of Los Angeles and an MS in Mathematics from San Jose University. Howard considers being married to his wife and being father of two boys and two girls to be his most important responsibility.

Mary Perry Smith
Mathematics, MESA Co-Founder

Mary Perry Smith is a fiercely committed educator who was an advocate for young people as a local high school teacher, and as co-founder of the Mathematics Engineering Science Achievement program (MESA). Mrs. Perry Smith is also a key figure in East Bay cultural institutions with her longtime involvement with the Oakland Museum of California and the Black Filmmakers Hall of Fame.

Morris L. Smith
Ret'd Proj. Leader for Emerging Tech., Chemistry

Senior Research Leader. His initial patents, issued in 1968, were for advanced printing ink that made printing designs on paper towelspossible that would not rub off on your hands. These products are biodegradable. He was a Senior Research Leader, responsible for Aesthetics technology development related to coloring, decorating, and fragrancing of sanitary paper, nonwoven, and related products. During his leadership, several patents were received by his aesthetics technology team, upgrading the process. In his position, he leads developments in new technologies which enhance the appearance, smell, and functionality of personal-care Scott paper products. In 1989, he received two additional patents.

Paul Smith
Retired Hospital V.P., Pharmacist

Paul Wellington Smith, Hospital Administrator, Pharmacist, Entrepreneur, and Photographer, was Vice President of Professional Services at Providence Hospital, Washington, D.C. (until his retirement in 2006). Mr. Smith was born in Jacksonville, Florida. His parents, Pauline a school teacher and William a businessman, are no doubt proud of their son. Mr. Smith is married to Dr. Gaurdia E. Banister who is Senior VP of Patient Care Services at Providence Hospital in D.C. He owned and operated an apothecary and photographic division while serving as a consultant to a major health care management and consulting firm. He also performed numerous consulting tasks for the American Society of Hospital Pharmacist and Planning and Human Systems, Inc. in Washington, D.C. He taught pharmacology at the School of Nursing in Catholic University, Washington, D.C.; was also a clinical instructor at the College of Pharmacy and Pharmaceutical Sciences at Howard University and also at the University of Maryland. Additionally, Mr. Smith was on the Board of Directors and Chairman of the Legislative and Regulatory Committee of the American Hospital Association Society of Ambulatory Care Professionals and was a founder of the Association of Black Hospital Pharmacists. He was also President of the Board of Pharmacy in DC.

Sonya Smith, Ph.D.
Mechanical Engineer

Dr. Smith joined the Howard University faculty in 1995 and is the first tenured female faculty member in the Department of Mechanical Engineering and recently became the first woman promoted to the highest academic rank of Professor (full) in this department at Howard University. Since joining the faculty, Dr. Smith has established an interdisciplinary theoretical and computational fluid dynamics research program. She obtained her Ph.D. in Mechanical and Aerospace Engineering from The University of Virginia (UVA) in Charlottesville, VA in 1995 and was also the first African-American woman to do so. She has received research grants from NASA, DOD, and The Boeing Corporation to conduct research on topics in Atmospheric Turbulence, Aeroacoustics, Vortex-Wake Aircraft Encounters, Simulation of Wake Vortex Dynamics, and Rotorcraft Icing Severity and Detection and has authored several articles on these topics. Dr. Smith also conducts research in computational neuroscience. For over four years she has collaborated with the Laboratory for Auditory Mechanics at the National Institute on Deafness and other Communication Disorders (NIDCD). Dr. Smith is actively involved in the Department of Mechanical Engineering, the College of Engineering, Architecture, and Computer Sciences (CEACS), and the Howard University Faculty Senate.

Tommy E. Smith, Jr., P.E.
Mechanical Engineering

Tommy E. Smith, Jr. has worked at the Lawrence Livermore National Laboratory since 1980. A registered professional mechanical engineer, Mr. Smith has worked on a number of projects relating to national security and energy use and analysis. In particular, Tommy worked on two of the three architectures initially under consideration by the Strategic Defense Initiative of the. This work included work on optical instruments in support of the Brilliant Pebbles program; (high-velocity kinetic energy interceptors). He also worked on the Free Electron Laser program. A highlight of Smith's work on this project is his receiving a patent on an electron energy spectrometer – a device developed to help determine the energy transfer between the drive laser and an undulating electron beam. Since 1994, Mr. Smith has turned his career focus on increasing the numbers of minority and female engineers and scientists by taking on the position of Director of Affirmative Action and Diversity at the Laboratory.

Lanny S. Smoot
Electronic Panning Camera Co-inventor

Mr. Smoot is credited with the invention and prototyping of the electronic panning camera for multi-user interactive applications and large screen teleconferencing. The panning camera allows networked subscribers unprecedented control over their individual views of remote sites. Large screen teleconferencing gives participants the feeling of direct intimacy and reality -- namely that other parties are actually just sitting across the table and not miles away. He is the Diector of Walt Disney Imagineering, the master planning, creative development, design, engineering, production, project management, and research and development arm of The Walt Disney Company and its affiliates. Representing more than 150 disciplines, its talented corps of Imagineers is responsible for the creation of Disney resorts, theme parks and attractions, hotels, water parks, real estate developments, regional entertainment venues, cruise ships and new media technology projects.

Henri H. Soclo, Ph.D.
Director General of the Environment, Ministry of Environment and Nature Conservation; Eco-toxicology Chemistry

Gnida Sossou, Ph.D.
Civil Engineering

Dr. Sossou earned his BS degree from Technical Lycee Eyadema, Lome, Togo (1981); his MS degree in Civil Engineering from the Zaporojie Industrial Institute in Ukraine (1988); his Ph.D. from the Dniepropetrovsk Civil Engineering Institute in Ukraine (1991). Currently he is a Senior Lecturer, Research Associate in Civil Engineering at Ghana's Kwame Nkrumah University of Science and Technology. Prior to this, he worked for 9 years as a Dosent, Research Associate and Interpreter at Dniepropetrovsk Civil Engineering Institute and National Mining University of Ukraine. Dr. Sossou's research has included theoretical and experimental analysis of the influence of concrete creep on the long duration nonlinear flexural characteristics and on the exponents of limit states of reinforced precast and prestressed concrete beams, slabs prestressed in both directions, columns, load-bearing wall elements, electric poles and prestressed concrete trusses. Dr. Sossou is a member of professional organizations and has written several papers for journals and books.

Sulayman K. Sowe, Ph.D.
Computer Science

Dr. Sowe has a wide teaching experience in computer science, software engineering, and physics in Africa, China and Europe. His research interests include Free/Open Source Software Development, Knowledge Management & Knowledge Sharing, Information Systems Evaluation, Human-Computer Interaction, Social and Collaborative Networks, Software Engineering Education, Digital divide and ICT for Sustainable Development. In The Gambia, he briefly worked with the ministry of education, where he functioned as a teacher, administrator and the director of information and communication technology/human resource development. He furthermore worked as an assistant registrar and system administrator for the West African Examinations Council (WAEC) in The Gambia, Nigeria, Ghana, Sierra Leone, Liberia and as a database manager for the Gambia's Medical Research Council (MRC), working on the RTSS malaria vaccine trial developed by Glaxo-Smithkline and funded by the Gates Foundation.

Marion R. Spenser, MS
Immunologist and Molecular Pathologist

Before retirement, she served as Chief Technologist of Immunology/Molecular Pathology at Los Angeles County/University of Southern California (USC) Medical Center. Ms. Spencer's work experience is varied and extensive. She served in several positions and disciplines during 28 years of employment at LAC-USC Medical Center, a 1500 bed County General Hospital. She has managed and supervised operations and staff of 32 members; performed research and engaged in development for hospital labora- tories; established Flow Cytometry Laboratory within the Immunology/Molecular Pathology Section; instructed and lectured at colleges, universities, semi- nars, and workshops; performed laboratory analyses in Biochemistry, Hematology, Microbiology, Blood Bank laboratories. She has evaluated new analyses-- most recently, methods for assuring a safe blood supply for transfusions. She has performed specialized techniques such as Fluorescent Antibody assays and Histocom- patibility screening/matching for kidney and bone marrow trans- plantations. Her endeavors seem endless.

Michael Gregg Spencer, Ph.D.
Electrical Engineer

Recent work has emphasized wide bandgap materials and Dr. Spencer group was the first to produce conducting AIN and thick films of beta SiC grown by the bulk sublimation technique. Dr. Spencer has over fourteen years of research experience in the epitaxial and bulk growth of compound semiconductors such as GaAs, SiC and AIN (growth techniques include molecular beam epitaxy, vapor phase epitaxy, liquid phase epitaxy, and sublimation), microwave devices, solar cells and electronic materials characterization techniques (including deep level transient spectroscopy and photoluminescence). His particular interest has been in the correlation of device performance with material growth and processing parameters. Dr. Spencer has served as a research scientist and/or consultant to General Electric, The Naval Research Laboratories, Jet Propulsion Laboratories, Lawrence Livermore National Laboratories and (NASA) National Aeronautics and Space Administration. Dr. Spencer has authored over 50 publications in the area of compound semiconductor research. He is currently one of the Directors of the NSF sponsored National Nano-fabrication network (NNUN). He currently has co-authored three U.S. patents with several patents pending.

Frank Staggers, Jr., M.D.
Addiction Medicine and General Medicine

Dr. Staggers is a practitioner of addiction medicine and general medicine and the senior drug detoxification specialist. He is also the former director of the alcohol, drug, and methadone programs at the West Oakland Health Center, CA. Dr. Staggers has been an investigator on multiple federal research grants, including research on the effects of the Transcendental Meditation program on cardiovascular disease. Dr. Staggers was also the Co-Principal Investigator on a four year study on stress in the workplace of Federal employees of the US Department of Health and Human Services.

Stephan Stanton
Dir., Software Test Engineering

As a software quality assurance manager, Stephan Stanton loves to dig into software. His employer provides enterprise monitoring software for large e-commerce sites. Determining how software works and making sure it meets end-user requirements is the daily challenge for Stanton and his team of software test engineers. Stephan graduated from California State University-Chico in 1986 with a BS in applied math and a heavy load of Computer Science courses. His first job was in telecommunications with Pacific Bell (eventually owned by AT&T). He spent three years as a project engineer in the telephone switching systems department, where he implemented digital and electronic switching systems. He moved over to the IT side in 1989, doing software testing and then software application support and troubleshooting. In 1993 he returned to software testing and QA. In 1998 Stephan left to do similar testing and QA for retailer Williams-Sonoma and Bechtel Corp. He joined his present employer in 2000, where he likes the diverse technical environment. "We run a lot of different operating systems," he says. "You get different flavors of Unix, Windows 2000 server and different databases. We have one of the biggest Oracle databases running anywhere."

Denise Stephenson-Hawk, Ph.D.
Associate Professor and Mathematician

Dr. Stephenson-Hawk is Chairman of the Stephenson Group, LLC and a science, policy, and education consultant. She is a former provost of Spelman College and professor at Clark Atlanta University, recently held a position as the NCAR associate director for the Societal-Environmental Research & Education Laboratory (SERE). Through her multifaceted career in academia, government, and the corporate arena, Stephenson Hawk has often worked at the interface between science, education, and policy. She holds a Ph.D. from Princeton University in geophysical fluid dynamics. While at Clark Atlanta, Stephenson Hawk served as founding director of the interdisciplinary Earth Systems Science Program and co-led a program to enhance the mathematics and science achievement of Atlanta public school students. She has served on many NSF, NASA, and NOAA science and education advisory committees, as well as on the NOAA Science Advisory Board and the UCAR University Relations Committee.

Frank Stewart
AABE President; Electrical Engineering

Frank was the U.S. Department of Energy Golden Field Office Manager He has made visits to such nations as Nigeria, Mozambique, South Africa and Ghana to advise governments on how using renewable energy technologies can meet some of their enormous electricity needs. On one of those trips, wielding pliers and a hammer, he actually helped install a solar-powered water purification system. As a federal employee for more than 25 years, he served on a number of state, national and international advisory groups. He has also served in various executive roles for U.S. delegations, including traveling to Rome, Cote d'Ivoire, India and Botswana. In 1996, he lped the delegation that concluded the first Memorandum of Agreement between the U.S. and Uganda. Prior to his work in Golden, CO, Frank worked for DOE in Washington, D.C., where he served as a Deputy Assistant Secretary in the Office of Energy Efficiency and Renewable Energy, directing grant programs and providing technical assistance to state and localities. Among these programs were the Institutional Conservation Program, State Energy Conservation Program, Weatherization Assistance Program and Inventions and Innovations Program. Currently, Frank Stewart is the President and COO of the American Association of Blacks in Energy, and Member, Joint Center for Political and Economic Studies Commission on Climate Change.

Sheila "Jewel" Stiles, Ph.D.
Research Geneticist, Fisheries, Marine Biology

As a research geneticist, Dr. Stiles currently is Team Leader of the Genetics Unit in the Biotechnology Branch of the Aquaculture and Enhancement Division. This Unit is concerned with the application of genetic technology to enhance and restore economically and ecologically valuable marine resources, specifically shellfish such as oysters, clams and scallops, with aquaculture, the farming of aquatic organisms. Approaches include selective breeding, population genetics or molecular analyses (DNA, RNA, protein) and field or performance evaluations. Results were presented in China and Denmark. In addition, she has worked on genetic effects of pollutants such as petroleum aromatic and PCB hydrocarbons and on reproductive success of winter flounder, clams and oysters. She developed a cytogenetic-cytological technique to assess the condition of bivalve larvae and other zooplankton from the field or in the laboratory. Earlier, Dr. Stiles planned and supervised genetic crosses for mutations (i.e. radiation), inbreeding and hybridization in oysters. She also conducted experiments on chromosome manipulation and genetic engineering to understand mechanisms involved in obtaining polyploids and clones of shellfish.

Gerald V. Stokes, Ph.D.
Microbiology, Tropical Medicine

His research interests have been directed at an important group of bacteria of the genus Chlamydia, obligate intracellular parasites. Some members of the group are responsible for causing over 4 million new cases of sexually transmitted infections each year in the U.S. They are the leading agents of pelvic inflammatory disease, cervicitis, urethritis, pneumonia, conjunctivitis and infertility in both men and women. Some strains cause blinding trachoma, a disease that affects millions of people in arid regions of north Africa and the Mediterranean. More recently chlamydiae have been implicated in coronary heart disease. Even though these organisms respond to antibiotics multiple drug resistant isolates have been reported. Vaccine therapy remains elusive primarily due to our lack of a detailed understanding of the molecular biology of the virulence factors possessed by these unusual bacteria. His department is now called 'Microbiology and Tropical Medicine'. They recently acquired new leadership and direction, focusing on those neglected, but important diseases which afflict millions of people in Africa, Asia and South America. Tropical (formally called 'Parasitic') Diseases alter or destroy the lives of the less fortunate, while neglected by the major targeted research programs.

David S. Summers, M.D.
Neurologist

Dr. Summers served as Assistant Chief of Neurology at the Landstuhl Army Medical Center in Germany, 1964-67. Medical Staff appointments at Williamsburg Community & Maguire VA Hospitals followed his discharge from USAR active military duties, and he was Assistant Professor of Neurology at the University of Rochester School of Medicine & Strong Memorial Hospital, 1967-72. He was recruited to the University of Utah Medical Center in Salt Lake City, where he was Assistant Professor of Neurology & Electroencephalographer, 1972-76, then began a private neurology practice in NW Pennsylvania with admitting & consulting privileges at St. Vincent, Hamot, Veterans Administration, Millcreek, & Doctors Osteopathic Medical Centers in Erie, and at the Meadville Medical Center & Warren State Hospital. Dr. Summers has been very active in civic and community activities, including the Human Rights Campaign, stem-cell, spinal cord & pain research, the Schomberg Center at the NY Public Library. He is the author of medical publications and a contributing author to The Black Humanist Experience, 2003. He has been Director of the Reflex Sympathetic Dystrophy Assn of NW PA & support of the Planetary Society, Menninger Society, Nat. Committee for Science Edu, NY Academy of Sciences, AAAS, ACLU and Americans United for Separation of Church & State.

Mark E. Swai, M.D.
Pediatrician, Dir. Of Hospital Services

Dr. Swai is the Director of Hospital Services of the Kilimanjaro Christian Medical Centre (KCMC), the largest hospital in the north of Tanzania. KCMC is a referral hospital for over 11 million people in Northern Tanzania. The hospital is a huge complex with over 450 beds, with hundreds of outpatients and visitors coming to the centre everyday. Over 1000 staff are employed at the centre. In addition to providing medical services to the local community it provides training for nurses, medical students, and other ancillary workers, under the auspices of the associated KCM College. It also accepts students from other countries for their 'elective' studies.

Douglas J. Sweeney
Security Department Project Manager, Security Engineering Group Leader

Douglas Sweeney is Project Manager for LLNL's Security Department. He is responsible for many high visibility security projects across the Laboratory. During his more than 20 year career at LLNL, Douglas has worked primarily as a systems engineer in the electronics engineering and technologies areas. His wide breadth of experience in systems integration and project management have been utilized by several Laboratory programs including the Laser Program, the Defense and Nuclear Technologies Program, the Safeguards and Security Engineering Program, and the National Ignition Facility. Douglas has been recognized for his many contributions to successful projects. He has been awarded the Director's Performance Achievement Award, the Nuclear Defense and Technologies Achievement Award, and the Nuclear Complex Guidance Team Performance Award.

Ramona Tascoe, M.D., MHSA
Internal Medicine, Global Health

Dr. Ramona Tascoe is an Internist, award-winning human rights advocate, and international public health leader. She was a member of the faculty of the University of California, Berkeley and San Francisco Schools of Medicine. She is the Inaugural Chair of the Women's Health Section to the Scientific Assembly of the National Medical Association (NMA) was the Chair of International Affairs for the NMA. As the elected California State Chair, she prepared California's 208 delegates on topics of Sustainable Development, for their participation in the historic National Summit on Africa held in Washington, DC in February 2000. She is the past president of the Kaiser African American Professional' Association for Northern California, during which time she contributed to the strategic plan for cultural competency designed to improve morbidity/mortality outcomes for patients of color. Dr. Tascoe recently completed an appointment to the National Expert Advisory Panel on Women's Health for the Department of Health and Human Services (DHHS), and was advisor the Task Force of the Office of Research on Women's Health (ORWH) of the National Institutes of Health (NIH). She is an ordained minister who mentors youth and young adults at the Allen Temple Math/Science Institute in Oakland, and the University of California School of Medicine in San Francisco.

Julius H. Taylor, Ph.D.
Physics

In 1945, Dr. Taylor was Chairman, Dept. of Physics, West Virginia State College. He later joined Morgan State as an Associate Professor in 1949, then went on to become the Dept. Chairman and Professor from 1951 - 1978. Dr. Taylor now serves as a contractor to NASA. He has researched and published widely about physcial nature of matter, including, but not limited to "Electrical and Optical Properties of Semi-Conductors Under Hydro-static Pressure", "Index Refraction of Liquids", and "the Forbidden Bandwidth in Tellurium". Dr Taylor has always been concerned about increasing the number of African Americans in Science and Engineering; he has published articles about this matter over 40 years. He edited The Negro in Science, Morgan State College Press, 1955. Dr. Taylor has mentored students in Junior and Senior High Schools in the Baltimore Public School system from 1987 - 1997.

Elorm Marcel K. Tchaou, Ph.D.
Environmental and Civil Engineering;GeoScience

The UNESCO Office in Dakar and Regional Bureau for Education in Africa, better known by the acronym BREDA, is the largest UNESCO office in Africa. A dual mandate assigned to it. As the Regional Bureau for Education, BREDA covers the entire sub-Saharan Africa, representing 46 countries. As a multi-country office, Dr. Tchaou assumed the representation of the Organization in four countries in West Africa: Cape Verde, Gambia, Guinea-Bissau and Senegal. For these countries, the liability extends to all areas of competence of UNESCO, namely, education, natural sciences, social sciences and humanities, culture, communication and information. BREDA partners are the Member States, the UN System, the Organizations Internationales (IGOs), SnoN Governmental Organization (NGO) and all persons and institutions engaged in activities in the areas of competence of the Organization.

Alain Djacoba Tehindrazanarivelo, M.D.
Neurologist, former Vice-Prime Minister in charge of Public Health

Dr. Tehindrazanarivelo, neurologist was been in Paris from 1988 to 1994 to become a neurologist while practicing as a Médecin attaché associé (Université Paris VI, University Hopital Pitié-Salpêtrière & Saint Antoine). In 1995, he went on in Madagascar, to become a Professor of Neurology, the Founder and Associate Director of the Neurosciences and Mental Health Center, the Founder and Editor in Chief of the Journal de Médecine et de Thérapeutique, the head of Department of Neurology & psychiatry and Associate Dean at University of Antananarivo Medical School. Alain has been Secretary General of the Ministry for Scientific Research (1999-2002). In 2009, after 7 years of exile in France, he left his position consultant neurologist at Lariboisiere Hospital (Paris) and senior neurologist at Louis Pasteur Hospital (Chartres), and went on in Madagascar to be appointed as Vice Prime Minister in charge of Public Health. Alain has been Reviewer and Editorial Board member for international, African and Malagasy medical journals. He is a member of the National Academy of Arts, Literature and Sciences of Madagascar, and is author and co-author of more than 150 scientific papers and book chapters. He is presently Professor of Neurology and Director of Neurosciences and Mental Health Center (University of Antananarivo Medical School) and is a Member of Madagascar's High Council for Transition.

Botlhale O. Tema, Ph.D.
Science Education; Biology

Dr. Tema is a member of the Advisory Panel of the Network for the Coordination and Advancement of Sub-Saharan Africa-EU Science and Technology (CAAST-Net). She is also Managing Director of African Creative Connections which sets out to facilitate and enhance African partnerships between South African institutions, companies and organizations with their counterparts in other African countries. My consultancy also mentors of public servants to improve their effectiveness and efficiency. From 2005-2007, she was Director, Department of Human Resources Science and Technology, African Union Commission, Addis Ababa, where she served as liaison with 53 AU Member States for the development and harmonization of policies and programmes in the fields of Education, Science and Technology, ICT and Youth for the African Union. Dr. Tema was General Manager (Chief Director): International Cooperation, Department of Science and Technology (220-2005), responsible for developing and implementing a strategy for science and technology bilateral cooperation between South Africa and other countries as well as managing South Africa's participation in multilateral organizations related to S&T.

Michel A. Tevoedjre
Engineering

Is an engineer with experiences in international Cooperation Program Management, Engineering and Science Education, Community Project Development, Industrial Project Management, and Alumina Production and Alumina Plant Design. Currently, he works as consultant on Project and Programme Development in the area of Science and Technology (Renewable Energy – Science and Technology Promotion). Earlier, he served as National Program Officer (NPO) in charge of UNESCO "Science and Technology" Cooperation Program, and as Office Chief for Accra UNESCO Sub Regional Office Branch in Benin (2004 – 2009). Early in his career, Michel worked for Martin Marietta Alumina as Process Engineer in Saint Croix (US Virgin Island), responsible of the Red Mud section - Plant Water Ingress –and Plant Energy Audit. He also worked for Kaiser Engineers (Oakland, California), responsible for Alumina Plant Assessment; Acted as Assistant to the Engineering Manager for Martin Marietta Alumina Plant Expansion in Saint Croix, US Virgin Island; and for Alumina Plant Construction on Bintan Island, Indonesia.

A. Babatunde Thomas, Ph.D.
Chairperson, NEPAD Science & Technology Forum; and Director for Africa, CURE International; former Presidential Adviser on Human Resources, Science & Technology, Office of the Nigeria President

Dr. Thomas has been the past Presidential Adviser on Human Resources, Science and Technology, Office of the past President of Nigeria. He earned his Ph.D. from Indiana University in Bloomington (1972), in Economic Development and Technological Change, Science & Technology Policy and Econometrics/Statistics. He is the author of three books, several monographs and numerous articles. He has taught in Nigerian and American universities for over three decades and was a tenured professor before taking up the post of Executive Director of the African Regional Center for Technology, a continental institution established by African Heads of State, providing research on post-harvest food technology and new and renewable energy technologies. Dr. Thomas later joined the United Nations and served in New York, Tanzania, Kenya and recently in Uganda, where he was the Resident Representative of the United Nations Development Program (UNDP) and UN Resident Coordinator for Operational Activities (1994 – 1999). Before going to Nigeria, he was Special Adviser/Coordinator of the UN System-Wide Special Initiative on Africa (1999 – 2000).

Lydia Waters Thomas, Ph.D.
Biology, Zoology, President & CEO

Dr. Thomas was recently President and CEO of a prestigious technology based corporation, responsible for the general management and direction of the company's overall technical, financial, and administrative activities. Previously, as Vice President for Civil Systems, she was center's Space Systems Division, the Advanced Information Systems Division, and the Energy Resources and Environmental Systems Division. In addition to her many corporate activities, she has served two terms on a seven-member Environmental Advisor Board to the Chief of Engineers, U.S. Army Corps of Engineers. Earlier, as Technical Director, she was responsible for the development of a coherent work program that was responsive to the Federal government's numerous energy resources and environmental efforts; for maintaining a highly qualified and technical and management team; and for opening a project and document quality assurance program. Dr. Thomas co-chaired the R&D Investment Panel for a Defense Science Board Summer Study on Defense Technology, and she served a three-year term on the Scientific Advisory Board of the U.S. Defense Department's Strategic Environmental Research and Development Program. In 2002, Dr. Thomas was appointed to serve as a member of the President's Homeland Security Advisory Council.

Valerie L. Thomas, Ed.D.
Retired Mathematician

Past Assoc. Chief of the Space Science Data Operations Office (SSDOO), NASA/Goddard Space Flight Center, Greenbelt, MD. Served as a leader, responsible for the development and operations of data and information systems that support processing, management, archiving and distribution of space physics, astrophysics, and other NASA data and information. She also managed NASA's first wide area network, the Space Physics Analysis Network (SPAN) (1986-1990) and the NASA Automated Systems Incident Response Capability Team, served as Technical Officer of SSDOO's Hughes STX On/Offsite technical support contract, and chaired SSDOO's Education Committee. Since joining NASA in 1964, Dr. Thomas has served as the Asst. Director of the National Space Science Data Center (NSSDC), Asst. Project Manager for the Pilot Land Data System (1984 - 85), and Goddard's leader for the multi-Agency (NASA, NOAA, AND USDA) Large Area Crop Inventory Experiment (LACIE). From 1970 - 81, Dr. Thomas managed the development of state-of-the-art pipeline processing software data systems, which supported the launch of Landsats-1, -2, and -3 and served as an international expert on Landsat digital products. During 1964 - 70, she developed real-time quick-look processor data systems for the Orbiting Geophysical Observatory (OGO) and Multi-Satellite Operations Control Centers.

Arthur N. Thorpe, Ph.D.
Physics, Astronomy

Dr. Arthur Thorpe is a professor of physics and is receiving support from NASA as director of Center for the Study of Terrestrial and Extraterrestrial Atmospheres (CSTEA). The Laboratory for Atmospheres at Goddard Space Flight Center (GSFC) and CSTEA at Howard University have been collaborators on research and graduate education since 1996. CSTEA is an interdisciplinary research center at Howard University, which sponsors research in Atmospheric Science and related areas. Some of his present fields of specialization are Solid State Physics and Low Temperature Physics with special emphasis on Magnetic and Thermal Properties of Solids. He is also involved with the evaluation and characterization of superconducting materials for space applications. he is interested on enhancing the current density of high-temperature superconductors (HTSC) by studying the effects of dopants (added impurities). He is also interested in the effect of prseodymium (rare earth ion Pr3+) as a dopant. Pr3+ ions suppress HTSC and may lead to formations of weak links for Josephson junctions. Dr. Thorpe has listed over 93 publications in journals such as the Journal of Geophysical Research 69, Physical Review, 1975 no.3, the Journal of Radiation Effects 19, and the Journal of Bioinorganic Chemistry 3.

Patrice Tognifode
Mechanical Engineering

Patrice Tognifodé is an inventor who holds Beninese citizenship and was born in 1968 in Bopa (Benin). Based in France since 1990, he is a professor and engineer in mechanical engineering, as well as the inventor of a pluvial-electric power plant (CENTRATOG) that produces electricity from rainwater. Patrice Tognifodé asserts that his device can store electricity by collecting rainwater, and that it operates continuously; which brings back the debate about energy conservation on the table. Patrice Tognifodé is not only a genius inventor. He is also a thinker and author of a book entitled Devoir de Vérité aux Noirs, Les Noirs Doivent se Prendre en Main published by Editions Antipode, his own publishing house.

Festus Tolo, Ph.D.
Microbiology

Dr. Tolo works at the Center for Traditional Medicine and Drug Research, Kenya Medical Research Institute as a Senior Research officer and Unit head, Biological Sciences Unit, CTMDR-KEMRI and Part time Lecturer, Department of Medical Microbiology-Karen Campus, Jomo Kenyatta University of Agriculture and Technology, Kenya. He Group Leader on the KEMRI/JICA Infectious Diseases Project: The Plant Drug Research group for antiviral agents; P.I. on the research of antiviral activity of Kenyan *Centella asiatica, Myrica salicifolia, Aloe secundiflora* and *Maytenus senegalensis* against human herpes viruses; *herpes simplex, varicella-zoster* and *cytomegalo* viruses; Proj. Mgr. on the WHO/TDR-KEMRI Project ID: An Investigation of Safety, Efficacy and Chemistry of Herbal Medicines used Traditionally for Treatment of Malaria; and Co-Investigator on Pre-clinical evaluation and formulation studies for development of safe, effective and standardized phytomedicines from selected Kenyan medicinal plants. Dr. Tolo also has 3 patents pending.

Glen O. Toney, Ph.D.
Senior Corp. Vice-President Emeritus, Computer Science

Dr. Toney retired in 2002 as Group Vice President, Corporate Affairs of Applied Materials, Inc., the leading worldwide supplier of semiconductor wafer fabrication equipment. Prior to that date, he was Group Vice President and Vice President, Global Human Resources since 1985. He first joined Applied Materials, Inc. in 1979. Prior to employment with Applied Materials, Dr. Toney held several positions in education and business industries. He worked as the Assistant Superintendent of Schools for the Palo Alto Unified School District, Assistant Superintendent of Schools for the Ravenswood City School District, and a Mathematician and Systems Analyst for Lockheed Missile and Space. Dr. Toney also served as Chairman of the Board of the 21st Century Education Initiative, part of the Joint Venture: Silicon Valley (JVSV) Network. Dr. Toney has two undergraduate degrees, a B.A. in Philosophy from California State University at Chico, and a B.S. with honors in Mathematics from San Jose State University. He received his M.A. in Instructional Technology from San Jose State University, and earned his Doctorate in Organizational Behavior from the University of Southern California.

Teotonio A. Torres
Civil Engineering

Teotonio has over twenty years of experience in project planning and management in both government and in private sector. These include construction, rehabilitation and expansion projects involving Sao Tome's International Airport, as well as numerous building and road constructions. He also worked extensively on project teams rehabilitating the water supply and drainage/sewage systems in cities internationally. While working for Sao Tome's (West Africa) Public Works Office, he served as a Civil Engineer and General Manager, developing plans and specifications for construction bids for Government projects; received and processed bids; supervised 100 plus employees and staff; and oversaw construction of a variety of projects such as roads, schools, government offices, and multi-level residents, etc. While working for SOGEA Group (French General Contractor) Angola (West Africa), he was Deputy General Manager responsible for developing construction projects worldwide. He researched, solicited and obtained construction projects in Angola. As a Project Manager for this company, he managed and coordinated five subcontractor construction of an international airport, consisting of tower, terminal, technical buildings and taxi-ways.

John Trimble, Ph.D.
Computer Science, Knowledge Mgmt.

Dr Trimble's experiences and research interests include System Dynamics: philosophy, teaching tools, knowledge acquisition; Expert Systems: knowledge acquisition, instructional expert systems; Software Engineering: software quality assurance, life cycle models; Modeling and Simulation: discrete and continuous models, Stella, Extend, Arena; Knowledge Management; Curriculum development in simulation and systems thinking; Appropriate Technology and System Dynamics. He has taught, given guest lectures and consulted extensively in Africa including Rwanda, Ghana, Mauritius, Zimbabwe, South Africa and Namibia. He spent a year as a Fulbright professor in Zimbabwe in 2003-2004.
  Dr. Trimble is an Associate Professor in systems and computer science at Howard University, but is currently on a two year leave until 2009 to serve as Dean of Information Communication Technology at Umutara Polytechnic University (a new university in Nyagatare Rwanda). He has been extensively involved in international work on 'appropriate technology' including serving as the chair of the international planning committee on the first two international conferences on appropriate technology hosted in Zimbabwe in 2004 and 2006.

Carlton M. Truesdale, Ph.D.
Physical Chemistry

Dr. Truesdale is a research fellow who was recognized for being one of the "Top 100 Most Important Blacks in Technology" at the Black Engineer of the Year Awards Conference in 2006. Additionally, he was named the Society of Black Engineers' Pioneer of the Year in 1998. He is widely recognized for his research in optical couplers, multimode fibers and waveguide processing. His current research activities include the nanomaterials processing for life sciences, specialty materials, and energy applications. He is on the Board of Advisors to the Jackson State University College of Science Engineering and Technology (CSET) and Howard University (CREST) Nanomaterials. He holds 22 patents and has authored numerous technical reports. In addition he has written a number of journal articles and made presentations at scientific conferences.

James M. Turner, Ph.D.
Deputy Assistant Secretary, NOAA; Physics

Dr. Turner is the Deputy Assistant Secretary of Commerce for International Affairs and Director of the National Oceanographic and Atmospheric Administration (NOAA) Office of International Affairs, leading NOAA's international scientific and environmental efforts associated with the global oceans, atmosphere, and space. Prior to joining NOAA, he was the Deputy Director of the National Institute of Standards and Technology (NIST). Earlier, he served as the Assistant Deputy Administrator for Nuclear Risk Reduction in the Department of Energy's National Nuclear Security Administration, being responsible for major projects in Russia to permanently shut down their last three weapons-grade plutonium-production reactors. He also worked with foreign governments and international agencies to reduce the consequences of nuclear accidents by strengthening their capability to respond to nuclear emergencies. Earlier, Dr. Turner managed one of DOE's San Francisco-San Jose-Oakland Bay Area, California Operations Office. He holds degrees in Physics from the Massachusetts Institute of Technology (Ph.D.) and Johns Hopkins University (B.A.). Prior to joining the DOE, he was an Associate Professor of Physics and Engineering at Morehouse College, where he researched in solar-terrestrial physics, magnetic fusion, and molecular biophysics.

Charles K. Twesigye, Ph.D.
Biology

Dr. Twesigye is the Head of the Department of Biological Sciences at Kyambogo University, and current chairman of the International Organization for Biotechnology and Bioengineering (**IOBB**) founded in 1968. He is President of the Uganda Society, a multidisciplinary organization founded in 1923 as the Uganda Literary and Scientific Society, and Chief Editor of the Uganda Journal, first published in 1934. Charles is a fellow of the East African Quaternary Research Association (**EAQUA**). He has over 60 publications including journal articles, book chapters and books covering Natural Resources Management, Remote Sensing Applications, Integrated Water Resources Management, Water Pollution Control, and Information Communication Technologies (**ICTs**). Dr Twesigye has been a Senior Researcher with the Inter-University Council for East Africa(IUCEA) under the Lake Victoria Research Initiative (**VICRES**) since 2004 and the Millennium Science Initiative (**MSI**) of the Uganda National Council for Science and Technology(**UNCST**) since 2008.

Mr. Lavell Tyler, Jr., P.E. RCDD
Electrical Engineering, Telecommunications

Lavell Tyler is licensed registered professional electrical engineer and a registered telecommunications engineer with technical expertise in interior building systems and exterior transmission and distribution systems. The systems include power, lighting, motor controls, security, voice, data, CATV, and many other types of systems. He has experience supervising and directing professional architects, engineers, contractors, and staff in the planning, design, and construction of buildings, site development, and utility systems. His general experiences include technical quality management, project management, construction management, and program management. Mr. Tyler's projects ranged in size and type from major new projects to multiple smaller alterations projects consisting of hospitals, medical clinics, educational research facilities, military research facilities, aircraft maintenance facilities, vehicle maintenance facilities, dormitories, office buildings, waste processing facilities, power transmission and distribution systems, voice and data centers, telecommunications systems, and other types of systems and facilities.

Henrietta Ukwu, M.D., FACP
Infectious Disease, Corp. Exec.

Dr. Ukwu is Vice President of Global Regulatory Affairs for a major pharmaceutical company. The extensive portfolio which she oversees spans all therapeutic areas of Wyeth, including Cardiovascular disorders, Neuroscience, Gastro-Intestinal disorders, Anti-Infectives, Metabolic Disorders, Women's Health, Biopharmaceuticals and Vaccines. Prior to joining Wyeth in 2004, Dr. Ukwu was the Vice President and Head of Worldwide Regulatory Affairs, Biologics/Vaccines, at Merck Research Laboratories where she started her pharmaceutical regulatory career in 1992. Dr. Ukwu was Chief of Infectious Diseases at the Alvin C. York Veterans Administration Hospital, Murfreesboro, TN immediately after completing an infectious diseases fellowship at Vanderbilt University Medical Center in 1991. There her research included HIV/AIDS pathogenesis and clinical research in potential HIV vaccines. Dr. Ukwu has served as consultant to the World Health Organization on the Global Program for AIDS. She completed her residency training in internal medicine at Baptist Hospital, University of Tennessee, after taking medical and surgical degrees in Nigeria. She has received many awards for her contributions to science, medicine, and industry.

Marcel Uzegbu, P.E.
Supervising Civil Engineer

Marcel Uzegbu is a registered Civil Engineer in the State of California and has been practicing Civil Engineering for over 20 years. As a Supervising Civil Engineer with City of Oakland, Mr. Uzegbu possesses extensive and team building, municipal engineering experiences which he has utilized effectively in working with other engineers, consultants, contractors and developers and his staff at City of Oakland. Marcel enjoys discerning viable solutions to engineering issues and land use complexities. Marcel Uzegbu has extensive experience in Construction Management, Project Management, Subdivisions Development, Civil Engineering Design and currently in charge of Right-of-Way Management Division under Community and Economic Development Agency. In May 18, 2001 Marcel received an award from American Public Works Association Northern California Chapter for his exemplary customer service and engineering contributions to Engineering Services, City of Oakland.

Thomas H. Via, CmfgE
Industrial Engineering Technology

Before Mr. Via started his own company, Via Technologies in 1985, he worked in manufacturing for 25 years. Initially, he went to work for Viking Steel as an ironworker/welder, then Tegal Corp. As an electro-mechanical technician. He later served as an instructor at Carbondale University, IL in 1985 and later as an instructor in welding, machine tools and business at Solano Community College, CA. Mr. Via has been a member of several professional associations, including Automated Imaging Assoc., Robotics International of the Society of Manufacturing Engineers.

Clarence W. R. Wade, Ph.D.
Chemistry, Professor

Dr. Wade's research experiences include serving as a Supervisory Research Chemist: Chief, Environmental Effects Division, US Army Medical Bioengineering Research and Development Laboratory, Ft Detrick, MD, responsible for the Army Surgeon General's development of data bases for the detection, estimation and analysis of toxic pollutants at US Army bases (1972 - 1986). During 1966 -1972, he was Supervisory Research Chemist: Chief, Materials and Applications Division, USArmy Medical Bioengineering Research and Development Laboratory, Walter Reed Army Medical Center, Washington, DC. He Supervised and directed research on the preparation, evaluation and use of biomaterials for use as prostheses, blood expanders, burn dressings, tissue adhesives, and tissue compatible materials for treatment of injuries to soldiers. From 1957 - 1966, Dr. Wade was a Research Chemist, National Bureau of Standards (now NIST, National Institute of Science and Technology). He developed 24 metallo-organic, oil-soluble standards for estimation of metals in oils which are currently distributed as certified standards. He pioneered synthetic chemical procedures for the labeling of simple sugars with tritium (H3) and carbon-14 (C14). Since 1972, Dr. Wade has been an Adjunct Professor of Chemistry, University of the District Of Columbia.

Atty. Paul Ware
Patent Attorney, Physicist

(- 2010) Prior to practicing as a Patent Attorney, his early work experience was that of Chairman of the Department of Physics at the then Alabama State College in Montgomery, AL. He worked as an Associate Physicist at Cornell Aeronautical Laboratory, developing methods for measuring and analyzing the radar cross sections of various shapes. He later went on to work for Litton Systems as a Senior Engineer; Principal Investigator in the Advanced Missile Systems for Radar Cross Section studies at Douglas Aircraft Company; Apollo Test and Operations Engineer at Space and Information Systems Division and Minuteman Systems Programmer at Autonetics Div., both at North American Rockwell; and Weapons Programmer at Hughes Aircraft Co. Atty. Ware, retired in 2002 from the California Institute of Technology with the title of Manager of Technology Utilization/Patents in the Office of Patents, where he reviewed and evaluated, with respect to intellectual property value issues, research output from Technical Members of the Staff. Prior to joining CalTech, Atty. Ware started practicing as a Patent Attorney while working at Hughes Aircraft Company, preparing and prosecuting patent applications and developing disclosures of inventions from technical personnel for patent action.

Herman Lecil Warren, Ph.D.
Plant Pathologist

In summary, Dr. Warren has an outstanding record of important contributions to scientific understanding and control of maize and sorghum diseases, to knowledge of the basic characteristics of fungus diseases of maize and to service to his profession and society. He. has received many notable awards and citations and has authored or co-authored more than 150 refreed publications, 65 abstracts, book chapters, proceedings, and other publications. Dr. Warren has released 4 inbred lines with resistance to Puccinia polysora (southern rust) in 1975. These lines serve as a worldwide source for use in germplasm improvement for southern rust resistance and are used as standards in southern rust research. Dr. Warren has released 11 inbred lines developed from an exotic composite which have multi-disease resistance and good combining ability. The release of these lines demonstrates that useful genes found from exotic corn can be transferred and adapted to local regions. The distribution of these inbred lines include over 250 public and private domestic and 100 international breeders/pathologists, respectively. Dr. Warren is recognized internationally and nationally as an authority on corn and sorghum disease. He has been involved in programs in Brazil, China, Egypt, India, Mexico, for Yugoslavia, and Zimbabwe, Croatia, Eritrea, Uganda, Kenya, and Ukraine.

Elbert Washington
Mathematics, Engineering

Recently supported the development of major Flight Projects with the Jet Propulsion Laboratory (JPL). As Supervisor of the Projects Cost Group, Mr. Washington supported the pre-project activities of the Advanced Planning Office for the development of new projects, with particular emphasis on systems engineering, implementation planning, scheduling, financial and cost analysis and risk considerations. Also, his responsibilities include the development of mathematical models and analyzing the political and budgetary conditions to assess the probability of JPL receiving a new start, based on a proposed project's cost and technical readiness. These projects have a total cost of $500 million dollars or more. Some of these projects included the Voyager, TOPEX (Ocean Topography Experiment), Mars Observer, SIRTF (Shuttle Infrared Telescope Facility), and Lunar Observer. "Our legacy is one of science, medicine, philosophy, and religion", says Mr. Washington. "We have built the pyramids of Egypt, designed and constructed the Great Stone City of Zimbabwe, and founded the greatest Universities of antiquity (such as Timbuktu and El Karnak). As parents we must feed this truth to our children. This knowledge will inspire our children and provide them with the inner strength to meet the challenges of life."

Warren M. Washington, Ph.D.
Director, Climate & Global Dynamics Division

He was the head of the Climate Change Research Section at the National Center for Atmospheric Research in Boulder, CO, which uses state-of-art computer climate models to study present and future climate change. His expertise is in atmospheric and climate research. These models are made up of atmospheric, ocean, land/vegetation, and sea ice components. His involvement in research for more than forty years has made him a much sought after individual for advice, testimony, and lecturing on global climate change. He has served on numerous committees and panels, among them the U.S. President's National Advisory Committee on Oceans and Atmosphere from 1978-1984. More recently, he has served on the National Science Board from 1994 to 2006 (Chair, 2002 - 2006). He has published over 100 publications and co-authored, with Claire Parkinson, a book considered a standard reference on climate modeling -- "An Introduction to Three-Dimensional Climate Modeling"(2005). Dr. Washington has many awards including being a member of the National Academy of Engineering, Presidency of the American Meteorological Society (1994), and a member of American Philosophical Society. President Barrack Obama awarded Dr. Washington the National Medal of Science, the highest honors bestowed by the U.S. government on scientists, at the White House Nov. 2010.

Charles B. Watkins, Ph.D.
Dean, School of Engineering, Mechanical Engineer

Current Research: experimentally investigates the interaction of a shock wave with homogeneous and isotropic turbulence. Specifically, the program focuses on the phenomenon of turbulence amplification in the vorticity mode by a moving shock wave propagating inside the flow. The experiments are being conducted in a new 12 in. dia. shock-tube facility and will cover interactions with relative Mach number 1.5 to 4.5.

Levi Watkins, M.D.
Cardiac Surgery, Assoc. Dean, School of Medicine

Dr. Watkins, Jr. is the Associate Dean of the Johns Hopkins University of School of Medicine and full Professor of Cardiac Surgery, where he is the first African American to achieve these positions. In 1966 he integrated the Vanderbilt University School of Medicine, becoming the first black ever admitted and the first black to graduate from the institution. In 2005 his portrait was unveiled at the School of Medicine. In 1970, he went to Johns Hopkins Hospital as a surgical intern and in 1978 became the first black chief resident in cardiac surgery at that institution. Between 1973 and 1975 he developed his research interest at the Harvard Medical School Department of Physiology. There he defined the role of the renin-angiotensin system during congestive heart failure. This and other work led to the clinical use of angiotensin blockers in the treatment of congestive heart failure today. He performed the first human implantation of the automatic implantable defibrillator in February of 1980 and subsequently developed several different techniques for the implant-tation of this device. To date, over 1 million devices have been implanted and the lives of approximately 2/3 of these patients have been saved with this treatment. He helped revolutionize the culture for postdoctoral education in America by working to establish the nation's first postdoctoral association. Today, over fifty associations now exist in America.

H. Geoffrey Watson, M.D.
Internal Medicine

Dr. Watson, President/C.E.O. of The James A. Watson Wellness Center, has served in a variety of medical rotations, including: inpatient - ICU, CCU, ER, cardiology, nephrology and infectious diseases; outpatient - neurology, dermatology, rheumatology, pulmonary endocrine, OB/Gyn. Besides being a member of countless professional organizations and receiving numerous awards, Dr. Watson serves the community in general and provides healthcare services to the poor via his "Men's Mobile Clinic" outreach program. He is the host of "HEALTH BEAT", a long running medical information TV program. The program airs via Network Cable TV in Oakland, California. Dr. Watson, besides serving a large office practice, also provides on-the-job learning opportunities for African-Americans in a variety of medical related fields including medical residency programs, physician assistance programs, medical assistance programs, nursing programs and general youth education programs, in his office. He is also affiliated and provides medical services via his "Medicine and Ministry" program throughout his community based church affiliations. He is an Associate Professor of Medicine for the University of California, San Francisco, Department of Medicine and has co-authored numerous research publications in connection with Annals of Allergy, Asthma and Immunology.

John A. Watson, Ph.D.
Professor Emeritus, Biochemistry and Biophysics

Dr. Watson, Ph.D joined the Department of Biochemistry and Biophysics at the University of California, School of Medicine, San Francisco in 1969. He participated and succeded in each of the areas consistent with being a member of the University of California Academy. His research was directed at identification of the sterol and non-sterol isopentenoid regulatory signal molecules that regulated mevalonic acid synthesis in eukarotic cells. A personal national and international reputation was built upon Dr.Watson's research effort. Dr. Watson received received recognition for his teaching in the classroom and laboratory. University Service by Dr. Watson was extensive. He served as Associate Dean of Medical School Admissions Chair and Vice Chair Medical School Admissions Committeee; Associate Dean, Medical Student Affairs Chair of Committtee for Academic Personnel, Chair of Chancellor's Advisory Committee on Diversity and a wide range of University California Systemwide Committees as Chair and / or member. Dr. Watson's Public Service included being a member of the American Heart Association Grants and Research Committee, Chair and member of several National Institutes of Health Study Sections and Chair and member of the Sigma Xi Distinguished Lectureship Committee.

Morgan Watson, P.E.
Engineering Company President; Mechanical Engineering

Mr. Watson is the President of MEL, Inc. He has served in various technical and administrative capacities during his many years of experience as a professional engineer. Not only has he worked on projects for oil companies and the Dept. of Energy, he has also served as Principal-in Charge or Project Manager on 44 contracts performed for the Corps of Engineers since 1978, responsible for client liaison, contract negotiations, project administration, and technical review. Under his supervision, over 2,100 surveys of various types were performed, nearly 300 quality assurance inspectors were provided to observe construction and debris removal activities at approximately 200 sites, and approximately 36 design and drafting support projects were performed, all for the Corps of Engineers. In the aftermath of Hurricane Gustav, he served as Project Manager on his company's debris removal monitoring services contracts and for the removal of hazardous trees, limbs and stumps in the public parks. He also served as Project Manager involving quality assurance debris removal and reduction services, demolition and selective salvage, and private property debris removal in the aftermath of Hurricanes Katrina and Rita.

Hamé M. Watt, Ph.D.
Water Supply and Sanitation

Dr. Hamé M. Watt founded the Africa Water Foundation to tackle the enormous and critical water challenges and help the less fortunate people meet their needs for water. He was Director of the Washington, D.C. Water Resources Research Center (WRRC), College of the Life Sciences, University of the District of Columbia. WRRC researchers have been dedicated to identifying and finding solutions to critical water concerns in the District of Columbia. Mr. Watt has a Ph.D. in education and civilization from the University of Paris 7 in Paris, France and was also a Professor at the University of Mauritania in Nouakchott. Dr. Watt is an internationally recognized authority on water resources development and water research management. Over the past 2 decades, he has served as a planner and manager for a wide range of water projects. He has conducted and coordinated over fifty multi-disciplinary water and energy-related projects.

Ellerson F. Weaver
Ret'd Pharmacist

(1936- 2009) Ellerson Weaver graduated in Pharmacy from Howard University in 1958. Shortly after residing in California, he established his pharmacy business to serve the Oakland, CA community. Ellerson was always present at his business, serving this community or 35+ years. Dr. Weaver a retired pharmacist was the President and Chief Pharmacist of the North Oakland Pharmacy for 45 years.

Frank C. Weaver, Ph.D.
EE, Engineering Co. Executive

Joining Boeing in 1998, Dr. Weaver is responsible for coordinating corporate requirements for frequency spectrum and developing strategies to secure licenses and approval for Unmanned Aircraft Systems from the Federal Aviation Administration, the U.S. congress, State Department, Federal Communications Commission, International Telecommunications Union, and the National Telecommunications and Information Administration. He has over 30 years of experience in government and private industry, and has marketed over $1 billion in communication satellites and launch vehicles to NASA, DOD, and the telecom industry. Dr. Weaver serves on the Board of Visitors at Howard University's Schools of Business and Engineering. He is Chairman emeritus of the Washington Space Business Roundtable and a board director of the U.S. Telecommunications Training Institute.

James L. Weaver, Jr., DDS
Dentistry

While Dr. Weaver has practiced General Dentistry in the downtown area of Oakland, California since 1990, he has a vast knowledge of resources of African Americans in science and technology. He holds membership in several professional and civic organizations, including the Alameda County Dental Society, California Dental Association, and the American Dental Association. He served on the Health Commission for the city of Berkeley, participated in Head Start Dental Advisory and screenings for Oakland, East Palo Alto and San Mateo County. Dr. Weaver has mentored youth through the Alameda County Probation Department and with the Kaiser Chemical Dependency Program.

Raymond B. Webster
Information Scientist

Mr. Webster has been involved for the past six years, in extensive research, consulting and publication efforts regarding the contributions of African Americans to science, invention and technology with the goal of incorporating such information into documented history of the United States. He has published a major volume and twenty-six articles and reports on this subject; appeared on radio/TV; and provided over seventy presentations locally/nationally. He also produced his own sixteen-segment TV show on Philadelphia Channel-52 that aired sixty-seven times. Previously, he was employed in private industry for ten years, prior to operating his own company for twenty-five years working on air/spacecraft programs, basic and applied research and information systems technology. Mr. Webster just completed the original design, development and implementation of CAASTIS, an information system comprising over seven hundred fifty-thousand data-facts on African American contributions to science, invention and technology, the largest ever.

Wayne P. Weddington, Jr., M.D.
Physician, Otolaryngology

Dr. Weddington has practiced as an Otolaryngologist (ear, nose, throat) for more than 40 years. He served with the Germantown Hospital and Medical Center, PA; Neuman Medical Center, PA; St. Christopher's Hospital, PA; and as owner and CEO of Weddington ENT Associates, PA. He has been a Fellow with the College of Physicians of Philadelphia since 1972.

James E. West, Ph.D.
Research Professor, Electrical & Computer Engineering

Dr. West is currently Research Professor at Johns Hopkins University, Department of Electrical and Computer Engineering. He was formally a Bell Laboratories Fellow, at Lucent Technologies. His pioneering research on charge storage and transport in polymers (the electrical analogy of a permanent magnet) led to the development of electret transducers for sound recording and voice communication. Almost 90% of all microphones built today are based on the principles first published in the early 1960s. This simple but rugged transducer is the heart of most new telephones and can be found in most microphone applications from toys to professional equipment. Dr. West holds more then 50 U.S. and about 200 foreign patents on various microphones and techniques for making polymer electrets and transducers. He was inducted into The National Inventors Hall of Fame in 1999 for the invention of the electret microphone. Dr. West is a member of the National Academy of Engineering; a Fellow, and past President, and past member of the Executive Council of Acoustical Society of America (1998-2001), and a Fellow of the IEEE. He is the recipient of an honorary Doctor of Science degree from New Jersey Institute of Technology (1997), an honorary Doctor of Engineering from Michigan State University (2006) and the National Medal of Technology (2006).

William L. West, Ph.D.
Biochemical Pharmacology, Endocrinology

Dr. William L. West is the Principal Investigator, the Center for Drug Abuse Research (CDAR), funded by the National Institute on Drug Abuse (NIDA). He is Emeritus Professor and Chair of the Dept. of Pharmacology. Not only has Dr. West been an instructor and Professor since the late 1940s, he has performed research in cellular and pharmacology/endocrinology; metabolic developments of the embryo and various chemical and radiation impacts on cancer. He has written peer reviewed publications ranging selected potential environmental contaminants to pharmacology in medicine.

Augustus A. White, III, M.D., Ph.D.
Orthopedic Surgery

Dr. White is an internationally renowned orthopedic surgeon and biomedical engineer. His mechanical studies of the human spine have helped to develop technologies and surgical systems that speed patients' recovery from spinal injuries. After graduating cum laude from Brown in 1957 (while playing football and lacrosse), he went on to earn his M.D. in 1961 at Stanford Medical School where he served as student body President and became the first African-American graduate of this medical school. He went on to Yale, where he completed his orthopedic residency and became the first African-American surgical resident at Yale University School of Medicine. After serving two years with the Army, Dr. White attended University of Gothenburg and at the Karolinska Institute, where he earned his Ph.D. in 1969 for research on the biomechanics of the spine. Returning to Yale Medical School, he became a full Professor of Orthopaedic Surgery and Director of the Engineering Laboratory for Musculoskeletal Disease. He has received countless awards and authored or coauthored more than 200 scientific and clinical publications. Most noted among them is the highly regarded work, "The Clinical Biomechanics of the Spine." While serving as a great surgeon, Dr. White has always been committed to issues of diversity and is nationally recognized for his work in medical education and issues of health care disparities.

Sandra L. White, Ph.D.
Immunobiology; Experimental Therapeutics and Hematopoiesis

Following her post-doctoral training, Dr. White joined the faculty of Howard University Medical School as an Assistant Professor. As a member of their Cancer Center, her research in pre-clinical experimental therapeutics focused on the immunomodulating effects of the novel anti-metastatic agent swainsonine. Her work showed that swainsonine had potential clinical application in the prevention and treatment of metastatic disease. Based on this work, the NCI selected it for "high priority development." In 1994, she accepted a position as an Associate Professor in the Duke University Adult Bone Marrow Transplant Program, Division of Hematology-Oncology, Department of Medicine, and member of the Cancer Center. She continued her research on the mechanism of the myeloproliferative properties of swainsonine and its potential use with high dose chemotherapy. After a five year stint at Duke, Dr. White accepted the position of Chair of Biology at North Carolina Central University where she now serves as the Director of the Center for Science, Math and Technology. She also continues to hold an adjunct appointment in the Cancer Center at Duke. She is actively involved in the mentoring and training of scientists, which focus on increasing the number of minority researchers in the biomedical behavioral disciplines, such as Cancer Control, as well as in interdisciplinary women's health research.

Alison P. Williams, Ph.D.
Chemistry

Alison Williams is a Senior Lecturer in the Chemistry Department at Barnard College in New York City. She began her scientific career in high school working at the Ohio State Agricultural Research and Development Center in Wooster, Ohio. She received her undergraduate degree in chemistry from Wesleyan University and her M.S. and Ph.D. in biophysical chemistry from the University of Rochester where she was a NSF graduate fellow. She taught at Swarthmore College, Wesleyan University, Princeton University before joining the faculty of the chemistry department at Barnard. Her research focuses on thermodynamic and kinetic properties of nucleic acids. Most recently her work emphasizes the role of ions in shaping the physical properties of oligonucleotides. She was an NSF ADVANCE Fellow and served as a Sigma Xi Distinguished National Lecturer. Dr. Williams has also received numerous recognitions for her teaching, outreach and mentoring activities for scientists of all ages.

Arthur L. Williams, Ph.D.
Biology

(1947 – 2010) Dr. Williams was a Professor of Biology and Chairperson at Morgan State University. Prior to joining Morgan, he served as Professor and Chairman of the Department of Biology at Howard University (1995-2001). During the past twenty-nine (29) years, he devoted substantial efforts to the education and training of minorities in the biomedical sciences. He received numerous honors and awards during his career such as Research Scientist, Teacher of the Year, Faculty of the Year, etc. He was a member of several prestigious scientific organizations; served as a member of national review panels, chaired several boards for undergraduate and graduate fellowships/scholarships; and is a former President of the Howard University Chapter of Sigma Xi, the Scientific Research Society. He generated over 30 papers published in peer-reviewed journals and received more than $3 million in extramural grant support. Subsequently, he was engaged in a brief period of postdoctoral research at NIH. Prior to joining the faculty at Howard University, Dr. Williams served on the faculties at Murray State University, University of Kentucky, and Atlanta University. His research interests included the regulation of gene expression in bacteria and fungi.

Eric Williams
Mechanical Engineer, Biotechnology

He founded a company Advanced Stent Technology which was purchased by Boston Scientific in 2004 for $120 million. Mr. Williams, an engineer and inventor, is renowned throughout the biotechnology industry for bringing concepts from the prototype phase to a finished product. He has played several pivotal roles in the company's development, including the start-up phase and co-inventing the SLK-View(tm) Stent and Delivery System. Prior to AST, Mr. Williams was with Advanced Cardiovascular Systems, now known as Guidant where he developed over-the-wire and rapid exchange catheters and co-invented the Ellipse catheter. Previously, he was at Boston Scientific in San Jose, California where he invented the Ultra Sound Atlantis Catheter, which is the smallest ultrasound delivery system currently in worldwide distribution. Mr. Williams is listed on 19 patents for cardiovascular stents, the miniature devices which have been implanted in millions of blood vessels in the past decade to prevent clogging.

Gwendolyn D. Williams, S M (ASCP) SBB (ASCP)
Blood Banking Consultant

Her experience includes living in Eritrea, East Africa where she provided blood banking consultation to the Minister of Health for the National Blood Transfusion System, National Reference Laboratory, province hospitals, health center laboratories and referral hospitals. Ms. Williams has also taught Immunohematology at the University of Asmara, Eritrea, conducted lectures and trainings at the national blood bank, provincial hospitals and health centers throughout Eritrea, Africa. She has also provided analysis and consultation to the Swiss Red Cross. Ms. Williams has had abstracts accepted and presented at the ISBT and American Association Blood Banks. Ms. Williams has over 30 years of experience supervising the blood bank for the University of California at Davis Medical Center, serving as an instructor at the University of California at David Medical Center School of Medical Technology. Ms. Williams is certified blood bank assessor from AABB, specialist in blood banking technology from AABB and American Society of Clinical Pathologists(ASCP), as medical technologist from ASCP, clinical laboratory scientist from California Department of Health Services, along with having a B.S. in Biological Science from Florida AMU. Ms. Williams maintains a home in Sacramento, California.

Henry N. Williams, Ph.D.
Microbiology

Dr. Williams was Director and Professor, Environmental Sciences Institute at Florida A&M University until his retirement in February 2010. Earlier in 1997, he was appointed Assistant Vice President (AVP) for Sponsored Programs at Morgan State University. Soon after earning his doctorate, he worked for the University of Maryland, Baltimore (UMB) Dental School in 1980 as an Assistant Professor of Microbiology and subsequently advanced through the ranks to full Professor and currently holds the position of professor emeritus. In 1993, he assumed the position of AVP for Research at UMB. Dr. Williams' research group is an international leader in studies on the predatory group of bacteria, the *Bdellovibrio* and like organisms, and the microbiological quality of dental unit water. His group has published over 100 scientific papers and abstracts. In 2003, Dr. Williams was elected to fellowship in the American Academy of Microbiology, an honor leadership group that recognizes excellence, originality and creativity in the microbiological sciences. From1980-81, he was Science and technology advisor to U.S. Senator Mathias, where Dr. Williams analyzed science and technology reports issued by the Office of Technology Assessment, other government agencies, and Congressional committees.

James H. Williams, Jr., Ph.D.
Professor, Mechanical Engineering

Dr. Williams is the School of Engineering Professor of Teaching Excellence, Charles F. Hopewell Faculty Fellow, and Professor of Applied Mechanics in the Mechanical Engineering Department at MIT. He is also Professor of Writing and Humanistic Studies in the School of Humanities, Arts, and Social Sciences. He consults and research in the mechanical characterization of advanced fiber reinforced composites; wave propagation in large space structures; in-process and post-process quality control; reliability; dynamic fracture; nondestructive evaluation with emphasis on acoustic emission, thermal, and ultrasonic responses of composites; dynamic behavior of structures subjected to seismic excitation; and the development of computerized data base systems for composite materials selection. Formerly, as a senior design engineer at the Newport News Shipbuilding and Dry Dock Company, he performed a broad range of mechanics calculations, for example, stress and dynamical analyses of catapults, turbines, and propulsion shafting on nuclear-powered aircraft carriers such as the USS Nimitz (CVN-68). He has also conducted major multi-year consultations for the US government and international corporations involving a multiplicity of structural systems on high-performance aircraft, automobiles, rockets, offshore oil platforms, and hydroelectric power generation stations.

Luther S. Williams, Ph.D.
Provost and V.P., SEM Education, Medicine

Dr. Williams is Vice President for Academic Affairs at Tuskegee University and serves as dean of graduate studies and director of the Integrative BioSciences Ph.D. Program. He has a distinguished career that ranges from faculty positions at major American universities to administrative roles in higher educational and government agencies, particularly in science and technology. He also previously served as Provost at the University. He will also continue to assist with the National Center for Bioethics in Research and Health Care. He has provided tremendous influence on directions of science education in the U.S. He served in the NSF as Asst. Dir. of Education and Human Resources; Deputy Director of the National Institute of General Medical Sciences for the National Institutes of Health; Associate Professor of Biology at MIT; Professor of Biology and Assistant Provost at Purdue University, IN; Professor of Biology and the Dean of the Graduate School of Arts and Sciences at Washington University, MO; Professor of Biology and Vice President of Academic Affairs at the University of Colorado, CO; and Professor of Biology and President of Atlanta University, GA. He also has many varied scientific publications on topics relating to some of his research interests about the Control of Gene Expression, Microbial Physiology, and Molecular Biology.

Willie Williams, Ph.D.
Physics

Dr. Willie Williams' is University Professor of Physics and Pre-engineering Program Coordinator, where he has served this university for over 30 years. He chaired the Physics Department and developed programs for the preparation of minority students for careers in Science, Engineering and Mathematics (SEM). Dr. Williams became the Principal Investigator for the nationally recognized Lincoln Advanced Science and Engineering Recruitment (LASER) Program, that identified, recruited, trained and prepared students for careers in SEM fields, graduate and professional school. The program provided an integrated set of components: Pre-freshman summer bridge program; Scholarship and fellowship support; Community College Program; Honors program; Student personal and career counseling; Student undergraduate research; Summer internships; Career and professional field trips; Tutorial services program; Graduate and Professional school prep. Over the years, Dr. Williams has served as a Research Scientist for the Department of Defense, where he managed the development of the power sub-systems associated with national satellite programs. In particular, he managed the development of the first mass-produced Gallium Arsenic solar cells and the development of significantly improved Nickel Hydrogen batteries.

Samuel P. Williamson
Meteorology

Mr. Williamson is the Federal Coordinator for Meteorological Services and Supporting Research, accountable to the U.S. Congress and the Office of Management and Budget for systematic coordination and cooperation among 15 Federal departments and agencies with meteorology programs or interests. He directs the analysis and evaluation of Federal weather programs, operational requirements, and supporting research to facilitate executive and legislative funding decisions for over $4.1 billion annually. He has been instrumental in bringing to the forefront important interagency programs including weather information for surface transportation, space weather, and phased array radar, designed to improve public safety and enhance economic well-being. He began his career as a weather officer in the U.S. Air Force's Air Weather Service and has served the National Oceanic and Atmospheric Administration (NOAA) in numerous key positions for over 32 years. For more than 12 years, he was the principal planner and ultimately director of the Joint System Program Office for the tri-departmental Next Generation Weather Radar (NEXRAD). A major scientific and technical breakthrough, the system significantly improved the nation's hazardous weather detection and warning capability. He has received the Presidential Rank Award and the NOAA Distinguished Career Award.

Bobby L. Wilson, Ph.D.
Chemistry

Dr. Wilson's tenure at Texas Southern University spans more than thirty years, as a noted academician and leader in higher education, where he has served as Professor and Chair of the Chemistry Department, Assoc. Dean of the College of Arts and Sciences, Interim Dean of the College of Arts and Sciences, Vice President for academic affairs, Provost, and Acting President. He serves as the Shell Oil Endowed Chair of Environmental Toxicology and L. Lloyd Woods Distinguished Professor of Chemistry. His experiences include being a visiting research professor at Exxon Research and Engineering and program director at the National Science Foundation. He has produced over seventy publications in scientific journals and books. He holds two patents and one international patent application pending, involving dispersion of nanotubes in polymeric composites. He is committed to close the gap and facilitate the increase in minority students within STEM through the Houston Louis Stokes Alliance for Minority Participation in which he is the campus Program Director. Dr. Wilson's research interest includes the synthesis of inorganic metal complexes and monitoring and assessing environmental and human health toxicants. Currently, he is concentrating his research efforts in modifying and characterizing carbon nanotubes, emphasizing the dispersion of nanotubes in polymeric composites.

Charles Wilson
Computer Science Co. Executive

Charles Wilson currently serves as President of Intellus, which he co-founded in 1998. Originally from Norfolk, Virginia, Charles is a graduate of Old Dominion University. While at Old Dominion, he was a member of the Data Processing Management Association, Black Student Alliance, and Kappa Alpha Psi Fraternity. Since his graduation, Charles has completed executive training programs at Kenan-Flagler Business School, University of North Carolina; Tuck School of Business, Dartmouth; Pacesetter Program, Raleigh Business and Technology Center. He began his professional career with IBM in Raleigh, and after 17 years of corporate experience in the information technology arena – Charles ventured out on his own to co-found Intellus. Intellus has provided solutions for commercial businesses, government entities, universities, and non-profit organizations. Companies like Verizon, Progressive Insurance, North Carolina Department of Transportation, Bristol-Myers Squibb, and University of North Carolina to name a few have achieved their desired results using Intellus software. Charles currently serves in the North Carolina Dept. of Transportation Minority Contractor Expansion Council; North Carolina Technology Assn.; Black Data Processing Assn.; Assn. of Information Technology Professional. He is also a Big Brother and volunteer and coach youth sports.

Ken Wilson
Electrical Engineer, Computer Science

Ken Wilson is the President and owner of Eagle Web Solutions Inc, a web design firm located in Raleigh, NC. His firm was started in 2003 and focuses on small businesses. EWS designs, builds and host attractive, state-of-the-art and industry specific web sites. Prior to that, Ken was a Senior Engineer, Manager at IBM in Research Triangle Park, NC. During his 33 year career at IBM, Ken had an opportunity to work on many leading edge projects, including an Inroute Traffic Control System for the FAA and some of the first computer systems for banks and retail stores. As a Manager at IBM, he lead teams working on IBM's first implementation of a Local Area Network, developing adapters that allowed IBM's personal computers and workstations to attach to the IBM Token Ring LAN. Teams working under his leadership also developed some of IBM's first ATM adapters that allowed IBM servers to connect to this new high-speed network. His teams also developed a line of low cost Ethernet switches that helped IBM to enter this competitive switch market. Ken's last projects were focused on helping IBM enter the Network Attached Storage arena, with the design and release of one of IBM first NAS servers. Ken is a graduate of the University of Pittsburgh with a BS degree in Electrical Engineering.

Vulindlela I. Wobogo, Ph.D.c
Chemistry, Physics

Vulindlela studied chemical engineering and physics while at San Jose and eventually earned a BS and MS in physical chemistry. While at SJS he became involved in radical Pan African activism which led involvement is the formation of several important political organizations, including the Black Panther party of Northern California. His involvement resulted in two trips to Africa. The first was in 1964 as a science delegate to the sixth Pan African Congress held in Dar es Salaam, Tanzania. From 1975 to 1991. He served as the first Manager of the East Palo Alto Sanitary District from 1985 1988. In 1991, Vulindlela returned to San Francisco State University as an Assistant Professor of Black Studies, where he specialized in ancient and modern African history and culture and science in ancient Africa. Vulindlela's science interests include cosmology, theories of everything science in ancient Africa. He also has a keen interest in the philosophy of science and the effects of technology on socialization and human rights in future society. He is currently working on a book regarding the latter subject. Vulindlela's other interests include social group dynamics in diverse societies, implications of quantum phenomena for human consciousness and the role of extended family in socialization within traditional and contemporary African society.

Charles E. Woodward, Ph.D.
Astrophysics

One focus of Dr. Woodward's research is the study of solar system comets, which are frozen reservoirs of primitive solar dust grains and ices. He analyzes the composition and size distribution of cometary dust grains from infrared imaging and polarimetry techniques using the LBT and Steward Observatory telescopes which support his Spitzer Infrared Telescope activities. In this way, he can determine the physical characteristics of the solid materials that constituted the primitive solar nebula, out of which planetesimals, then planets were formed. His published research and been concerned with infrared spectroscopy, star formations, novae, and comets. In 1997, he co-authored an article on the baffling halo emission from Galaxy NGC5907 in the revered British science journal *Nature*. Woodward and collaborators participated in the NASA Deep Impact mission, providing real time, ground-based near-and mid-infrared remote sensing spectroscopic support as detailed a series of articles published in 2005 in the leading American journal "Science."

Oscar Wright
Civil Engineering

Not only has Mr. Wright practiced civil engineering and construction over 35 years, he often speaks of his passion: helping African American children to be and do their best. Born in 1923, he entered Alcorn State University where he excelled academically, while playing football (elected All-American) and basketball. He organized the first African American Conservation League in Mississippi and a Charter Member of Old Miss' first African American Credit Union. He was the President of Emerville, CA's NAACP (Meger Evers was Mr. Wright's first college roomate). In 1986, he founded the "The Black United Front for Educational reform". In 1993, he filed a complaint with the U.S. Dept. of Education Office of Civil Rights, alleging that African American Students were being tracked in the lowest academic classes, and disciplined, suspended and expelled at a far greater rate than other races, for similar issues. After investigation, this Department found the allegations to be true and issued a decree to the Oakland, CA Public School District to provide equal access to educational resources. Mr. Wright is currently the Co-Chair of the African American Education Task Force. He reminds us all through his quote: "It is not about you and it is not about me; it is about our children".

James H. Wyche, Ph.D.
University Provost; Biochemistry, Cell Biologist

Dr. Wyche is Howard University's Provost and Chief Academic Officer. He is a distinguished cell and molecular biologist, cancer researcher and university administrator. Spanning four decades, Dr. Wyche's research and academic career includes appointments as Vice Provost for Academic Affairs and Professor of Biochemistry and Molecular Biology at the University of Oklahoma Health Sciences Center; Vice Provost and Dean of the College of Arts and Sciences and Professor of Biology and Molecular Pharmacology, School of Medicine, University of Miami; Associate Provost and Professor of Medical Science, Department of Molecular Biology, Cell Biology and Biochemistry at Brown University; and Visiting Professor and Scholar-in-Residence at other institutions. During the 2001-2002 academic year, Dr. Wyche served as interim president of Tougaloo College. The focus of his research interest is the transduction of apoptotic signals and characterizing the molecular mechanisms by which various agents elicit cell death in cancer cells and the use of natural products and their analogues and examining their structure function effect(s) on specific cell death pathways in target cancer cells. In addition to publishing over 100 articles and abstracts on his research in peer-reviewed journals, Dr. Wyche holds patents for gastrointestinal stem cell markers and pancreatic cancer serum markers.

Patrice O. Yarbough, Ph.D.
Infectious Diseases

Dr. Yarbough earned a Ph.D. in Biochemistry from the University of Houston in 1985. After a NIH Post-Doctoral fellowship, she held positions in research and research administration at biotech companies Genelabs Technologies Inc. and Tanox, Inc. She is co-inventor on eight U.S. patents for the hepatitis E virus and has published over 40 publications on Hepatitis E and the virus that causes disease. At the University of Texas Medical Branch at Galveston, she was responsible for promoting the growth of basic and clinical research programs. Dr. Yarbough joined the Universities Space Research Association's (USRA) Division of Space Life Sciences (DSLS), which supports NASA's needs for understanding and counteracting the physiological changes that accompany space flight. Based at USRA Houston, the DSLS manages extramural research programs, administers educational programs, coordinates a visiting/staff scientist program, and enhances collaboration between NASA and academic institutions. She serves USRA as Deputy Project Scientist for the Flight Analog Project in the Human Adaptation and Countermeasures Division. Dr. Yarbough is married and has two children.

Peter O. Yimbo, Ph.D.
Science Applications

Dr. Yimbo earned his doctorate in Environmental sciences. Over the years he has worked for SAIC as a Senior EMS Consultant, Lawrence Livermore Laborator-y and NASA.

Clarence E. Younger
IT Management

Appendix

Alphabetical List of ASI Fellows

Dr. Shaukat Ali Abdulrazak
Exec. Sec., National Council for Science and Technology; AgriScience

Dr. Albert Cosmas Achudume
Toxicology

Dr. Adetunji Adelekan
Nephrologist, Internal Medicine

Dr. Clement Oladapo Adewunmi
Parisitology; Veterinarian; African Medicinal Plants

Dr. John Afele
Plant Breeding/Biotechnology

Dr. Abolade S. Afolabi
Plant Biotechnology & Molecular Virology, Bio-Safety and Diagnostics

Valentin Agon
Green Medicine

Justin Ahanhanzo
Physical Oceanography

Gboyega Aladegbami
Civil Engineering

Dr. Edward Cleve Alexander
Chemistry

Dr. Joan Olubunmi Amarteifio
Biochemistry

Kenneth R. Anderson
Electrical Engineering

Ediang Okuku Archibong
Meteorology and Climatology

Dr. Moses T. Asom
Opto-electronics

Dr. Osama Awadelkarim
Engineering Science and Mechanics, Nanotechnology

Virgil A. Baker, PE
Geotechnology

Dr. Sharon J. Barnes
Chemistry; NOBCChE National Secretary

Dr. Harry S. Bass, Jr.
Biology

Dr. Dankyi Augustine Beeko
Consultant Neurosurgeon

Dr. Adolfo O'Biang Biko
Civil Engineering, Proj. Mgmt.

Dr. Adigun Ade Abiodun
Satellite Remote Sensing; Space Sciences

Dr. Ebenezer Adebisi Adebowale
National Universities Commission; Animal Science

Dr. Sunday Adeniji Adesuyi
Chemist

Dr. Olanike Kudirat Adeyemo
Veterinary Medicine, Aquatic Pathobiology

Dr. Kouadio Affian
GeoScience; Remote Sensing

Dr. Abel A. Afouda
Mathematics

Louzolo (Augie) Agostinho
Senior Petroleum Engineer

Dr. Joseph Owolabi Ajayi
Hydrogeology, Engineering Geology

Dr. George E. Alcorn
Physics

Dr. Aliyageen M. Alghali
University Vice Chancellor; Agricultural Entomology

Dr. Reginald L. Amory
Civil Engineering

Tikisa M. Anderson
Electronics Engineering

Dr. Shem Arungu-Olende
Secretary General of the African Academy of Sciences

Dr. Ojonigu F. Ati
Climatology/Physical and Biogeography, Remote Sensing and GIS

Gregory P. Bagley
Research Engineer

Dr. Olusanjo A. Bamgboye
GeoScience

Dr. Nabil H.H. Bashir
Entomology; Pesticides & Toxicology

Dr. Clayton W. Bates, Jr.
Material Science, Electrical Engineering, Physics

Dr. Carl C. Bell
Psychiatry

Dr. Harriette Howard-Lee Block
Molecular Biology

Babagana Abubakar
Geology

Dr. Jimmy Adegoke
Geosciences

Mayen Adetiba
President of Association of Consulting Engineers of Nigeria; Civil Engineering

Dr. Adeyinka A. Adeyiga
Chemical Engineering

Godwin Kwaku S. Aflakpui
Rector, Wa Polytechnic, Ghana; Crop and Plant Physiology; Agronomy

Dr. Georges A. Agbahungba
Soil Science

Jones Fairfax Agwata
Water Resources and Environmental Science

Dr. Kemji Ajoku
Technology Management; Microbiology

Dr. Sam Olatunji Ale
Mathematics

James E. Allen
Mgr., Lab Space Flight Operations – *Deceased*

Dr. Gloria Long Anderson
Professor Emeritus; Chemistry

Dr. Kweku Andoh
Ethnobotanist, Botanist, Proprietor

Dr. Modupe Fisayo Asaolu
Toxicology and Clinical Biochemistry

Donna Auguste
Software Engineering, Electrical Engineering, Renewable Energy, E-learning

Shelly Nathan Bailey, PE
Civil Engineering

Dr. Gaurdia Banister
Hospital V.P, Specialist in Psychiatric Nursing

Dr. Gibor Basri
Vice Chancellor for Equity and Inclusion; Astronomy

Gerald Bauldock
Chemistry

Dr. Lawal Bilbis
Biochemistry

Dr. Damase Bodzongo
Director General of Health, Thoracic Surgeon

Dr. Ntoelioong Bohloko
Pharmacy

Hamilton Victor Bowser, Sr., PE
Civil Engineering

Dr. Christopher S. Boxe
Environmental Science and Engineering

Dr. Clarence A. Boyd, Jr.
Orthopedic Surgeon

Dr. Robert "Pete" Bragg
UC Prof. Emeritus, Material Scientist, Physicist.

Dr. Haruna Braimah
Crop Pest Management/Biological Control

Dr. Albert Bridgewater
Particle Physics

Dr. Randolph W. Bromery
Geophysics Professor Emeritus; Former Chancellor

Delroy Brown
Biology, Nutrition Research

Dr. William T. Brown
Physics

Lee F. Browne
Science Educator and Chemist, Lecturer Emeritus

Dr. Aaron L. Brundage
Mechanical Engrg., Nanoscale & Reactive Processes

Herbert L. Byrd, Jr.
IT Management

Dr. Lisa Cain
Neuroscience and Cell Biology

Kevin Canada, PE
Civil Engineering, Proj. Mgmt.

Dr. George R. Carruthers
Astrophysics

Dr. Benjamin S. Carson, Sr.
Pediatric Neurosurgery

Dr. Hattie Carwell
Health Physics

Dr. Les E. Casher
Biology, Entomology, Ecology

Dr. Gilbert B. Chapman II
Physicist, automobile product specialist

Dr. Gilbert B. Chapman II
Physicist, automobile product specialist

Dr. Bwire Chirangi
Medical Officer

Lee O. Cherry
ASI President & CEO, Engrg., Proj. Mgmt.

Bernard E. Chove, Ph.D.
Food Science and Processing

Yvonne Y. Clark, PE
Professor, Mechanical Engineering

Xernona Clayton
President and Founder of Trumpet Awards

Dr. Milton Cofield
Chemistry

Dr. Timothy W. Conner
Plant Genomics

Dr. Edward S. Cooper
Physician

Dr. George Cooper
Chemistry

Lois Louise Cooper, PE
Civil and Transportation Engineering

Dr. Walter Cooper
State University Regent Emeritus, Chemist

Mildred Crear, RN, MPH
Nursing, Maternal & Child Care

Dr. Frank Alphonso Crossley
Material Science

Dr. Lesia L. Crumpton-Young
Industrial Engineering

Hardiman D. Cureton, II
Science Education

Dr.. Richard H. Djoble D'Almeida
Chief Medical Officer

Dr. Dennis E. Daniels
Epidemiology

Dr. Christine M. Darden
Ret'd NASA Langley Senior Project Engineer

Dr. Rufus Benton Darden, PE
Civil Engineering

Dr. Calvin A. Davenport
Microbiologist

Carolyn S. Davis
Biology

Ifeyinwa Davis
Environmental Scientist

Dr. John H. Day, Jr.
Chief, Electrical Engineering Div., Physics

Joseph Debro
Chemistry; Engineering; Project Dev.

Dr. Peter J. Delfyett, Jr.
Trustee, Chair, Professor, Optics, ECE, & Physics

Dr. Cheick Modibo Diarra
Chairman for Africa at Microsoft Corp.; Aerospace Engineering

Dr. Lincoln I. Diuguid
President, Chemical Lab & Mfr.

Dr. Felix Djembo-Madingou
Regional Director of Medicine

Dr. James A. Donaldson
Mathematics

Raymon Dones
Engrg and Constuction, Renewable Energy

Dr. Ikechukwu N.S. Dozie
Medical Microbiology and Parasitology

Eddie Dunbar
Entomology

W. Paul Dunn
Civil & Aerospace Engineering

James Ealey
EE, Computer Science

Dr. Archie W. Earl, Sr.
Mathematics

Dr. Julian Earls
Ret'd Dir., NASA-Lewis, Health Physicist

Dr. Omotayo O. Ebong
Pharmacology

Dr. Oghenetsavbuko Todo (O. T.) Edje
Cropping Systems Agronomy

Dr. Robert V. Edwards
Chemical Engineering

Dr. Mustafa El Tayeb
Ret'd Dir., UNESCO Div of Science Analysis & Policy; Geophysics

Dr. Dimi Elisa
Research and Planning, Public Health

Dr. Amani Eltayb
Pharmacology

Dr. A. Egrinya Eneji
Agronomy

Dr. Andrew Achuo Enow
Agricultural Sciences (plant pathology)

Dr. Justin Epelu-Opio
Secretary General, Uganda National Academy of Sciences (UNAS); Veterinary Medicine

Dr. Aprille J. Ericsson
Mechanical Engineering, Aerospace Engineer

Dr. Augustine O. Esogbue
Dir., Intelligent Systems & Controls Lab

Dr. Herman E. Eure
Ecological Animal Parasitologist

Dr. Fabian I. Ezema
Physics

Dr. Jonathan D. Farley
Mathematics

Dr. Doudou D. Faye
Entomology; Agronomy

Dr. Lloyd N. Ferguson
Chemist, Prof. Emeritus, author of 7 chem. books

Terry L. Few
Mechanical Engineering

Dr. Mark J. Finch
Infectious Diseases

Dr. Essex E. Finney, Jr.
Agriculture Science

Dr. Edward G. Fisher
Physician, Surgeon

Dr. Kweku David Fleming
Mechanical and Electrical Engineering

Vernon C. Floyd
Broadcast Engineer

Dr. Joseph Ibikunle Folayan, PE
Civil, Structural, Water and Geotechnical Engineering

Dr. Regina Folorunsho
GeoScience; Climatology and Remote Sensing/GIS

Dr. John W. Forje
African Science and Technology Policy

Dr. Alvin G. Foster
Veterinarian

Dr. Norma Francisco
Educator, Administrator, Entrepreneur

Dr. Renty B. Franklin
Biomedical Science

Dr. Bert Fraser-Reid
Chemistry

Dr. Edward H. Freeman
Technical Dir., Adv. Knowledge Sys. Research

Dr. Kamau Gachigi
Material Scientist, Ceramics

Ilene Patricia Garner
Engineering Management, Chem/Math.

Dr. Julius W. Garvey
Thoracic, Cardiothoracic Vascular Surgery; son of Marcus Garvey

Dr. Yaye Kene Gassama
Biotechnology and Plant Physiology

Dr. Dianne D. Gates-Anderson
Environmental Engineering

Dr. Akpa Raphael Gbary
WHO Representative to Benin; Medicine

Dr. Andemariam Gebremichael
Associate Dean, and Dean of Academic, Student, and Research Affairs; Medicine

Dr. Mack Gipson, Jr.
Professor of Geology - *Deceased*

Dr. Lynford L. Goddard
Physics, Electrical Engineering - Lasers and Photonics Research

Edgar Goff
Futurist and Research Development

Dr. Ernest J. Goodson
Orthodontics

Dr. Odell Graham
Physics, Electrical & Aerospace Engineering

Bradford C. Grant, AIA, NOMA
Architecture

Julius Grant
Physics

Dr. Clarence C. Gray, III
Agriculture Research - *Deceased*

Gerald Green
Mechanical Engineering, Proj. Mgmt.

Dr. James L. Green
Clinical Associate of Ophthalmology and Visual Science

Dr. Barbara Green-Ajufo
Epidemiologist

Dr. Kevin C. Greenaugh
Nuclear Engineering

Dr. Lionel O. Greene, Jr.
Research Scientist

Dr. Henry Randall Grooms
Engineering Manager; Civil Engineer

Dr. Ameenah Firdaus Gurib-Fakim
Pro-Vice-Chancellor and Prof. Organic Chemistry

Arif Gursel
Tech Evangelist, Business Dev @ Microsoft, CS

Dr. Adugna Haile
Entomology, Integrated Pest Management

Robert D. Hammie
Mathematics, Nat'l Chess Master

Dr. Ernest C. Hammond, Jr.
Physics

Dr. Delon Hampton, PE
Civil and Structural Engineering and Program/Construction Management

Dr. Marc R. Hannah
Past V. P. and Chief Scientist of SGI, Comp. Sci.

Dr. Mark G. Hardy
Biology

Anthony ("Tony") Harris
Mechanical Engineer, NSBE CoFounder

Dr. Gary L. Harris
Electrical Engineering, Nanotechnology

Dr. Geraldine E. Harris
Microbiologist

Dr. Jim Harris
Nuclear Chemist and Researcher - *Deceased*

Dr. Wesley L. Harris
Past NASA Assoc. Admin. for Aeronauctics

William (Bill) Harris
Nano-Technology, Computer Chip Processor

Dr. Djuana M. E. Harvell
Biochemistry

Dr. L. Julian Haywood
Cardiologist

Dr. David Rice Hedgley, Jr.
Mathematician

Dr. Nadia Hegazy
Computer Science; Communications Engineering

Dr. M. Nidanie Henderson
Chemistry, Molecular Biophysics

Dr. Marvin B. Hendricks
Genetics Research, Molecular Biology

Hon. Olden Henson
Physicist; City Councilman

Dr. William Henson
Ret'd Prof. of Agriculture and Univ. Admin.

Brandon L. Hewitt, PE
Civil Engineering

Dr. Ray A. Hill
Botany; Biology

Dr. Lynne M. Holden
Pres. Mentoring in Medicine, Emer. Medicine

Denise Holland
President, Black Data Processing Associates (BDPA); Computer Science

Kerrie L. Holley
CTO, IBM Web Services Ctr

Franklin Hornbuckle
COO, Satellite Aerospace Corp., EE

Napoleon Hornbuckle
Ret'd Corp. VP, Diversified Technologies, EE

Dr. Norbert Hounkonnou
Quantum Theory; Mathematical Physics; Orthogonal Polynomials and Special Functions

Dr. Clifford W. Houston
Microbiology and Immunology, Immediate Past President of the American Soc. of Microbiology

Dr. A. Chidi Ibe
Physical Oceanography, Geology, Ocean Governance

Dr. Felix I. Ifeanyi
Biology; Veterinarian

Dr. Peter Intsiful
Physics

Dr. Deborah Jackson
Opto-Electronics Communications

Dr. Assan Jaye
Veterinary Medicine; Viral Diseases

Dr. Bill Jenkins
Epidemiologist

Dr. George W. Johnson, Jr.
Cardiothoracic & Vascular Surgery, Physician

Dr. Albert Jose Jones
Enviromental Science, Marine Biology

Dr. Marshall G. Jones
Laser Technology, Research, Physicist

Frederick E. Jordan, PE
Pres., Consulting Engineering Co., Const. Mgmt.

Jacqueline Kakembo
Nursing

Dr. Jane-Frances Kengeya Kayondo
Epidemiology; Tropical Diseases

Howard E. Kennedy
President, Fragrance and Flavoring Co.

Dr. James King, Jr.
Ret'd Dir, Tech Divs. at NASA-JPL.; Chemistry

Pierre M. Labossiere
Agriculture Science

Carl N. Lester
Former Dir., Alameda County Public Healthcare

Dr. Mwananyanda Mbikusita Lewanika
Founding President of the Zambia Academy of Sciences; Biochemistry; Microbiology

William Lucy
Ret'd Sec-Treasurer of AFSCME; Civil Engineer

Dr. John W. Macklin
Chemistry

Dr. Eiman A. Mahmoud
Pathologist, Infectious Diseases

Dr. Johnny L. Houston
Mathematics, Computer Science

Dr. Oyewusi Ibidapo-Obe
President of the Nigerian Academy of Science; Civil Engineering; Mathematics

Dr. Saidiq Bello Ikharo
Facilities Engineering and Management

Dr. Adrian J. Isles
Computer Science

Dr. Keith H. Jackson
Physics, VP of Univ Sponsored Research

Dr. Ambrose Jearld, Jr.
Chief, Research Planning & Eval, Marine Biology

Dr. Anthony M. Johnson
Distinguished Research Physicist; Photonics

Dr. Marian C. Johnson-Thompson
Dir., Office of Institutional Dev; Biologist

Gregory P. Jones, PE
Civil Engineering

Dr. Rena T. Jones
Microbiology

Dr. Soodursun Jugessur
Chairman, University of Mauritius; Chairman, Mauritius Research Council; President of the Mauritius Academy of science and Technology; Physics, Electrical Engrg.

Dr. Alafuele M. Kalala
Chemistry; Biochemistry

Larry D. Keith
Biology, Anatomy, Medical Education Development – *Deceased*

James M. Kennedy
Computer Networks

Dr. Sandra A. Knight
Physician, U.S. CDC in Jamaica; Medical Officer at the Ministry of Health

Dr. Elaine LaLanne
Physics

Dr. William A. Lester, Jr.
Chemistry Research

Dr. Ronald W. Lindsey
Trauma and Spine Surgery

Dr. Phindile E. Lukhele-Olorunju
Plant Breeding and Virology

Dr. Bereneice McClentton Madison
Clinical and Public Health; Pathogenic Microbiology/Immunology

Dr. Dominic W. Makawiti
Deputy Vice-Chancellor (Academic Affairs); Biochemistry

Dr. Samuel Hunter
Physician and Biochemist

Dr. Elham M. A. Ibrahim
Commissioner For Infrastructure And Energy Of the African Union Commission; Electrical Engineering

Dr. Victor Akpan Inem
Family Physician; Primary Health Care

Dr. Saadou Issifou
Medicine; Medical Parisitology; Molecular Biology

Dr. William Jackson
Chemist. Photodissociation Dynamics

Dr. Yemisi Adefunke Jeff-Agboola
Food Mycotoxicology/Phytopathology; Food Microbiology

Dr. Denise Johnson
Oncologists; Cancer Research

Wallace O. Johnston, PE
Mechanical Engineering

Dr. Lovell A. Jones
Biochemistry & Molecular Biology

Venita A. Jones, RN
Nursing

Dr. Calestous Juma
Science and Technology Policy at Harvard; Founding Director of the African Centre for Technology Studies in Nairobi

Abu Bakarr Kamara, PE
Civil Engineering; Proj. Mgmt.

Dr. Harmon Kelley
OB/GYN, Physician

Dr. Stranger Kgamphe
Biology and Anthropometry

Dr. Wade M. Kornegay
Chemistry; Retired Division Head, MIT Lincoln Laboratory

Dr. Michael LeNoir
Physician

Dr. James C. Letton
Chemistry

Janice Lord-Walker
Science Education

John L. Mack
Telecommunications

Dr. Elizabeth J. Maeda
Agriculture Research

Sello T. Makoa
Water Distribution Technology and Construction

Mosibudi Mangena
Former Minister of Science and Technology: Republic of South Africa, 2004 – 2008

Dr. Philip J. Marion
Physician

Dr. Tshilidzi Marwala
Exec. Dean, Faculty of Engineering and the Built Environment at the University of Johannesburg, South Africa; Mechanical Engineering

Dr. Robert A. Matthews
Professor Emeritus, Geologist- *Deceased*

Alphonse Mboussa
Director General, Engineering

Dr. Alston B. Meade, Sr.
Senior Research Biologist

Dr. Francis Mensah
Theoretical and Mathematical Physics

Dr. Ronald E. Mickens
Physics

Dr. Robert B. Mims
Physician; Enocrinology

Dr. Raphael Mmasi
Engineering Science

Dr. Stanislas Ebata Mongo
Director, Disease Control

Gregory B. Morrison
Corp. Vice President and CIO

Dr. Sospeter M. Muhongo
Tectonics, Structural geology, Petrology, Geochronology and Economic Geology

Dr. Edith Eliakim Ndemanisho
Agriculture Science

Dr. Roland Ndip
Medical Microbiology

Mbangiseni P. Neptumbada
Soil Physics

Dr. Magnus Ngoile
Large Marine Ecosystems; fisheries; coastal management; marine protected areas

Dr. Godfrey O. Nunoo
Medicine; Chiopractor

Rudo Nyachoto
Chemical Engineering

Joseph Oakley, Jr., PE
Civil and Structural Engrg., Const. Mgmt.

Dr. Eric O. Odada
Earth System Science; Climatology

Dr. Samwel V. Manyele
Chemical and Process Engineering

Dr. Wayne J. Martin
Environmental Science, Geochemistry

Dr. Verdiana G. Masanja
Applied Mathematics

Dr. James A. Mays
Physician, Hypertension, Cardiology

Dr. Victor R. McCrary
Chemistry

Dr. Linda C. Meade-Tollin
Biochemistry

Dr. Debra Meyer
Biochemistry

Gregory Miller, RN
Nurse, Health Educator and Consultant

Dr. James W. Mitchell
Chemistry and Chemical Engrg.

Dr. Aberra Mogessie
Metamorphic, Igneous Petrology, Geochemistry and Economic Geology

Ulysses J. Montgomery, PE
Civil Engineering, Proj. Mgmt.

Edmond Moukala
Civil Engineering; Personal Assistant to the Chairman of the Executive Board, UNESCO Paris

Dr. Kassim S. Mwitondi
Data Mining and Business Intelligence

Dr. Ahmadou Lamine Ndiaye
Veterinary Science

Dr. Eddie Neal
President, Engineering Consulting Firm, Proj. Mgmt.

Dr. Mortimer H. Neufville
Agriculture Scientist

Dr. Victor Anomah Ngu
Ret'd Surgeon; Former Public Health Minister; former President of the Cameroon Academy of Sciences

Dr. Emmanuel A. Chukwuedo Nwanze
University Vice-Chancellor; BioChemistry

Dr. Ntahondi Nyandwi
Marine Sciences

Dr. Theresa Nkechi Obiekezie
Research Physics

Dr. Tolu Odugbemi
Medical Microbiology and Parisitology

Dr. Benjamin Siyowi Mapani
Geologist

Dr. Judy Martin-Holland, RN
Nursing

Dr. Jonathan Ihoyelo Matondo
Civil Engineering; Hydrology

Dr. Wilfred F. Mbacham
Biochemistry; Molecular Parasitology; Tropical Public Health

Gene McGowen, RN
Resource RN, Flight Nurse

Dr. C. Ralph Melton
Urologist

Dr. Carolyn W. Meyers
University President; Engineering

John W. Milton
Engineering and Law

Willie Mitchell
Environmental Science, Health and Safety Officer

Michel F. Molaire
Senior Research Associate Chemist

John P. Moon
Corp. Vice President, Computer Imaging Products

Dr. Hassina Mouri
Metamorphic Petrologist; Secretary General of the Geological Society of Africa

Dr. M. Paul Nampala
Executive Secretary, Uganda National Academy of Sciences (UNAS); Entomology; Crop Science

Dr. Lucy Mande Ayamba Ndip
Director, Laboratory for Emerging Infectious Diseases; Biochemistry and Microbiology

Dr. Claire A. Nelson
Futurist; Industrial Engineering; Founder and President of the Institute of Caribbean Studies

Dr. Jane Catherine Ngila
Analytical and Environmental Chemistry

Dr. Obed Norman
Science Education

Dr. Bertram Ekejiuba B. Nwoke
Public Health Parasitology & Entomology

Dr. Tebello Nyokong
Medicinal Chemistry and Nanotechnology

Dr. Chuma Obiudu
Pomology; Agriculture Education

Dr. Ferdinand A. Ofodile
Plastic & Reconstructive Surgery

Dr. Olugbenga Okunlola
Geology

Dr. Ken Olden
former Director of the National Institute of Environmental Health Sciences (NIEHS) and the Nation Toxicology Program (NTP), 1991-2005; Cell Biology and Biochemistry

Dr. Abiodun Francis Oluwole
Nuclear Physics; Environmental Science

Dr. Soji F. Oluwole
Medical Surgery

Dr. Josiah Ouma Omolo
Chemistry

Dr. Peter Azikiwe Onwualu
CEO, Raw Materials R & D Council; Agricultural Engineering

Dr. C.O.E. Onwuliri
Vice-Chancellor and Professor of Zoology; Parasitology

Dr. John Onam Onyatta
Environmental Soil Chemist

Dr. Theophilus A. Ossei-Anto
Science Education

Dr. Kwadwo Osseo-Asare
Material Science; Metallurgy

Dr. Chidi G. Osuagwu
Biochemistry

Dr. Rose Uzuma Osuji
Solar Energy Physics

Dr. Alfred Oteng-Yeboah
Environmentalist

Dr. Neville A. Parker
Transportation Systems; Civil Engineering

Paul E. Parker
Mechanical Engineering

Richard Patterson
Nuclear Waste Management

Anthony R. Pegram, PE
Civil and Structural Engineering, Proj. Mgmt.

Arnold Perkins
Public Health

Dr. Waverly J. Person
Geology; "Mr. Earthquake"

Dr. Linda Phaire-Washington
Cell Biology; Immunology; Molecular Biologist

Denis Sekoja Phakisi
Mechanical Engineering

Barry Pierce, PLS
Chief Surveyor, Software Developer

Karl Pierce
Urban Planning, GIS Mgmt. Project Mgmt.

Dr. Lasha Kim Pierce
Obstetrics & Gynecology, Surgeon

Wiley Pierce, PLS
Proj. & Construction Mgmt., Surveying

Dr. Derrick H. Pitts
Astronomy

Brent D. Pogue
Nuclear Engineering, Proj. Mgmt.

Dr. Richard H. Pointer
Biochemistry

Anthony J. ("Tony") Polk
Pathology, Blood Testing and Mgmt. Services

Dr. Clarence A. Porter
Retired V.P. and Provost, Parisitology

James Pringle
Electrical Engineering

Dr. Nathanial R. Quick
Material Science and Engineering

Dr. Clyde T. Raby
Veterinarian

Dr. Melvin R. Ramey
Civil and Environmental Engineering

Gen. Bernard Randolph
Four Star General, Electrical Engineer

Cordell Reed
Ret'd VP, Utility Co., Fossil & Nuclear Fuel

Dr. Kennedy Reed
Theoretical Physicist

Dr. Madison F. Richardson
Chief Head and Neck Surgeon

Dr. Lee Riley
BioResearch, Infectious Diseases

Shelly W. Riley, II
Ret'd Fighter Aircraft Mission Simulations

Dr. Stephen S. Robinson
Physician

Dr. Joan Robinson-Berry
Aerospace Engineering

Dr. Christopher Rose
Electrical & Computer Engineering

Wallace Russell, PE
Mech. Engrg., Co-Founder LACBPE - *Deceased*

Dr. Rashid Saeed
Communications and Network Engineering

Dr. Papa Ibra Samb
Plant Pathology

Dr. Bernard Sammons
Plant Pathology

Dr. Henry T. Sampson
Ret'd Aerospace Engineer, Blacks In Film Expert

Dr. John B. Sampson
Neuroanesthesia and Critical Care Medicine

Dr. Barbara A. Sanders
Advanced Automotive Engineer

Dr. Robert B. Sanders
Biochemistry

Dr. Cheryl L. Scott
Former U.S. CDC Dir. in Tanzania, Physician

Michael Seals, PE
Civil Engineering

Dr. Mesgun Sebhatu
Physics

William A. Shanks, RN
Ret'd Oncology Clinical Nurse Specialist

Dr. Earl D. Shaw
Physics, Optical Lasers

Dr. Umaru Shehu
Medicine; Public Health

Dr. Hazle Jeffries Shorter
Pediatrician; Pharmaceutical Research Physician

Dr. Omega C. Silva
Physician

Benito A. Sinclair, PE
Civil Engrg. Co. Executive, Structural Engrg.

Dr. Todd Singleton
Electrical Engineering

Norma M. Sklarek, FAIA
Architect Fellow

Dr. John B. Slade, Jr.
Physician

Patricia C. Sluby
Author; Chemistry; Registered Patent Agent

Howard Smith
Company CEO, Math, Computer Science

Mary Perry Smith
Mathematics, MESA CoFounder

Morris Smith
Ret'd Proj. Leader for Emerging Tech; Chemistry

Paul Smith
Retired Hospital V.P.; Pharmacist

Dr. Sonya Smith
Mechanical Engineering

Tommy E. Smith, Jr., PE
Mechanical Engineering, Nat'l Lab Administrator

Lanny S. Smoot
Electronic Panning Camera Co-inventor

Dr. Henri H. Soclo
Eco-toxicology Chemistry

Dr. Gnida Sossou
Civil Engineering

Dr. Michael Gregg Spencer
Electrical Engineer

Dr. Denise Stephenson-Hawk
Mathematician

Dr. Gerald V. Stokes
Microbiology, Tropical Medicine

Douglas J. Sweeney
Electrical Engineering, Project Management

Dr. Elorm Marcel K. Tchaou
GeoScience

Michel A. Tevoedjre
Engineering

Dr. Valerie L. Thomas
Retired Mathematician

Dr. Festus Tolo
Microbiology

Dr. John Trimble
Computer Science

Dr. Charles K. Twesigye
Biological Sciences

Thomas H. Via
Industrial Engineering Technology

Dr. Herman Lecil Warren
Plant Pathologist

Dr. Charles B. Watkins
Dean, School of Engrg., Mechanical Engineer

Dr. John A. Watson
Biochemistry; Biophysics

Ellerson Weaver
Pharmacist – *Deceased*

Raymond B. Webster
Research Scientist

Dr. William I. West
Biochemical Pharmacology, Endocrinology

Dr. Alison P. Williams
Chemistry

Gwendolyn D. Williams
Blood Bank Specialist

Dr. Luther S. Williams
Provost and V.P., SEM Education, Medicine

Dr. Bobby L. Wilson
Chemical Engineering

Dr. Vulindlela I. Wobogo
Chemistry, Physics

Dr. Sulayman K. Sowe
Computer Science

Dr. Frank Staggers, Jr.
Physician; Addiction Medicine

Frank Stewart
AABE Presdent; Electrical Engineering

Dr. David S. Summers
Neurologist

Dr. Ramona Tascoe
Internal Medicine; Global Health

Dr. Alain Tehindrazanarivelo
Neurologist, former Deputy Prime Minister in charge of Public Health

Dr. Adebisi Babatunde Thomas
Chair, NEPAD Science & Technology Forum; and Director for Africa, CURE Int'l; former Nigeria President's Adviser on Human Resources, Science & Technology

Dr. Arthur N. Thorpe
Physics

Dr. Glen O. Toney
Senior Corp. VP Emeritus; Computer Science

Dr. Carlton M. Truesdale
Physical Chemistry

Lavell Tyler, Jr., PE
Electrical Engrg., Telecommunications Engrg.

Dr. Clarence W. R. Wade
Chemist and Professor

Elbert Washington
Mathematics and Engineering

Dr. Levi Watkins, Jr.
Cardiac Surgery, Assoc. Dean, School of Med.

Morgan Watson
Engineering Company President; Mechanical Engineering

Dr. Frank C. Weaver
EE; Engineering Company Executive

Dr. Wayne P. Weddington, Jr.
Physician, Otolaryngologist

Dr. Augustus A. White
Orthopedic Surgery

Dr. Arthur L. Williams
Biology - *Deceased*

Dr. Henry N. Williams
Microbiology

Dr. Willie Williams
Physics

Charles Wilson
Computer Science

Dr. Charles E. Woodward
Astrophysics

Marion R. Spencer
Immunologist and Molecular Pathologist

Stephan Stanton
Dir., Software Test Engineering

Dr. Sheila ("Jewel") Stiles
Research Geneticist, Fisheries, Marine Biology

Dr. Mark E. Swai
Pediatrician, Dir. of Hospital Services

Dr. Julius H. Taylor
Physics

Dr. Botlhale O. Tema
Science Education; Biology

Dr. Lydia Waters Thomas
Ret'd Corp. Pres.& CEO; Biology and Zoology

Patrice Tognifode
Mechanical Engineering

Teotonio A. Torres
Civil Engineering

Dr. James M. Turner
Deputy Assistant Secretary, NOAA; Physics

Marcel I. Uzegbu, PE
Supervising Civil Engineer

Atty. Paul Ware
Patent Attorney; Physicist - *Deceased*

Dr. Warren M. Washington
Climate & Global Dynamics

Dr. H. Geoffrey Watson
Internal Medicine

Dr. Hamé M. Watt
Water Supply and Sanitation

Dr. James L. Weaver, Jr.
Dentistry

Dr. James E. West
Research Prof., Electrical & Computer Engrg

Dr. Sandra L. White
Immunobiology; Therapeutics, Hematopoiesis

Eric Williams
Mechanical Engineer; Biotechnology

Dr. James H. Williams, Jr.
Professor, Mechanical Engineering

Samuel P. Williamson
Meteorology

Ken Wilson
Computer Science, Electrical Engineering

Oscar Wright
Civil Engineering

Dr. James Howard Wyche
University Provost; Biochemistry; Cell Biologist

Dr. Sankare Yacouba
Marine Biology

Dr. Patrice O. Yarbough
Infectious Diseases

Dr. Peter Oriwa Yimbo
Science Applications

Clarence E. Younger
IT Management

ASI Fellows By Discipline

Aerospace

W. Paul Dunn
Aerospace and Civil Engineering

Franklin Hornbuckle
COO, Satellite Aerospace Corp., EE

Dr. Odell Graham
Physics, Electrical & Aerospace Engineering

Dr. Cheick Modibo Diarra
Chairman for Africa at Microsoft Corp.;
Aerospace Engineering

Dr. Henry T. Sampson
Aerospace, Blacks In Film Expert

Shelly W. Riley, II
Fighter Aircraft Mission Simulations

Dr. Christine Darden
Ret'd Project Engineer at NASA Langley

Dr. Aprille J. Ericsson
Aerospace and Mechanical Engineering

Dr. Wesley L. Harris
Aeronauctics and Astronautics

Dr. Adigun Ade Abiodun
Satellite Remote Sensing; Space Sciences

Agriculture

Dr. Clarence C. Gray, III
Agriculture Research - *Deceased*

Dr. Essex E. Finney, Jr.

Dr. Timothy W. Conner
Plant Genomics

Dr. Shaukat Ali Abdulrazak
and Exec. Sec., National Council for Science
and Technology

Dr. Oghenetsavbuko T. Edje
Cropping Systems Agronomy

Dr. M. Paul Nampala
Executive Secretary, Uganda National
Academy of Sciences (UNAS); Entomology;
Crop Science

Godwin Kwaku S. Aflakpui
and Rector, Wa Polytechnic, Ghana; Crop
and Plant Physiology

Dr. Andrew Achuo Enow

Dr. William Henson
Ret'd Agriculture Prof. & Univ. Admin.

Dr. A. Egrinya Eneji

Dr. Herman Lecil Warren
Plant Pathologist

Dr. John Afele
Plant Breeding/Biotechnology

Dr. Elizabeth J. Maeda

Dr. Chuma Obiudu
Pomology; Agriculture Education

Dr. Phindile E. Lukhele-Olorunju
Plant Breeding and Virology

Dr. Edith Eliakim Ndemanisho

Dr. Mortimer H. Neufville

Pierre M. Labossiere

Dr. Bernard Sammons
Plant Pathology

Dr. Aliyageen M. Alghali
University Vice Chancellor; Agricultural
Entomology

Dr. Papa Ibra Samb
Plant Pathology

Dr. Peter Azikiwe Onwualu
CEO, Raw Materials R & D Council;
Agricultural Engineering

Dr. Haruna Braimah
Crop Pest Management/Biological Control

Bernard E. Chove, Ph.D.
Food Science and Processing

Astronomy & Astrophysics

Dr. George R. Carruthers

Dr. Gibor Basri
and Vice Chancellor for Equity and Inclusion

Dr. Charles E. Woodward

Dr. Derrick H. Pitts

Biochemistry

Dr. William L. West
Biochemical Pharmacology, Endocrinology

Dr. Debra Meyer

Dr. Sandra L. White
Immunobiology; Experimental Therapeutics
and Hematopoiesis

Dr. Richard H. Pointer

Dr. Linda C. Meade-Tollin
Biochemistry

Dr. Robert B. Sanders

Dr. Luoy Mande Ayamba Ndip
Director, Laboratory for Emerging Infectious Diseases; Biochemistry and Microbiology

Dr. James H. Wyche
and University Provost; Cell Biologist

Dr. Ken Olden
former Director of the National Institute of Environmental Health Sciences (NIEHS) and the Nation Toxicology Program (NTP), 1991-2005; Cell Biology and Biochemistry

Dr. Mwananyanda M. Lewanika
and Founding President of the Zambia Academy of Sciences; Microbiology

Dr. Dominic W. Makawiti
and Deputy Vice-Chancellor (Academic Affairs)

Dr. Wilfred F. Mbacham
and Molecular Parasitology; Tropical Public Health

Dr. Lucy Mande Ayamba Ndip
Director, Laboratory for Emerging Infectious Diseases; Biochemistry and Microbiology

Dr. Emmanuel A. C. Nwanze
and University Vice-Chancellor

Dr. Joan Olubunmi Amarteifio

Dr. Modupe Fisayo Asaolu
and Toxicology

Dr. John A. Watson
and Biophysics

Dr. Djuana M. E. Harvell

Dr. Lawal Bilbis

Dr. Chidi G. Osuagwu

Biology

Dr. Harry S. Bass, Jr.

Dr. Les E. Casher
and Entomology

Dr. Sheila ("Jewel") Stiles
Research Geneticist, Fisheries, Marine Biology

Dr. Lydia Waters Thomas
Corp. Pres.& CEO

Dr. Clarence A. Porter
Retired V.P. and Provost, Parisitology

Dr. Marvin B. Hendricks
Senior Genetics Research Scientist

Dr. Ray A. Hill
Botany

Dr. Alston B. Meade, Sr.
and Ho. Jamaica Counselor

Dr. Arthur L. Williams

Dr. Ambrose Jearld, Jr.
Chief of Research Planning and Evaluation, Marine Biologist

Dr. Marian C. Johnson-Thompson
Director, Office of Institutional Development

Dr. Herman E. Eure
Ecological Animal Parasitologist

Dr. Albert Cosmas Achudume
Toxicology

Eddie Dunbar
Entomologist

Dr. Albert Jose Jones
Marine Biology, Enviromental Science

Dr. Kweku Andoh
Ethnobotanist, Botanist, Proprietor

Dr. Abolade S. Afolabi
Plant Biotechnology & Molecular Virology, Bio-Safety and Diagnostics

Dr. Rena T. Jones
Microbiology

Dr. Calvin A. Davenport

Dr. Nabil H.H. Bashir
Entomology; Pesticides & Toxicology

Dr. Harriette Howard-Lee Block

Delroy Brown

Carolyn S. Davis

Dr. Ikechukwu N.S. Dozie
Medical Microbiology and Parasitology

Dr. Doudou D. Faye
Entomology; Agronomy

Dr. Yaye Kene Gassama
Biotechnology and Plant Physiology

Dr. Adugna Haile
Entomology, Integrated Pest Management

Dr. Mark G. Hardy

Dr. Geraldine E. Harris

Dr. Clifford W. Houston
and Immunology, Immediate Past President of the American Soc. of Microbiology

Dr. Yemisi Adefunke Jeff-Agboola
Food Mycotoxicology/Phytopathology; Food Microbiology

Dr. Lovell A. Jones
and Molecular Biology

Dr. Stranger Kgamphe
Biology and Anthropometry

Dr. Sankare Yacouba
Marine Biology

Dr. Charles K. Twesigye

Dr. Roland Ndip
Medical Microbiology

Dr. C.O.E. Onwuliri
Vice-Chancellor and Professor of Zoology; Parasitology

Dr. Linda Phaire-Washington
Cell Biology; Immunology; Molecular Biologist

Dr. Tolu Odugbemi
Medical Microbiology and Parisitology

Dr. Festus Tolo

Dr. Henry N. Williams

Dr. Kemji Ajoku
and Technology Management

Chemistry

Dr. Sunday Adeniji Adesuyi

Dr. Lincoln I. Diuguid
President, Chemical Lab & Mfr.

Dr. William Jackson
Photodissociation Dynamics with Velocity Ion Imaging

Dr. Lloyd N. Ferguson
and author of 7 chemistry books

Dr. Gloria Long Anderson
Professor Emeritus; Chemistry

Dr. Edward Cleve Alexander

Gerald Bauldock

Dr. James C. Letton

Dr. Alafuele M. Kalala
Chemistry; Biochemistry

Dr. Sharon J. Barnes
and NOBCChE National Secretary

Patricia C. Sluby
and Author; Registered Patent Agent

Dr. Tebello Nyokong
Medicinal Chemistry and Nanotechnology

Dr. Bert Fraser-Reid

Dr. James W. Mitchell
and Chemical Engrg.

Dr. Jim Harris
Nuclear Chemist and Researcher - *Deceased*

Dr. Carlton M. Truesdale
Physical Chemistry

Morris Smith
Ret'd Proj. Leader for Emerging Tech. and Chemistry

Michell F. Molaire
Senior Research Associate Chemist

Dr. Milton Cofield

Dr. John W. Macklin

Dr. M. Nidanie Henderson
Chemistry and Molecular Biophysics

Dr. Ameenah Firdaus Gurib-Fakim
and Pro-Vice-Chancellor

Dr. Henri H. Soclo
Eco-toxicology Chemistry

Dr. Josiah Ouma Omolo

Dr. Clarence W. R. Wade

Howard E. Kennedy
President, Fragrance and Flavoring Co.

Dr. William A. Lester, Jr.
Professor, Chemistry Research

Dr. James King, Jr.
Ret'd Director, Tech Divs at JPL, Professor Emeritus

Lee F. Browne
Science Educator and Chemist, Lecturer Emeritus

Dr. Walter Cooper
and Ret'd State University Regent

Dr. George Cooper

Dr. Alison P. Williams

Dr. Vulindlela I. Wobogo
and Physics

Dr. Victor R. McCrary

Dr. Jane Catherine Ngila
Analytical and Environmental Chemistry

Computer Science

Thomas H. Via
Computer Integrated Manufacturing

James M. Kennedy
Computer Networks Co. President

Dr. Adrian J. Isles

Dr. John Trimble

John P. Moon
Corp. Vice President, Computer Imaging Products

Arif Gursel
Technical Evangelist, Business Dev. at Microsoft, Computer Scientist

Stephan Stanton
Dir., Software Test Engineering

Dr. Sulayman K. Sowe

Clarence E. Younger
IT Management

William ("Bill") Harris
Nano-Technology, Computer Chip Processor

Dr. Marc R. Hannah
Past V. P. and Chief Scientist of SGI

Charles Wilson

James Ealey
Computer Science, EE

Kerrie L. Holley
CTO, IBM Web Services Ctr

Dr. Nadia Hegazy
and Communications Engineering

Dr. Kassim S. Mwitondi
Data Mining and Business Intelligence

Herbert L. Byrd, Jr.
IT Management

Donna Auguste
Software Engineering, Electrical Engineering, Renewable Energy, E-learning

Dr. Edward H. Freeman
Tech. Dir., Adv. Knowledge Sys. Research

Ken Wilson

Howard Smith
Computer Science, EE

Gregory B. Morrison
Corp. Vice President and CIO

Denise Holland
and President, Black Data Processing Associates (BDPA)

Engineering

Chemical

Dr. Adeyinka A. Adeyiga

Dr. Robert V. Edwards

Dr. Bobby L. Wilson

Rudo Nyachoto

Dr. Samwel V. Manyele

Civil and Stuctural

Frederick E. Jordan, PE
Civil and Structural Engineering Co.
President

Dr. Neville A. Parker
and Transportation Systems

Benito A. Sinclair, PE
Civil and Structural Engineering Co.
President

Teotonio A. Torres
Civil Engineering

Ulysses J. Montgomery, PE

Oscar Wright

Anthony R. Pegram, PE

Michael Seals, PE

Dr. Reginald L. Amory
And Dean of Civil Engineering Faculty

Dr. Oyewusi Ibidapo-Obe
President of the Nigerian Academy of
Science; Civil Engineering; Mathematics

Dr. Gnida Sossou

Dr. Melvin R. Ramey
Prof. Emeritus and Environmental
Engineering

Shelly Nathan Bailey, PE
and Concrete Specialist

Lois Louise Cooper, PE
and Transportation Engineering

Kevin Canada, PE

Hamilton Victor Bowser, Sr.

Dr. Henry Randall Grooms
and Engineering Management

Brandon L. Hewitt, PE

Mayen Adetiba
and President of Association of Consulting
Engineers of Nigeria

Dr. Joseph Ibikunle Folayan, PE
Civil, Structural, Water and Geotechnical
Engineering

William Lucy
and Ret'd Sec-Treasurer of AFSCME

Edmond Moukala
and Personal Assistant to the Chairman of the
Executive Board, UNESCO Paris

Joseph Oakley, Jr., PE
Civil and Structural Engineering Co.
President

Dr. Adolfo O'Biang Biko

Abu Bakarr Kamara, PE

Dr. Rufus Benton Darden
Civil and Structural Engineering

Alphonse Mboussa
and Co. Director General

Marcel Uzegbu, P.E.

Gregory Jones, PE
and Mechanical Engrg., Gen'l Contractor

Gboyega Aladegbami

Dr. Delon Hampton, PE
Civil and Structural Engineering and
Program/Construction Management

Marcel I. Uzegbu, PE

Dr. Jonathan Ihoyelo Matondo
Civil Engineering; Hydrology

Electrical

Napoleon Hornbuckle
Ret'd Corp. Vice President, Diversified
Technologies

Dr. Michael Gregg Spencer

Raymon Dones
Engineering and Constuction, Renewable
Energy

Tikisa M. Anderson

Lee O. Cherry
and Project Management

Dr. James E. West
Research Professor, Electrical & Computer
Engrg.

Dr. Frank C. Weaver
and Engineering Company Executive

Frank Stewart
and AABE Presdent

Cordell Reed
Ret'd Vice Pres., Utility Co., Fossil &
Nuclear Fuel

Dr. John H. Day, Jr.
Chief, Electrical Engineering Div., Physics

Dr. Todd Singleton

Dr. Frank C. Weaver
and Engineering Company Executive

Dr. Gary L. Harris
and Nanotechnology

Dr. Christopher Rose
and Computer Engineering

Gen. Bernard Randolph
and Four Star General

James Pringle

Lavell Tyler, Jr., PE
and Telecommunications Engineering

Dr. Kweku David Fleming

Kenneth R. Anderson

Gen. Bernard Randolph
Four Star General, Engineer

Douglas J. Sweeney
and Project Management

Dr. Elham M. A. Ibrahim
Commissioner For Infrastructure And Energy
Of the African Union Commission; Electrical
Engineering

Dr. Todd Singleton

Mechanical

Eric Williams
and Biotechnology

Anthony ("Tony") Harris
and NSBE CoFounder

Yvonne Y. Clark, PE
Professor

Dr. Charles B. Watkins
Dean, School of Engineering

Tommy E. Smith, Jr., PE

Dr. Sonya Smith

Terry L. Few

Gerald Green

Wallace O. Johnston, PE

Paul E. Parker
and ret'd Asst. Dean, Univ Engrg and Dir. of MEP

Dr. Tshilidzi Marwala
and Exec. Dean, Faculty of Engineering and the Built Environment at the University of Johannesburg, South Africa

Patrice Tognifode

Dr. Eddie Neal
President, Engineering Consulting Firm

Dr. James H. Williams, Jr.
Professor

Wallace Russell, PE
and Co-Founder LACBPE - *Deceased*

Dr. Aaron L. Brundage
Nanoscale & Reactive Processes

Morgan Watson
and Engineering Company President

Denis Sekoja Phakisi

Other

Dr. Barbara A. Sanders
Advanced Automotive Engineer

Gregory P. Bagley
Research Engineer

Dr. Moses T. Asom
Opto-electronics

Lanny Smoot
Electronic Panning Camera Co-inventor, Imagineering

Dr. Saidq Bello Ikharo
Facilities Engineering and Management

Barry Pierce, PLS
Surveying, Construction Mgmt., Software Developer

Dr. Osama Awadelkarim
Engineering Science and Mechanics, Nanotechnology

Michel A. Tevoedjre
Engineering

Dr. Raphael Mmasi
Engineering Science

Virgil A. Baker
Geotechnology

Joseph Debro
Chemistry; Engineering; Project Dev.

Wiley Pierce
Surveying and Construction Mgmt.

Ilene Patricia Garner
Engineering Management, Chem/Math

Dr. Lesia L. Crumpton-Young
Industrial Engineering

Joan Robinson-Berry
Aerospace Engineering, VP Boeing

Dr. Kevin C. Greenaugh
Nuclear Engineering

Dr. Claire A. Nelson
Futurist; Industrial Engineering; Founder and President of the Institute of Caribbean Studies

Vernon C. Floyd
Broadcast

Brent D. Pogue
Nuclear Engineering

Dr. Augustine O. Esogbue
Dir., Intelligent Systems & Controls Lab

Dr. Carolyn W. Meyers
University President; Engineering

Dr. Dianne D. Gates-Anderson
Environmental Engineering

Louzolo (Augie) Agostinho
Senior Petroleum Engineer

Dr. Hamé M. Watt
Water Supply and Sanitation

Dr. Rashid Saeed
Communications and Network Engineering

Geology *and* Earth Science

Dr. Wayne J. Martin
Environmental Science, GeoChemistry

Dr. Georges A. Agbahungba
Soil Science

Dr. Joseph Owolabi Ajayi
Hydrogeology, Engineering Geology

Dr. Christopher S. Boxe
Environmental Science and Engineering

Dr. Jimmy Adegoke
Geosciences

Jones Fairfax Agwata
Water Resources and Environmental Science

Dr. Ojonigu F. Ati
Climatology/Physical and Biogeography, Remote Sensing and GIS

Ifeyinwa Davis
Environmental Scientist

Dr. Kouadio Affian
GeoScience; Remote Sensing

Justin Ahanhanzo
Physical Oceanography

Dr. Olusanjo A. Bamgboye
GeoScience

Dr. Mustafa El Tayeb
Ret'd Dir., UNESCO Div of Science

Dr. Regina Folorunsho
GeoScience; Climatology and Remote Sensing/GIS

Dr. A. Chidi Ibe
Physical Oceanography, Geology, Ocean Governance

Dr. Elorm Marcel K. Tchaou
GeoScience

Dr. Sospeter M. Muhongo
Tectonics, Structural geology, Petrology, Geochronology and Economic Geology

Dr. Ntahondi Nyandwi
Marine Sciences

Dr. John Onam Onyatta
Environmental Soil Chemist

Dr. Waverly J. Person
Geology, "Mr. Earthquake"

Dr. Mack Gipson, Jr.
Professor Emeritus of Geology – *Deceased*

Dr. Aberra Mogessie
Metamorphic, Igneous Petrology, Geochemistry and Economic Geology

Mbangiseni P. Neptumbada
Soil Physics

Dr. Eric O. Odada
Earth System Science; Climatology

Dr. Alfred Oteng-Yeboah
Environmentalist

Analysis & Policy; Geophysics

Dr. Robert A. Matthews
Professor Emeritus, Geologist - *Deceased*

Dr. Benjamin Siyowi Mapani
Geologist

Dr. Hassina Mouri
Metamorphic Petrologist; Secretary General of the Geological Society of Africa

Dr. Magnus Ngoile
Large Marine Ecosystems; fisheries; coastal management; marine protected areas

Dr. Olugbenga Okunlola

Babagana Abubakar

Material Science

Dr. Frank Alphonso Crossley

Dr. Nathanial R. Quick
and Co. President

Dr. Clayton W. Bates, Jr.
and Electrical Engineering, Physics

Dr. Kwadwo Osseo-Asare
Metallurgy

Dr. Kamau Gachigi
Ceramics

Dr. Robert ("Pete") Bragg
Univ. Prof. Material Science Dept. Chair Emeritus

Mathematics

Dr. Denise Stephenson-Hawk

Elbert Washington
and Engineering

Dr. Valerie L. Thomas

Dr. Abel A. Afouda

Dr. Jonathan D. Farley

Dr. David Rice Hedgley, Jr.

Dr. Johnny L. Houston
and Computer Science

Robert Hammie
and National Chess Master

Dr. Sam Olatunji Ale

Dr. Norbert Hounkonnou

Dr. Archie W. Earl, Sr.

Mary Perry Smith
and MESA CoFounder

Dr. Glen O. Toney
and Senior Corp. Vice-President Emeritus

Dr. James A. Donaldson

Dr. Verdiana G. Masanja

Medicine and Health

Dr. Denise Johnson
Cancer Research

Dr. Levi Watkins, Jr.
Cardiac Surgery, Assoc. Dean, School of Medicine

Dr. George W. Johnson, Jr.
Cardiothoracic & Vascular Surgery

Dr. Madison F. Richardson
Chief Head and Neck Surgeon

Dr. Stanislas Ebata Mongo
Director, Disease Control

Dr. Gaurdia Banister
Hospital V.P. and Specialist in Psychiatric Nursing

Marion R. Spenser
Immunologist and Molecular Pathologist

Dr. Mark Finch
Infectious Diseases

Dr. H. Geoffrey Watson
Internal Medicine

Dr. Ramona Tascoe
Internal Medicine, Global Health

Dr. Judy Martin-Holland, RN
Nursing

Venita A. Jones, RN
Nursing

Mildred Crear, RN
Nursing, Maternal & Cild Care

Dr. Clarence A. Boyd, Jr.
Orthopedic Surgeon

Dr. Alain Tehindrazanarivelo
Neurologist, former Secretary General of Science Ministry

Dr. Damase Bodzongo
Natl Dir. Gen'l of Health, Thoracic Surgeon

Dr. Dimi Elisa
Natl Dir. of Research and Planning, Public Health

Dr. Bill Jenkins
Epidemiologist

Dr. Hazle Jeffries Shorter
Pediatrician and Pharmaceutical Research Physician

Dr. Michael LeNoir
Allergist, Asthma Specialist

Dr. John B. Slade, Jr.
Physician

Dr. Wayne P. Weddington, Jr.
Otolaryngologist

Arnold Perkins
Public Health

Gene McGowen, RN
Resource Nurse, Flight Nurse

Dr. C. Ralph Melton
Urologist

Dr. Mark E. Swai, M.D.
Pediatrician, Dir. Of Hospital Services

Dr. Renty B. Franklin
Biomedical Science

Richard H. Djoble D'Almeida
Chief Medical Officer

Dr. Lynne M. Holden
President, Mentoring in Medicine, Emergency Medicine

Dr. Lasha Kim Pierce
Obstetrics & Gynecology, Surgeon

Dr. Norma Francisco
Dental Hygiene, Kumon Math and Reading

Dr. Dankyi Augustine Beeko
Consultant Neurosurgeon

Dr. Amani Eltayb
Pharmacology

Dr. Andemariam Gebremichael
Associate Dean, and Dean of Academic, Student, and Research Affairs; Medicine

Dr. Saadou Issifou
Medicine; Medical Parisitology; Molecular Biology

Dr. Sandra A. Knight
Physician, U.S. CDC in Jamaica; Medical Officer at the Ministry of Health

Ellerson Weaver
Pharmacist – **Deceased**

Dr. Godfrey O. Nunoo
Chiopractor

Dr. Adetunji Adelekan
Nephrologist, Internal Medicine

Dr. David S. Summers
Neurologist

Dr. Bwire Chirangi
Physician

Dr. Phillip J. Marion
Physician

Dr. Robert B. Mims
Enocrinologist

Dr. Edward G. Fisher
Physician, Surgeon

Dr. Felix Djembo-Madingou
Regional Director of Medicine

William A. Shanks
Ret'd Oncology Clinical Nurse Specialist

Dr. Lee Riley
Infectious Diseases

Dr. Carl C. Bell, M.D.
Psychiatry and Public Healthe

Dr. Gerald V. Stokes
Microbiology, Tropical Medicine

Dr. James L. Green
Clinical Associate of Ophthalmology and Visual Science

Jacqueline Kakembo
Nursing

Dr. Stephen S. Robinson
Physician

Dr. Lisa Cain
Neuroscience and Cell Biology

Dr. Ntseliseng Bohloko
Pharmacy

Dr. Julius W. Garvey
Thoracic, Cardiothoracic Vascular Surgery; son of Marcus Garvey

Dr. Samuel Hunter
Physician and Biochemist

Larry D. Keith
Biology, Anatomy, Medical Education Development – *Deceased*

Dr. Ronald W. Lindsey
Trauma and Spine Surgery

Dr. Augustus A. White
Orthopedic Surgery

Dr. Eiman A. Mahmoud
Pathologist, Infectious Diseases

Anthony J. ("Tony") Polk
Pathology, Blood Testing and Management Services

Dr. Benjamin S. Carson, Sr.
Pediatric Neurosurgery

Dr. Edward S. Cooper
Physician

Dr. Omega C. Silva
Physician

Dr. James A. Mays
Hypertension, Cardiology

Dr. Luther S. Williams
Provost and V.P., SEM Education, Medicine

Gregory Miller, RN
Health Educator and Consultant

Paul Smith
Retired Hospital V.P., Pharmacist

Gwendolyn D. Williams
Blood Bank Specialist

Dr. James L. Weaver, Jr.
Dentistry

Dr. Ernest Goodson
Orthodontics

Dr. Barbara Green-Ajufo
Epidemiologist

Carl N. Lester
Former Dir., Alameda County Public Healthcare Services

Dr. Cheryl L. Scott
Former U.S. CDC Director in Tanzania, Physician

Valentin Agon
Green Medicine

Dr. Dennis E. Daniels
Epidemiology

Dr. Akpa Raphael Gbary
WHO Representative to Benin; Medicine

Dr. Victor Akpan Inem
Family Physician; Primary Health Care

Dr. Harmon Kelley
OB/GYN, Physician

Dr. Bereneice McClentton Madison
Clinical and Public Health; Pathogenic Microbiology/Immunology

Dr. Patrice O. Yarbough
Infectious Diseases

Dr. John D. Campson
Neuroanesthesia and Critical Care Medicine

Dr. Bertram Ekejiuba B. Nwoke
Public Health Parasitology & Entomology

Dr. Omotayo O. Ebong
Pharmacology

Dr. Frank Staggers, Jr
Physician; Addiction Medicine

Dr. Ferdinand A. Ofodile
Plastic & Reconstructive Surgery

Dr. L. Julian Haywood
Cardiologist

Dr. Victor Anomah Ngu
Ret'd Surgeon; Former Public Health Minister; former President of the Cameroon Academy of Sciences

Dr. Soji F. Oluwole
Medical Surgery

Dr. Umaru Shehu
Medicine; Public Health

Physics

Dr. Anthony M. Johnson
Distinguished Research Physicist, Photonics Research

Dr. Wade M. Kornegay
Div. Head, Radar Measurements

Dr. Albert Bridgewater
Particle Physics

Dr. George E. Alcorn

Dr. Mesgun Sebhatu

Dr. James E. Turner
and Deputy Director, NIST

Dr. Julian Earls
Ret'd Director at NASA-Lewis, Health Physicist

Julius Grant
Physics

Dr. Francis Mensah

Dr. Fabian I. Ezema

Dr. Theresa Nkechi Obiekezie

Dr. Soodursun Jugessur
Chairman, University of Mauritius; Chairman, Mauritius Research Council; President of the Mauritius Academy of science and Technology; Physics, Electrical Engrg.

Dr. Hattie Carwell
Health Physics

Dr. Marshall G. Jones
Laser Technology Through Optical Fiber Research

Atty. Paul Ware
Patent Attorney, Physicist - *Deceased*

Dr. William T. Brown

Dr. Julius H. Taylor

Dr. Earl D. Shaw
Optical Lasers

Dr. Randolph W. Bromery
Geophysics Professor Emeritus, Former Chancellor

Olden Henson
and City Councilman

Dr. Kennedy Reed

Dr. Ernest C. Hammond, Jr.

Dr. Abiodun Francis Oluwole
Nuclear Physics; Environmental Science

Dr. Lynford L. Goddard
Physics, Electrical Engineering - Lasers and Photonics Research

Dr. Deborah Jackson
Opto-Electronics Communications

Dr. Gilbert B. Chapman, II
Physicist, automobile product specialist

Dr. Ronald E. Mickens

Dr. Willie Williams

Dr. Keith H. Jackson
X-Ray Optics, Sponsored Research

Dr. Peter J. Delfyett, Jr.
Trustee, Chair, Professor, Optics, ECE, & Physics

Dr. Peter Intsiful

Dr. Arthur N. Thorpe

Dr. Elaine LaLanne

Dr. Rose Uzuma Osuji
Solar Energy Physics

Veterinary/Animal Science

Dr. Clyde T. Raby, DVM

Dr. Clement Oladapo Adewunmi
and Parisitology; African Medicinal Plants

Dr. Felix I. Ifeanyi
and Biology

Dr. Alvin G. Foster, DVM

Dr. Olanike Kudirat Adeyemo
and Aquatic Pathobiology

Dr. Ahmadou Lamine Ndiaye

Dr. Ebenezer Adebisi Adebowale
and National Universities Commission

Dr. Justin Epelu-Opio
and Secretary General, Uganda National Academy of Sciences (UNAS)

Dr. Assan Jaye
and Viral Diseases

Weather & Climatology

Dr. Warren M. Washington
Climate & Global Dynamics

Samuel P. Williamson
Meteorology

Ediang Okuku Archibong
Meteorology and Climatology

Other

Edgar Goff
Futurist and Research Development

Richard Patterson
Nuclear Waste Management

Willie Mitchell
Environmental Science, Health and Safety Officer

Dr. Lionel O. Greene, Jr.
Research Scientist

Dr. Raymond B. Webster
Research Scientist

Bradford C. Grant, AIA, NOMA
Architecture

James E. Allen
Ret'd Mgr., JPL Space Flight Operations Facility - *Deceased*

Dr. Peter Yimbo
Science Applications

Dr. Obed Norman
Science Education

Dr. Shem Arungu-Olende
Secretary General of the African Academy of Sciences

Xernona Clayton
President and Founder of Trumpet Awards

Hardiman D. Cureton, II
Science Education

Norma M. Sklarek, FAIA
Architect Fellow

Karl Pierce
Urban Planning, GIS Mgmt. Project Mgmt.

Dr. John W. Forje
African Science and Technology Policy

Dr. Calestous Juma
Science and Technology Policy at Harvard; Founding Director of the African Centre for Technology Studies in Nairobi

Janice Lord-Walker
Science Education

John L. Mack
Telecommunications

Mosibudi Mangena
Former Minister of Science and Technology: Republic of South Africa, 2004 – 2008

Dr. Adebisi Babatunde Thomas
Chair, NEPAD Science & Technology Forum; and Director for Africa, CURE Int'l; former Nigeria President's Adviser on Human Resources, Science & Technology

Dr. Botlhale O. Tema
Science Education; Biology

Dr. Theophilus A. Ossei-Anto
Science Education

John W. Milton
Engineering and Law

Sello T. Makoa
Water Distribution Technology and Construction

Welcome to the……

African Scientific Institute

U.S. Administration: P.O. Box 12161, Oakland, California, 94604, USA
voice: (510) 653-7027
website: www.asi-org.net
email: asi@quixnet.net

ASI U.S. Offices: Oakland/San Francisco, CA • San Jose, CA •
Hollywood, CA • Washington, DC • Cambridge, MA
International: Accra, Ghana • Lagos, Nigeria • Nairobi, Kenya

African Scientific Institute

The African Scientific Institute (ASI) was founded in 1967. It is a non-profit organization representing a network of scientists, engineers, technologists, and health professionals, as well as young people aspiring to enter the world of science and technology.

ASI OBJECTIVES

- Expose and motivate more minorities to pursue careers in science and technology. Through various programs and events sponsored by ASI, young people have an opportunity to learn about the possibilities and rewards in scientific and technical professions. They will be welcomed. Minorities represent an untapped resource to satisfy the increasing demand for professionals in science and technology.

- Foster the professional development of its network of scientists and technologists, as well as their participation in their communities.

- Develop, organize and provide study, tutoring and counseling centers and other facilities and programs for use by young people.

- Develop programs and projects to help solve problems of developing countries, with emphasis on healthcare, infrastructure and economic, technology exchange, and development of appropriate sustainable technologies.

- Develop laboratories for technical professionals who have ideas and talent, but are without the resources to develop them. The various disciplines of science and technology are becoming more interrelated. ASI, as an interdisciplinary organization, is a forum for the exchange of technical information and expertise.

OUR METHOD OF IMPLEMENTATION

The objectives of ASI are implemented through:

• Publishing literature • Sponsoring conferences, seminars, workshops • Research and Consulting services • Lectures before various types of audiences • Making Radio and Television appearances • Counseling and providing special support services for scientifically motivated youth • Community Involvement projects—such as Achievement Award Banquets • Co-operative projects with private and governmental sectors—such as job fairs. • Maintaining a climate of high acceptance so that as increased needs require increased budgets, donors and volunteers, whether they be public, private, governmental, national or international, will join with ASI to provide the needed funds and services to maintain and continue the worthwhile objectives of the organization. • Employment Matching Program

Historically, ASI has concerned itself primarily with motivation programs for minorities entering scientific/ technological areas. However, over the past few years, ASI has expanded its objectives to become project development oriented. Also, ASI renders consulting and research services, which are rendered on a fee basis.

We are involved..........

PUBLISHINGS: Since 1967, we have produced and distributed publications free to keep both the scientific and lay communities aware of developments in science and technology. We have produced *SCITECH News* newspaper (distributed to 25,000+ nationally), *Technology Transfer* magazine and the BLACKS IN SCIENCE CALENDAR. ASI now enjoys participation on an electronic information system to present the world of science and technology to those having access to computers.

PARTNERING: We work closely with many organizations to efficiently address common concerns. Projects in which ASI has been involved as a partner include Oakland, CA School District's "Magnet School Program" and Math Dept.; BASTEC (Bay Area Science and Technology Education Colloquium) – a joint venture of the U.S. Dept. of Energy, Oakland, CA School District, and Community Based Organizations; the Urban League's Calif. Bay Area Chapter; NAAAHR (National Association of African Americans in Human Resources) in presenting its 2003 national conference as well as regional Calif. partnering efforts.

SCIENCE AND TECHNOLOGY AWARENESS PROGRAM: This program (STAP) helps keep the public aware of developments in Science and Technology through projects such as our Science and Technology Awareness Fairs and Technology and Environment Camp. By becoming a Constituent for Science and Technology Awareness, this program also offers individuals an information resource conduit.

CONFERENCES, SEMINARS, WORKSHOPS: ASI presents information as an individual organization or in partnership with others.

AFRICA INPUT: A program to assist in Africa's enhancement through the ASI AFRICA RELIEF FUND, Save the "African Rainforest Project", as well as partnering with other institutions to effectively engage in worthwhile programs such the AFRICA FOCUS Series, Constituency Development. Currently, ASI is assisting to sustain Dolisie Hospital in Congo Brazzaville.

PROJECTS RESOURCES NETWORKING: ASI puts resources together to accomplish tasks, whether they are generated by ASI CORE members or others interested in mutual objectives.

INNOVATION and TECHNOLOGY EXCHANGE: Throughout ASI activities, one theme remains constant…… innovation and cognizance of development in science and technology. Each of us needs to help to aid others towards achieving their aspirations. We must be able to lead. We must also know where we are going. ASI stresses the importance of staying abreast of worldwide technological developments to give us the best "feel" possible about future directions.

AFRICAN SCIENTIFIC INSTITUTE CORE PROGRAM: Regional and local involvement in ASI activities is supported and implemented through a group of dedicated individuals who are interested in furthering ASI objectives. These individuals also work on the ASI Fellows Program, International African Science Conferences (IASC), Constituent for Science and Technology Awareness Program, SciTech News, Building Fund, ASI Africa Relief Projects, Speakers Bureau, and Partnering efforts. We are flexible to incorporate activities that are of particular interest to an individual, or a group of individuals. ASI acts as a clearinghouse of resources to connect people together to achieve goals.

ELECTRONIC ACCESS TO: Attending meetings can be too time consuming, frustrating, and even boring. Effective time management is always important to busy people. If you want to participate in ASI activities, or partner with ASI, or simply want to know about ASI and keep abreast of its developments, you may do so without leaving your home or office.

Contact ASI via our website: www.asi-org.net, or email us at: asi@quixnet.net.

ENGAGING LOCAL, NATIONAL, INTERNATIONAL POLICY MAKERS: Throughout ASI's history, we have worked with Nobel Prize winners, local, national, and international politicians and dignitaries to help assure developments in science and technology were at the very forefront of their policies to ensure that sustainable usage of science and technology was transferable to those in need.

RESEARCH AND CONSULTING: Both for Profit and Non-Profit activities alike, ASI engages in research and consulting (RC) on a fee basis. Usually non-profit RC is performed as a result of in-house concerns; the results are then marketed. Profit motivated RC results from responses to outside requests for ASI services, or ASI responds to 'requests for proposals' from others.

African Scientific Institute: P.O. Box 12161, Oakland, California, 94604, USA • (510) 653-7027
• www.asi-org.net • email: asi@quixnet.net

www.ingramcontent.com/pod-product-compliance
Lightning Source LLC
Chambersburg PA
CBHW080738230426
43665CB00020B/2784